THE
Sound *of* Money

Also by Darrell M. West
Air Wars: Television Advertising in Election Campaigns, 1952–1996 (Second Edition)
Crosstalk: Citizens, Candidates, and the Media in a Presidential Campaign (with Marion R. Just, Ann N. Crigler, Dean E. Alger, Timothy E. Cook, and Montague Kern)

Also by Burdett A. Loomis
The Contemporary Congress
The New American Politician

THE
Sound *of*
Money

How Political Interests Get What They Want

———

DARRELL M. WEST
Brown University
and
BURDETT A. LOOMIS
University of Kansas

W. W. NORTON & COMPANY
NEW YORK·LONDON 1998

Copyright © 1999 by W. W. Norton & Company, Inc.

The text of this book is composed in Janson.
Composition by PennSet, Inc.
Manufacturing by The Courier Company.
Book design by Chris Welch Design.

Library of Congress Cataloging-in-Publication Data
West, Darrell M., 1954–
    The sound of money : how political interests get what they want /
by Darrell M. West and Burdett A. Loomis.
        p.   cm.
    Includes bibliographical references and index.
    ISBN 0-393-97338-7 (pbk.)
    1. Lobbying—United States.   2. Pressure groups—United States.
3. Advertising, Political—United States.   4. Communication in
politics—United States.   I. Loomis, Burdett A., 1945– .
II. Title.
JK1118.W47   1999
324'.4'0973—dc21   98-25573

W. W. Norton & Company, Inc., 500 Fifth Avenue, New York, N.Y. 10110
                        http://www.wwnorton.com
W. W. Norton & Company Ltd., 10 Coptic Street, London WC1A 1PU

1 2 3 4 5 6 7 8 9 0

To Happy and John Hazen White, Sr.,
for their tireless efforts to improve the political process;
and
to Murray Edelman, democrat and scholar

Contents

Acknowledgments

We are grateful to many people for their assistance on this project. A number of individuals in Washington and elsewhere took time out of their busy schedules to share with us their thoughts about the political dynamics of recent policy controversies. We could not have written this book without the insights of each of these people.

Steve Dunn, our editor at Norton, deserves a big thank you for his help in refining our ideas and clarifying our language. The book is much better for his comments. Kate Lovelady did a wonderful job copyediting the book.

In addition, we benefitted from the research assistance of Richard Francis, Chris Goodwin, and Diane Heith, and the helpful commentary of Ross Cheit on several chapters of this book. Likewise, Eric Sexton, Allan Cigler, and Bob Wallace (of *CQ Weekly*) provided extensive assistance.

Portions of chapters 4 and 5 appeared earlier, respectively in "Harry and Louise Go to Washington," *Journal of Health Policy, Politics, and Law*, Vol. 21, no. 1, (Spring, 1996), co-authored with Diane Heith and Chris Goodwin; and "Electronic Advocacy: Interest Groups and Public Policymaking," *PS* (March, 1996), pp. 25–29, co-authored with Richard Francis.

Some material was also drawn from "Choosing to Advertise: How Interests Decide," with Eric Sexton, in *Interest Group Politics*, 4th ed., Allan J. Cigler and Burdett A. Loomis, eds. (Washington: CQ Press, 1995).

For their assistance on this project, we would like to thank the Department of Political Science and the John Hazen White, Sr., Public Opinion Laboratory of the A. Alfred Taubman Center for Public Policy and American Institutions of Brown University and the Political Science Department and the Hall Center for the Humanities at the University of Kansas.

THE
Sound *of*
Money

Chapter One

Prelude

The New Sound of Influence

Money is like water. If there is a crack, water will find it.
—*Clinton presidential assistant Harold Ickes commenting on
the 1996 campaign finance scandals.*[1]

On December 17, 1992, the United States, Canada, and Mexico embarked on a new era of trade relations among their countries by signing a historic pact known as the North American Free Trade Agreement (NAFTA). Subject to legislative approval by each nation, this treaty proposed to drop all trade barriers among the three countries by January 1, 1994, and in the process create a $6.5 trillion market made up of 360 million people. Since the legislation had the support of outgoing President George Bush, incoming President Bill Clinton, leading businesses, and academics and journalists who favored free trade principles, it looked like a smooth route to ratification in Congress, which remained under Democratic control.

From all outward appearances, the treaty signaled that free trade had triumphed throughout all of North America.

In short order, both Canada and Mexico ratified the agreement. In the United States, though, ratification got off to a slow start. Newly inaugurated President Clinton pledged to move quickly to assure congressional action, yet other issues kept impinging on his policy agenda, including deficit reduction, the crime bill, and his massive effort to remake the health care system. Then, labor and environmental groups demanded "side agreements" to the treaty that would insure fair working conditions and stronger environmental safeguards in Mexico and Canada. These interests sought to redefine the issue and call attention to possible job losses and ecological degradation.

By spring 1993, the early optimism of treaty proponents had faded. NAFTA was in big political trouble. The agreement was being criticized by Ross Perot in 30-second "infomercials," the kind the Texan had popularized during his $60 million presidential campaign in 1992.[2] Using a research study by pact opponent Pat Choate, Perot claimed NAFTA would cost the United States 5.9 million jobs, which would be moved to Mexico and Canada. In a line that would become his mantra, Perot repeatedly referred to the "giant sucking sound" of jobs being moved to Mexico in order for employers to escape the more stringent labor, safety, and environmental rules of the United States.[3]

Perot was not alone in these criticisms. On May 13, two dozen members of the U.S. House of Representatives announced that they had formed an "anti-NAFTA" caucus. No matter what side agreements were negotiated, these legislators pledged not to support NAFTA. Later that month, the AFL-CIO labor federation launched a "nix it or fix it" advertising campaign criticizing the treaty's lax protections for American workers. The ratification "air war" was in full force. Anti-NAFTA groups were running ads, holding press conferences, and citing critical research studies. Meanwhile, forces sympathetic to NAFTA used a group called the U.S. Alliance for NAFTA to promote a "yes" vote. Made up of state governments, local officials, and private businesses, this coalition established a $2 million budget to seek passage of the treaty.

The object of much of this advertising and news activity was the general public. And according to a CNN/*Time* magazine survey, anti-NAFTA forces were scoring points. Ordinary citizens became aware of NAFTA only in the context of the negative advertising and coverage; in that situation, they had grave doubts about the agreement. Sixty-three percent of Americans thought the trade pact "would encourage U.S. firms to move jobs to Mexico." Only one in four believed "NAFTA would create U.S. jobs."[4]

A stricken Clinton White House moved into high gear. On September 14, Clinton arranged for former Presidents Gerald Ford, Jimmy Carter, and George Bush to come to the White House to announce their support for the treaty. Ronald Reagan could not attend, but he sent a note proclaiming his approval of the agreement. The White House named William Daley, a member of the prominent Chicago political family (and subsequently, Secretary of Transportation), as "NAFTA czar." Under his direction, cabinet secretaries hit the road, giving speeches and explaining why the treaty would be good for America.[5]

In November 1993, after months of protracted discussion, Congress narrowly approved the treaty, thus assuring the creation of the free trade zone. It had not been the easy victory originally anticipated. Opponents had "gone public" through speeches, debates, ads, and infomercials. They nearly had turned what should have been a "slam dunk" ratification into a close call for the president. More generally, the highly visible treaty debate signaled the emergence of a new era of interest-group politics in the United States.

In this book, we examine the new "sound" of influence in American politics. The noisy debate that surrounded the NAFTA ratification effort now has become common in American politics. Just witness the following recent examples of interest-group activity:

1) In 1996, the AFL-CIO spent $22 million on public education ads (and $35 million overall) in targeted efforts to publicize the health, education, and labor voting records of three dozen House Republicans, mostly freshmen.

2) During the 1996 campaign, conservative nonprofit organizations, such as Americans for Tax Reform and the National Right to Life Committee, received more than $4 million from the Republican National Committee in order to organize last-minute mailings, phone calls, and ads.[6]

3) With the Republican takeover of Congress, business groups dramatically shifted their campaign fund-raising toward the GOP. Whereas in 1994, Democrats received 51 percent of all individual and political action committee contributions from business interests and Republicans 49 percent, by 1996, 63 percent of business money went to the GOP and 37 percent to the Democrats.[7]

4) On issues from health care and tort reform to telecommunications and tobacco, there has been extraordinary interest-group spending on advertising, public relations, and grassroots lobbying to sway the policy process.

Although such tactics did not begin with the NAFTA fight, the power of public lobbying to produce an effective story line became clear with that battle. Treaty opponents moved the conflict into the public's consciousness and almost pulled victory from the jaws of what should have been an overwhelming defeat. By drawing on communications technologies from television ads to 800 numbers to the Internet, interest groups demonstrated that they could alter public attitudes, elite opinion, and, on occasion, the preferences of a few key decision makers.

Even though NAFTA won ratification, rarely in politics is anything settled permanently. Interest groups and politicians alike learn from experience. The labor and environmental interests antagonistic to contemporary free trade policies discovered that their arguments resonated not only with broad segments of the public at large, but also with lots of rank-and-file congressional Democrats. While they could do little to alter the North American trade zone, anti-NAFTA lobbyists articulated a set of messages that affected later trade discussions. In 1997, the central issue was whether or not to give back to the president "fast-track" authority, which would disallow Congress to make amendments to trade legislation. By limiting the House and Senate to an "up-or-down" vote, fast-track would strengthen the president's hand vis-a-vis Congress in future trade discussions.

With NAFTA, the Clinton Administration had dominated the initial stages of the public debate. Outside interest groups, such as labor and environmental organizations, were forced, in political scientist E. E. Schattschneider's terminology, "to expand the scope of the conflict" to the general public. By appealing to ordinary citizens through dire predictions of job loss and increasing pollution, these groups attempted to sow seeds of doubt regarding the virtues of free trade.[8] The 1997 fast-track debate, however, reflected an almost complete reversal of roles, with trade skeptics dominating the discussion. As the *National Journal* reported, "the Administration ha[d]n't found a way to counter the opponents' arguments that fast track is nothing more than a referendum on the North American Free Trade Agreement."[9] Given a mixed bag of studies, often generated by the interested parties, the overall data suggested that NAFTA had produced neither job losses nor great economic benefits. In terms of policy discussions, though, the stories of job loss, lower wages, unfair competition, a collapsing peso, and environmental degradation dominated, thereby displacing the pro-NAFTA, free trade story line of 1993.

With their Democratic allies in the House and the overwhelming backing of the labor movement, which had become much more vocal in the years following NAFTA, fast-track opponents redoubled their efforts. The AFL-CIO spent $2 million in fall 1997 running television ads in twenty key congressional districts. According to labor spokeswoman Denise Mitchell, "we saw this as a battle for the soul of the country." The union federation set up 800 numbers that free trade skeptics could call in order to complain to members of Congress. It was estimated that as a result of such mobilization efforts, the steelworkers union alone sent 160,000 handwritten letters to Congress.[10]

In response, the Clinton Administration, through the New Democrat group known as the Democratic Leadership Council, spent $200,000 on television spots touting the virtues of free trade and the need to reinstate the fast-track process. AIG, a leading international insurance and finance company, purchased advertisements in the Washington political trade press (*CQ Weekly*, *National Journal*, and *Roll Call*, among others) that sought to equate "fast-track" with growth in exports.

But the last-minute reply was not effective. Unlike the

labor effort, which pushed a simple yet compelling message, the free trade argument was lengthy and cumbersome. It was informative in a way, but not a ready-made explanation that a wavering member of Congress could use back home with his or her constituency. In the end, free trade advocates were unable to redefine the terms of the debate. An exasperated President Clinton conceded to a small group of Democratic party supporters: "According to every public opinion survey, I have completely failed to convince a substantial majority of American people of the importance of trade to our economic development."[11]

For observers of the political process, the question arising from this and other contemporary cases is "What does all this activity mean for American democracy?" Is this new group activism the flowering of representative democracy or a fundamental threat to the integrity of our system? Has a plural society, long thought to characterize American life, been replaced by an age in which noisy group interests overwhelm the political system and dominate public policy making?

To address these questions, we study four recent examples of interest group politics: Clinton's effort at comprehensive health care reform, the Republican Contract with America "devolution revolution," telecommunications reform, and recent attempts to reform Medicare and health care insurance. Running through each of these case studies are a series of important questions: How do groups attempt to influence the political process? What lobbying strategies work? How are new communications technologies affecting the way groups behave? What types of interests are best able to take advantage of changes in the political process? In particular, given the glut of information that washes over citizens and decision makers alike, how do interest groups cut through the noise to make their case most effectively?

Increasingly, we see large, well-funded interests crowding out smaller consumer groups, public interest groups, political parties, and even broad-based social movements. As always, some groups are better organized and have access to better resources than others. In an era of instantaneous communications and an onslaught of information, financial resources are more important than ever. From the AARP to Zenith, major interests can commission polls and research studies, run ads, sponsor phone banks, contribute generously to charities, and organize affiliated tax-exempt groups. All of this puts them in a strong position to influence policy making. In many respects, this new group activism deeply affects—and may even threaten—the viability of representative government.

Our book consists of three parts. Part 1 lays out our theory of interest group activism. Chapter 2 examines how interest groups develop influence in contemporary politics. Drawing on several different literatures, both within and beyond the study of political communication, we suggest that the key to power today is the ability to generate and repeat a consistent set of attractive, coherent messages. In an era of new communications technologies and information overload, the ability to deliver a message has become increasingly dependent on the ability to pay for that delivery as well as to create content. Well-organized, well-funded interest groups are in an advantageous position to define problems, set agendas, and construct alternatives that serve their own policy goals. Indeed, the ability to develop persuasive story lines often determines the success of a group in influencing politics and policy making.

Chapter 3 builds on this framework by reviewing the tactics of influence in a high-tech era. Groups have advanced beyond traditional public relations strategies to large-scale advocacy, elite advocacy, grassroots organizing,

independent expenditures, issue advocacy, and stealth campaigns. Each of these tactics allows groups to generate
themes that advance their positions in policy debates. In
part, it is the development of new communications technologies that has widened the gap between rich organizations and all others.

In part 2, we present four case studies of group activism:
the comprehensive Clinton health care reform effort
(chapter 4), the devolution movement and tort reform
(chapter 5), telecommunications reform (chapter 6), and
Medicare and limited health care reform (chapter 7). Using
interviews, internal memos, polling results, news reports,
and other sources, along with examinations of focus groups,
ads, phone bank operations, and mailings, we investigate
how organized interests have conveyed particular points of
view as policy making unfolded. From the framing of messages to the substance of communications, we assess what
worked, what didn't, and why.

In these analyses, we use the differing politics of the four
cases to see how major changes in interest groups and their
political environment over the past decade have affected
groups and public policy making.[12] In a period of just a few
years, we have seen a historic change in party control of
Congress, major alterations in the personal popularity of
leading public officials such as President Clinton and
Speaker Newt Gingrich, and a remarkable shift in the
overall political agenda from government regulation to
market-based policy making. The cases that we have studied represent invaluable opportunities to see how groups
define the issues, set the policy agenda, and influence decisions on Capitol Hill.

Part 3 steps back from the details of these case studies
and looks at the broader ramifications of our study. In
chapter 8, we discuss how some interest groups have

achieved great power in contemporary politics. We look at alternative sources of power in American politics, from elections, political parties, and social movements to journalists and government officials, and show how interest groups have gained power at the expense of these countervailing political institutions. Based on our analyses, we argue that it is no longer clear in all circumstances that narrow groups can be overcome at election time, be beaten by more broad-based organizations such as political parties or social movements, or be held in check by journalists or government officials.

We conclude our book in chapter 9 by discussing the larger lessons of interest-group politics for American politics. In a world of information overload, we argue that moneyed interests are able to construct stories more clearly and effectively than poorer organizations. In a policy-making game that rests heavily on paid media, public relations, and targeted communications, well-heeled interests from corporations and trade groups to labor unions are going to fare much better than small interests. The paradox of the contemporary period is that the heavenly chorus of interest groups sings with more of an upper-class accent than ever before. By running stealth campaigns, relying on new technologies, and obtaining favorable news coverage, these affluent interests raise a host of problems for American democracy.

Part I

New Arrangements for the Same Old Songs

Chapter Two

Interests and Influence

Always a Story to Tell

No company illustrates the new "sound of money" better than General Electric, the $91 billion corporate giant whose products and services range from consumer goods, plastics, and broadcasting to pollution control, banking, stock brokerage, and jet engines. As described compellingly by author William Greider, GE is, with its wide array of concerns, "a conglomerate that functions as a ubiquitous political organization."[1] So far-reaching is the corporation's stake in different economic sectors that its "bottom line depends directly on the political outcomes—not just now and then, but *continuously*, every day, every year," Greider writes.[2]

GE's political and charitable activities range far and

wide: lobbying by two dozen Washington representatives; contributions from an active, well-financed political action committee; philanthropy through tax-exempt foundations in support of colleges, policy-oriented advocacy groups, and mainstream think tanks such as the Brookings Institution and the American Enterprise Institute; sponsorship of television public affairs shows such as the *McLaughlin Group* and *Meet the Press*; membership on the Business Roundtable, dozens of trade associations, and numerous ad hoc coalitions; policy advocacy through The Committee on the Present Danger (defense issues) and the Center for Economic Progress and Employment (product liability); general image advertising; and corporate ownership of the NBC television network and its cable subsidiaries, the financial channel CNBC and the news channel MSNBC.[3]

A corporation such as GE both represents and, perhaps more importantly, claims to represent millions of individuals, from its own employees and subcontractors to stockholders and communities in which plants are located. As secretary of defense and former chairman of General Motors Charles Wilson put it famously in 1957, "What's good for the country is good for General Motors, and vice-versa."[4] Ditto for GE in the 1990s.

General Electric is not alone in their efforts to influence the public dialogue. Organized interest such as Philip Morris, the AFL-CIO, and the Sierra Club have lobbied extensively inside Washington's corridors of power. Such interests (or their surrogate PACs, which donate to political candidates) have contributed hundreds of millions of dollars to congressional candidates and political parties. Still, the amounts spent on campaign contributions reflect only a part of the expenditures made by these interests as a whole. For example, in 1993–94, grassroots lobbying came to about $790 million, and corporate image advertising amounted to about a billion dollars.[5] These figures compare to the record profligacy of the 1996 elections, which absorbed a total of a billion dollars for all races. Thus, although tobacco companies contributed almost $7 million in political contributions to the major parties in 1995–96, they spent more than $4.8 billion in advertising and promotion during 1995 alone.[6] And much of that went not to sell cigarettes, but to burnish the image of the tobacco industry and to promote their complex set of public policy messages.

The politics of influence has never been cheap, but as increasing numbers of interests enter the fray and as the stakes of decisions reach historic proportions (for example, telecommunications reform touched about one-seventh of the total gross domestic product), the need to make clear and convincing arguments has never been greater. In the context of multiple, interested voices and a subsequent overload of information,[7] moneyed interests, ranging from tobacco companies to Archer Daniels Midland to health insurers, are able to convey their messages more clearly and effectively than less affluent groups or organizations. This capacity, we argue, often changes the nature of policy debates and allows those who control the narrative, in both public and private arenas, to determine the policy.

To be sure, political parties, populist movements, and public-interest groups can communicate coherently and powerfully at times. Each has experienced some real success in shaping both policy agendas and final decisions. In the end, however, those interests that can *generate and repeat a consistent set of messages*, publicly and privately, are most likely to define problems, set agendas, and construct alternatives that serve their own needs. Increasingly, the ability to generate and repeat messages depends on huge amounts of money.

Changes in the World of Interest Groups: More Voices and More Uncertainy

Writing in 1960, political scientist E. E. Schattschneider combined two insights to produce a powerful argument about interest group activity. First, dominant interests wish to restrict the scope of conflict while prospective losers often seek to expand it, with each side understanding that *"the definition of alternatives is the supreme instrument of power."*[8] Second, the struggle to define alternatives is not a fair fight. Rather, "the flaw in the pluralist heaven is that the heavenly chorus sings with an upper-class accent" when alternatives are ultimately selected.[9]

Although some observers have found "signs of . . . decline of special interest influence,"[10] such observations depend on emphasizing contests over the distribution of tangible policy benefits, such as military contracts, bridges, and dams. If we look beyond governmental largesse— toward regulation, the devolution of authority, and the privatization of governmental functions—there is little question that the politics of organized interests have involved more groups in more arenas since Schattschneider made his observations several decades ago. Uncertainty over policy outcomes and over the potential for groups to influence results has increased, in part because, during an era of tight budgets, more and more policy decisions create winners and losers, rather than simply distribute particular benefits.

In looking at changes in the world of interest groups, various general trends seem well established:

1) *The number of organized groups has increased steadily* over the past forty years, as illustrated by the more than four-fold growth of associations,[11] as well as a great increase

in public interest groups and professional organizations.[12] Although not all segments of society have shared in this trend, interest groups are more representative of the country than in previous decades.

2) *Organized interests have engaged in more activities seeking to influence governmental policies*, but in general, until recently, these have been "more of the same" techniques that have been used for decades, such as establishing personal ties and testifying at congressional hearings.[13]

3) *Organized interests and government decision makers share needs for high-quality information, both about policy alternatives and political prospects*. In a complex policy-making environment, "interest groups find themselves dependent upon government to obtain the information they so desperately need to effectively pursue their goals"; at the same time, there is "an increased congressional dependency upon interest groups for information."[14]

4) *The distinction between "inside" lobbying of members of Congress and "outside" strategies based on grassroots mobilization has diminished, largely due to technology*. Although differences remain between the "old-breed" lobbying of insider access and a "new breed" that emphasizes public relations techniques directed at the general public,[15] communications technologies frequently blur the boundaries. Consider, for example, the sophisticated work of the Thursday Group, a coalition of business associations that met weekly with Rep. John Boehner (R-Ohio), the fourth-ranking GOP leader, whose members "bought television, radio, and newspaper ads, faxed 'action alerts' to their members to stir up calls and letters, and for the tax [cut] bill, even arranged a bulletin board on the Internet."[16]

5) *Organized interests' investments in (mostly incumbent) candidates through political action committees have grown steadily*, and these have served to maintain access and complement

lobbying efforts. Not only have contributions for each election risen past $200 million, but a recent systematic study of PAC decision making concludes that, despite a great diversity among the groups, "most . . . spent their funds in a way that was designed to maintain access to important decisionmakers . . . [which] suggests that most PACs are involved in electoral politics to advance lobbying goals instead of to influence the outcomes of elections."[17] Recent campaigns illustrate that influencing election results and advancing lobbying efforts are difficult to separate in an era of highly partisan, issue-oriented national politics, as witnessed by the AFL-CIO's $35 million largely unsuccessful 1996 campaign against many of the Republican freshmen elected in 1994. Despite intense opposition by labor unions, nearly two-thirds of the targeted freshmen were reelected in 1996.

6) *The regulations designed to limit the ways in which interested money flows to politics have been rendered almost obsolete* by various Supreme Court rulings on soft money, the growth of independent expenditures on campaigns, and increases in issue advocacy advertising. Money in politics has come to resemble a "Wild West" where anything goes. The few rules that are in place are widely flouted, and efforts to limit abuses and reform campaigns have failed to win broad support in Congress.

7) *Business became more politically active during the 1970s and 1980s*, in response to growing government controls and the success of public interest groups in setting the national policy agenda.[18]

8) *Compared to thirty years ago, there are fewer policy monopolies involving cozy triangles among interest groups, bureaucrats, and congressional committees, and more broad, permeable policy communities known as issue networks in which a variety of groups can participate.*[19] Particular groups or coalitions surely desire to create policy monopolies to achieve dominance

and certainty, but most often they have to contend with an array of interests that compose the policy community.[20] Overall, many tight relationships that encompassed large policy domains have loosened over the past fifteen to twenty years[21] to the point at which the system covers many different types of linkages.[22]

9) *More and more decisions are perceived as redistributive (or zero-sum)* in an era of budget deficits and reductions in spending (or in the growth rate of spending). Both within economic sectors (weapons systems and military base closings) and between them (winterization program cutbacks to balance a visitor center's construction in Oregon), competition for scarce resources has increased. Likewise, generations frequently find themselves at odds over entitlements, borrowing, and deficits. Redistributional considerations increase uncertainty over outcomes and bring more players into the game, which further increases uncertainty. The stakes of policy decisions thus may increase for most interests, even as the resource pie shrinks. In addition, regulatory policy decisions can redistribute benefits, even if no governmental spending is at stake.[23]

10) *Proposed large-scale policy changes, such as health care reform, telecommunications regulations, or devolution of responsibilities to the states, increase the stakes of decisions that establish new rules for competition and policy making.* As political scientists Frank Baumgartner and Bryan Jones note, the dynamics of policy making during periods of major change are very difficult to direct.[24] Yet the stakes are extremely high, which encourages myriad interests to seek to affect change, even if their chances are slim and the causal relationships between their efforts and results are tenuous at best.

In short, organized interestes have grown more numerous, more active politically, and more representative of the entire society. Increasingly, they have come to operate in highly uncertain environment—broad policy communities rather than tight relationships in which certain groups could (and did) monopolize decision making. Moreover, the contemporary policy stakes are high, first as a result of budget deficits that have produced, through a series of congressional actions, more zero-sum decisions, and second as large-scale policy change looms on such issues as tort reform, welfare reform, and electric utility deregulation.

The Shift Toward Problem Definition

With all these changes in the world of interest groups, it is little surprise that interest groups have shifted their lobbying strategies. Although organized interests continue to lobby in time-honored ways within the corridors of Washington institutions such as Congress and bureaucratic agencies, they have begun to spend more time shaping public perceptions of problems and political agendas.[25] In addition, they are devoting more and more attention to earlier stages of policy formulation—especially the fundamental defining and redefining of issues. Academic writers Roger Cobb and David Rochefort have noted that narrowing or broadening participation are key goals of activists and organized interests.[26] Indeed, successfully defining conditions as problems (such as smog, learning disabilites, or global warming) often represents the single most important step in changing policies.[27]

Influencing final governmental decisions is ordinarily very difficult for all but a few political players and even fewer of the best-connected interest-group representatives. When major changes occur, especially in an era of divided government, a small "gang" of executive and legislative personnel hammer out the eventual solution.[28] In this situation, access must be limited, or decision making will grind to a halt.

But in the politics of problem definition, everyone can play by calling a press conference, releasing a study, going on a talk show, commissioning a poll, or buying an advertisement. There is no shortage in Washington of well-defined problems or potential solutions. Indeed, the capital is awash in arguments and evidence that seek to define probblems and set agendas. What is more difficult to understand is how certain definitions come to prevail within the context of political institutions that often, though not always, resist the consideration of new—or newly packaged—ideas.

We do have some clues, however. Baumgartner and Jones have sought to study agenda setting within the context of political institutions, both in terms of how items get considered and what implications may flow from agenda change. Issue definitions remain crucial, but they are placed within the framework of "policy image" and "policy venue," both of which have roots in Schattschneider's concept of expanding political conflict to more and more people in order to increase the odds of winning.[29] The construction of policy images, such as those debating whether slowing the growth of Medicare spending reflects an actual cut in the program, lies at the heart of policy formulation. But the search for a hospitable decision-making venue is scarcely less important.

Policy venues can range from the state and federal courts to U.S. Senate committees to state legislatures. They are crucial in understanding how the politics of problem definition and agenda setting relate to political institutions. As has been demonstrated in environmental and agricultural issues, venue change is central to understanding the evolution and impact of issue networks on policy outcomes.[30]

The growth of government has expanded the number of venues, as well as their diversity. Multiple venues offer widely carried opportunities for shaping issues in broader arenas such as elections, or narrower ones such as congressional subcommittees.

As problem definition, agenda status, and venue shopping become increasingly important elements of policy making, organized interests have stepped up their attempts to expand, restrict, or redirect conflict. Consumer and environmental movements of the 1960s often led the way in understanding these elements of political life, leaving business to catch up in the 1970s and 1980s.[31] Based on this development, Jeffrey Berry, a long-time student of public interest groups, has concluded that citizen groups have driven the policy agenda since the 1960s, thus forcing business interests to respond to sets of issues developed by groups such as Common Cause and environmental organizations.[32]

Following on the heels of these agenda successes by public interest groups has been the institutionalization of interests within the government, especially when broad public concerns are at stake.[33] For instance, many of the 1995 battles over the Contract with America placed legislators in sharp conflict with programs supported by members of government agencies, such as the Environmental Protection Agency.

And there's the rub. *As more interests seek to define problems and push agenda items, more messages emanate from more sources.* For threatened interests, whether corporate, environmental, or professional, the decision to "socialize" a conflict requires capturing the public's attention, which becomes more difficult as more groups try to get their messages out. Even Ralph Nader, the past master of using the press to expand the scope of conflict, has recently found it difficult to attract media attention.[34] In 1996, this long-time crusader for safety and environmental issues was forced to run for president as a Green party candidate to generate coverage of his message. Some interests can cut through the cacophony of voices; in particular, those in Schattschneider's "heavenly chorus" can—at a price—get their message across by spending lavishly on public relations campaigns or by buying advertisements. Moreover, if such messages are directed toward legislators who have received substantial campaign contributions from these same interests, they typically reach an audience already inclined toward receptivity.

Shaping Policy in an Uncertain World

The emphasis on problem definition looms large when public policy is on the table. In policy controversies, tremendous uncertainty is unleashed within the political process. Lots of substantive interests are in play, many competing scenarios are put forward, legislative decisions are always contingent, and public policy outcomes are often filled with unanticipated consequences.[35] As cozy policy-making triangles have been replaced by loose, ill-defined policy communities, decision making under conditions of great uncerainty has become more common.[36]

In policy battles, the capacity to obtain information and control its dissemination is the most important political power of all. Political scientist James Thurber makes the Schattschneider-based argument that if participants cannot resolve conflict on their own turf, " 'outsiders' from other committees, agencies, bureaus, groups, the media, or the general public will take the issue away from them."[37] This "scope of conflict" perspective is extremely important to

TABLE 2.1 SCOPE AND IMPACT OF GROUP-RELATED CONFLICT

Number of people/ interests affected	Scope of conflict	
	Narrow	*Broad*
Few	Niche politics (e.g., weapons procurement)	Symbolic politics (e.g., flag-burning amendment)
Many	Policy community politics (e.g., banking)	Public confrontation politics (e.g., abortion)

the dynamics of policy formulation, and a source of the greatest type of uncertainty of all—conflict redefinition, in which new players or new arenas are brought into the conflict.

As shown in table 2.1, there are different types of group conflict centering on two factors: 1) the scope of conflict and 2) the breadth of impact, that is, the number of people and interests affected. In previous decades, interest groups active on weapons procurement could count on the policy conflict being restricted to niche politics, a narrow scope of conflict affecting just a few interests. And an issue such as abortion illustrated the politics of public confrontation, namely a broad conflict affecting many people.

From the standpoint of interest groups, the beauty of these types of controversies was that they were stable and therefore predictable. Conflicts that started out as one type generally stayed in that domain. There were few efforts at conflict redefinition and even fewer cases of successful redefinition.

Today, the situation is radically different. Changes in the contemporary political process give groups more strategic options. Depending on their self-interest, groups can seek to reduce or expand the scope of conflict. At some points in time, it may be advantageous to restrict conflict to small policy niches in which certain interests can dominate. At other times, a group might embrace the competition among many interests in a more open policy community to make their political points. Whatever the policy issue, considerable effort must go into strategic calculations regarding the costs and benefits of changing the scope of conflict.

It is here that policy making is most uncertain. Groups interested in particular issues never know exactly what the venue will be, which factors will shape the institutional arena, or how the conflict will develop. Particular controversies can metamorphose overnight into the realm of symbolism, policy niches, or public confrontation, each necessitating very different kinds of political approaches.

An example of this type of strategic redefinition occurred in the 1980s with savings and loan institutions. The politics of this industry traveled relatively quickly from its traditional low-profile niche to a vigorous debate over its proper role within the financial policy community. By the late 1980s, the conflict broadened as the savings and loan "problem" won the label of a full-fledged "disaster" with a potential $500 billion price tag.[38] At this point, interests far beyond the financial community became involved, especially given the huge budgetary implications of hundreds of billions in bailout funding. However, the complex nature of the problem and the requirement of a timely response discouraged extended public discussion (in contrast to issues such as abortion or gun control, which can generate unlimited debate).

In the wake of the 1989 establishment of the Resolution Trust Corporation, the savings and loan issue moved simultaneously back to the financial policy community and into the realm of symbolism, where electoral politics would sort out the apportionment of blame. More than anything else, the involvement of President George Bush's son, Neil, in a failed savings institution personalized the politics of S&Ls. During the crisis, the contending interests—banks, savings and loans, federal regulators, and other financial actors—had to work through the myriad difficulties of implementing the restructuring of the savings industry in the face of tremendous uncertainty about the strategic arena.[39] Finally, in the 1990s, savings and loan politics returned to conventional policy-community politics, as the banking industry sought to redefine itself in a new financial era.

High Stakes/Great Costs: The Logic of (Seemingly) Exorbitant Lobbying Expenditures

The high stakes of recent policy controversies and the uncertainty under which those battles have taken place have generated incredible amounts of spending on lobbying public officials.[40] Any estimate of the funds expended to affect the outcomes of these broad sets of prospective policy changes—as with the $100 million estimates for health care in 1993–94—is likely to be too low, largely because many corporate interests and trade associations devoted substantial parts of their nonlobbying budgets to defeating the Clinton plan. Although neither health care reform nor telecommunications deregulation fell into the category of "winner-take-all" decisions,[41] both did propose to affect about one-seventh of the national economy (roughly speaking, a trillion dollars for each of them). The stakes were extremely high and perceived as such by virtually all in-volved. And in some instances, the policy stakes reflected an actual "winner-take-all" choice, especially for specific industries, such as medium-sized health insurers, some of which viewed their very survival as at stake in the health care debate. Nor were these policy changes especially un-usual; recent trade policies such as NAFTA, tort reform, and securities and banking legislation all fall into the cat-egory of high-stakes policy decisions, as do continuing ef-forts at electric utility deregulation.

Although some corporate interests (such as Microsoft, prior to intense federal scrutiny in the 1990s) have resisted involvement in Washington politics, there has been a surge of corporate political activity since the late 1970s.[42] As Jef-frey Birnbaum has observed, the growth of corporate (and trade association) lobbying makes good economic sense: "[Even] in relatively small changes to larger pieces of leg-islation . . . big money is made and lost. Careful *investment* in a Washington lobbyist can yield enormous returns in the form of taxes avoided or regulations curbed—an odd negative sort of calculation, but one that forms the basis of the economics of lobbying."[43]

The nature of high-stakes decisions makes such invest-ment almost mandatory, given the potential for tremen-dous gains and losses. In addition, the usual cost-benefit logic that applies to most managerial decisions—lobbying extensively versus building a new plant or embarking on an ambitious new research project—does not apply in high-stakes circumstances, because the potential benefits and/or costs are so great that virtually any expenditure can be jus-tified, even if its chance to affect the outcome is minuscule. Ironically, the need to establish a clear link between a cer-tain lobbying tactic or strategy and some bit of policy suc-cess is not very important, in that a) such linkages are difficult to demonstrate in the best of circumstances and b) a single overall strategy may include myriad tactical initiatives, to the point that objectively assessing the success of individual actions is impossible.

Two implications flow directly from this state of affairs. First, firms and their representatives enter the lobbying fray with high hopes and low expectations. As one lobbyist put it, referring to a major issue, "If I throw in a million here or a million there, I may get a hundred million back. And there are probably enough cases like that so [my clients] keep throwing money in."[44] Second, lobbyists and corporate strategists find such circumstances extremely attractive in that there is virtually no accountability for the way immense amounts of money are spent. Indeed, spending on a host of tactics—from election contributions to insider access to public relations campaigns—may represent a strategy designed as much to protect lobbyists from criticism by their corporate or trade association employers as to influence a given decision. As one veteran Washington representative described such high-stakes maneuvers: "Lots of money is spent externally for internal reasons—to cover your ass. The defense boys are the best in the world at that—of course they live and die on a few contracts."[45]

Vivid examples of the value of spending can be found in *Golden Rule*, a book by Thomas Ferguson that presents an "investment theory" of party politics.[46] According to his perspective, large investors (those who lobby and donate to political parties) hold natural advantages both in acquiring and analyzing information. He posits the control of political parties (and the party system in general) as a goal of these investors, who seek a hefty return on their capital. Even in an era of weak parties, such an interpretation offers real insights, especially given the proliferation of corporate soft money that has flowed to both Republicans and Democrats. Still, major economic interests rarely place all their bets on a single set of institutions, and political parties represent only one option among many within the political marketplace. Interests also will invest directly in individual politicians, through campaign contributions, and in various lobbying initiatives. This is especially true for corporations in concentrated industries, in which investment—by either one firm or a tightly knit trade association—will provide tangible dividends. Moreover, many industries, such as weapons/aerospace, combine the marketing of their products to the government with efforts to influence policy decisions.[47] Boeing and McDonnell-Douglas long have engaged in such activities.

It may be a mistake to make too much of a distinction between an organized interest investing in candidates through contributions, on the one hand, and providing information to elected officials through lobbying, advertising, or public relations campaigns, on the other. Interests employ a wide array of tools in pressing for advantage.[48] Nevertheless, information exchanges between interest groups and legislators can be seen as distinct from the seeking of influence through contributions or favors. One scholar, John Wright, has noted that interests "achieve influence in the legislative process not by applying electoral or financial pressure, but by developing expertise about politics and policy and by strategically sharing this expertise with legislators through normal lobbying activities. . . . [Organized interests] can and do exercise substantial influence even without making campaign contributions and . . . contributions and other material gifts or favors are not the primary sources of interest group influence in the legislative process."[49]

Even if information, and not favors or contributions, reflects the basis for interest group influence, does that mean that money is unimportant? Or that all information is equal? Hardly. Inevitably, some interests have much greater resources to develop information that shapes policy debates. For this reason, a disproportionate share of the policy and political information that is collected reflects the views of well-heeled interests that subsidize think tanks, pay for surveys, and engage public relations firms.[50]

The Crucial Role of Information

Much attention has been placed on the alleged exchange of material benefits between interests and office-holders: interest groups have provided campaign contributions, trips to Palm Springs and other lush resorts, and (formerly) honoraria to legislators in exchange for favorable treatment in the legislative process. Although the impact of these activities has proved difficult to pin down in extensive studies of congressional votes, we occasionally get revealing glimpses of these exchanges in the openly political operations of the agricultural giant, Archer Daniels Midland, whose jets were routinely used to ferry then–Senate Majority Leader Bob Dole (R-Kans) around the country, or in the journal entries of former Senator Bob Packwood (R-Ore.). In his private diary, Packwood made clear connections between contributions he received (such as campaign donations and a job for his spouse) and tax or business provisions he introduced on behalf of outside interests. Moreover, such influence may well exist below the surface of congressional operations, within the confines of informal deliberations in committees, subcommittees, or private conversations.[51]

Without dismissing the importance of corporate investments in political parties and politicians' careers, we emphasize another set of exchanges—the information that passes, almost continually, between legislators (and their staffs) and organized interests. The world of legislative politics is an uncertain one, and reliable information, especially on complex, politically thorny issues, is always at a premium, both for interests and lawmakers. Lobbyists need information that they can glean only from careful monitoring of the legislative process. "Lobbyists," writes Jeffrey Berry, "are the nerve endings of an interest group, [as they] spend most of each day carrying messages back and forth between their environment and their organization."[52]

Information that can be easily obtained is of little worth; in contrast, scarce and (apparently) reliable information in uncertain situations is highly valued. Indeed, uncertainty is the governing condition of much legislative activity, in that agendas, bill content, legislative strategies, constituent responses, and interest group reactions often are unpredictable on a single complex bill, to say nothing of the confusion generated by a host of difficult issues, considered simultaneously.

Although policy expertise is important, other intelligence can be equally useful. In the interaction between interest groups and Congress, there are three types of valuable information: policy, political (reelection), and procedural (internal to the legislative process).[53] Legislators and lobbyists continually attempt to reduce uncertainties by seeking out all of these kinds of information and engaging in long-term relationships to remain well-informed. Lobbyists frequently convey policy and political information to congressional enterprises (made up of the member and staff), and lobbyists will often provide regular communication linkages among a number of members' enterprises.[54]

At the same time, lobbyists garner policy and procedural

information from legislators and staff. In particular, knowledge of key procedural moves can only be obtained from congressional sources near the heart of the legislative process. The mutual, long-term needs of groups and lawmakers to reduce uncertainties often forge strong bonds between them, ties that would be cut if either partner seriously misinformed the other. Such information-based relationships supplement earlier descriptions of associations between lobbyists and legislators, in which organized interests were seen as "service bureaus" that communicated with only those members of Congress who agreed with them.[55]

Traditionally, lobbyists and political scientists have put forward the notion that a lobbyist cannot afford to lie to a legislator (or get caught in a lie). Describing the highly professional California legislature of the 1970s, William Muir concludes: "A lobbyist was welcome to enter any legislative office—unless he had lied, and virtually no lobbyist did that."[56] In a similar vein, Alan Rosenthal emphasized the trusting relationships—personal ties—that form between legislators and lobbyists: "If, through a relationship, a lobbyist proves to be a credible, loyal, empathetic, and reliable person, he or she will have made the grade; the path of direct lobbying will have been made smooth."[57]

In communicating with undecided or opposing lawmakers, however, lobbyists may gain by shading the truth in two distinct ways. First, they simply may exclude pieces of information or alter the truth, somewhere short of flat-out lying. Second, the very act of constructing policy narratives to present a persuasive argument often distorts the information that is being conveyed. Although some strong personal relationships do transcend lobbying, most exist so that information can be conveyed. And that information is interested, even as it must be accurate, roughly speaking. As we shall see, narratives become especially relevant in such a context. The stories that convey the information may make all the difference. Despite general agreement that trusting relationships are important, many lobbyists have great incentives to misrepresent the truth, especially when deception is unlikely to be discovered.[58]

In fact, lobbyists are expected to present information that favors their employers. We argue that shading the facts often comes in the context of storytelling that supports the lobbyist's client, whether as a private anecdote, a dramatic piece of testimony, a well-publicized piece of research, or an oft-repeated advertisement. One recent example of this truth-shading came in the context of congressional debate over "partial-birth" abortions—the term itself a powerful example of the politics of language. When a prominent pro-choice lobbyist admitted he had manufactured figures on the number of such procedures undertaken (he had deliberately underestimated the total), it became a powerful rallying argument for opposition forces.

This kind of information may be difficult to check factually, given the personal or general or contingent nature of the assertion. We could not, for example, know in advance how many individuals would be thrown out of work (or find new jobs) in the United States due to the enactment of NAFTA. So union lobbyists could cite studies and tell stories that maximized the potential impact, even if most objective observers viewed their estimates as exaggerations.

Narratives: How Information Is Put Together into Stories

With information so crucial to lobbying success, it is little wonder that groups devote major efforts to pulling information together into coherent stories. Stories provide a way of organizing diverse information into a form that can easily be understood by a variety of audiences. Writing more than three decades ago, Schattschneider pointed out the importance of audience in establishing the outcome of conflicts between competing interests. He proposed that "the outcome of *every* conflict is determined by the extent to which the audience becomes involved in it" and that "the most important strategy of politics is concerned with the scope of the conflict"—that is, the extent to which the conflict is socialized (broadened) or privatized (narrowed).[59]

If this assumption is even close to being correct, then the relationships between political actors and various audiences lie at the core of understanding who wins and loses in American politics. As issues develop, problems emerge, agendas become established, and alternatives take shape, the linkages between audience and actors are forged through narratives—stories about what is a problem, what the problems look like, and what solutions might exist.[60]

In a 1996 *New Yorker* article, Bill Buford explained the value of stories this way: "stories also protect us from chaos, and maybe that's what we, unblinkered at the end of the twentieth century, find ourselves craving. . . . We have returned to narratives—in many fields of knowledge —because it is impossible to live without them."[61]

No other political figures, not even legislators, have more at stake than lobbyists in polishing policy narratives that will work to their advantage. In an age of instant communications, the ability to package information is a very important skill.[62] The best take on this development comes from Jeffrey Birnbaum's close-up account of contemporary lobbying, as various professionals combine to convey messages that will resonate beyond the Beltway and echo back to Capitol Hill: "There are still plenty of gladhanders and fundraisers. But right behind those classic types of lobbyists are people with more targeted and potentially more potent skills: economists, lawyers, direct-mail and telephone salespeople, public relations experts, pollsters, and even accountants. All these skills play a role in information gathering. . . . [Moreover,] lobbyists see it as their job to persuade lawmakers that voters are on the lobbyists' side. To that end, *Washington has become a major marketing center.*"[63] More generally, Birnbaum argues that due to their pervasiveness, "Lobbyists provide the prism through which government officials often make their decisions."[64]

For elected officials, audiences come in all shapes and sizes; a legislator may pay attention to a few local notables, the district's constituents, a single important organized interest, or a set of political action committee managers. In virtually every instance, the linkage is cemented through a common understanding, based on a narrative that ties the legislator to the audience. Rarely is there a single dominant narrative or one given story that necessarily dictates a legislator's position. Rather, a good tale will include the fodder for an acceptable explanation to given sets of voters or interests. As Richard Fenno points out, a legislator must stockpile many explanations for a whole range of actions, especially votes. "There isn't one voter in twenty thousand who knows my voting record," he quotes one House member, "except on the one thing that affects him."[65]

In a related vein, legislators use stories to think through issues of justice and morality—matters that they may decide to approach head-on. Even sophisticated policy makers, such as lawmakers, process information in truncated form.[66] The virtue of narrative is that it "supplies cognitive shortcuts, provides an organization for the other, more specific organizations of attitudes, and places them in a familiar context. It tells us what items of information are to be treated as evidence and what items are irrelevant. It also invests the information with both meaning and purpose."[67]

Organized interests of all stripes take seriously the task of providing material for congressional explanations. Lobbyists and grassroots activists offer up stories that members can incorporate in their communications with constituents, such as tales of workers denied health benefits. Legislators and their staffers may draw upon public themes articulated by interests through advertisments and public relations campaigns such as "Just Say No" to drugs. To the extent that their stories are adopted, interests tend to claim credit for influencing the policy discourse.[68]

Such a perspective fits with Schattschneider's notion of drawing the audience into a conflict. There always is the possibility that the less powerful can use numbers to counteract position and wealth. Still, narratives are spun out by a wide variety of interests in a crowded and competitive political world. It is this competition that explains why some narratives work while others do not.

A study of the 1992 presidential campaign shows how important narratives have become to electoral communications. Candidates try to build stories that resonate with audiences.[69] For example, Clinton tried to portray himself as caring and compassionate in the face of a deep economic recession. Perot was the bulwark against ballooning government deficits. Bush was the strong leader who had won the Persian Gulf War. Much of campaign strategizing involves efforts to build narratives, tell stories, and control the candidate's overall campaign message in the face of powerful counternarratives from the opposition.

In a policy context, Deborah Stone observes that, in order to cut through the multitude of voices and rhetoric, "causal stories" play an increasingly important role in shaping agendas and making particular decisions.[70] Such stories are usually more specific than the narratives that are put forward to organize the discourse (and structure the conflict) within broad policy communities. Indeed, many causal stories are spun out in relatively private settings of congressional subcommittees or executive agencies, in which sophisticated, complex arguments can be made and understood.

If narratives are powerful, what is the nature of that power? Jay Clayton sees their strength as "not individual but neither . . . precisely collective; it arises from one's participation in established networks of expertise. . . ."[71] Still, many actors and interests participate within dozens, even hundreds, of distinct networks. Participation allows an individual or interest the chance to employ narrative powerfully. All messages are not created—or delivered—equally. Resources are crucial in developing and conveying meaningful communication. Survey research and focus groups help determine what message is most palatable or most powerful. Political consultants, public relations firms, and advertising professionals craft themes that appeal to policy makers, partisans, and the public, though rarely to all simultaneously.

How Narratives Affect the Political Process

In the end, we do not adopt the position that the "only thing left to examine [in policy controversies] are the different stories."[72] Different policies have objective dimensions, and other potential elements of influence, such as campaign contributions, congressional structure, and presidential involvement, that can and do make a difference. Still, the framing of past and future policies remains central to most struggles over important decisions.

In terms of shaping policy making, two types of competition among narratives come into play. First, there are competing "causal stories" that imply every different policy choices on such issues as welfare, violence, and trade. Second, and equally important, are those narratives that socialize (expand) or privatize (limit) the scope of conflict.

Narratives are important on both of these dimensions (causality and socialization of conflict) because they ordinarily mix together empirical and normative elements. Thus, causal stories both "purport to demonstrate the mechanism by which one set of people brings about harm to another set" and "blame one set of people for causing the suffering of others."[73] It is no wonder that so many narratives flow from Washington think tanks with distinct ideological leanings (such as the conservative Heritage Foundation, the libertarian CATO Institute, or the "New Democrat" Progressive Policy Institute). Almost invariably, we get either social science with a point of view (for example, Brookings) or a point of view with some social science trappings (for example, Heritage Foundation). Stripped bare, however, the analyses are both stories in themselves and the grist for many other stories—as with Charles Murray's welfare studies presented in *Losing Ground* and *The Bell Curve* and the many responses inspired by these works.

Lobbyists appeal to legislators and other policy makers because of their preferences for communicating through stories much of the time. Although data and related analyses are plentiful and important, anecdotes often provide both lobbyists and legislators with a way to blend both policy and political information as well as to combine empirical and normative approaches to a problem.[74] Even when addressing elites, interests often condense their stories and present them publicly through advertisements or public relations campaigns.

For example, an advertisement by Business Roundtable (in *Roll Call*, a Capitol Hill newspaper) opposed the expansion of health care benefits to include mental illness. Although this ad, entitled "First, Do No Harm," was directed at the congressional community, rather than toward a mass audience, its story line is simple; it uses medical terminology and the Hippocratic Oath to caution Congress against doing harm. The Roundtable, identified only at the bottom of the ad as the sponsor, borrows the normative authority of the medical profession while noting the empirical accounting ("Price Waterhouse") conclusion that 1.7 million people would lose their employer-sponsored health care benefits under a federal mental health mandate.

The same study predicts a steep rise (8.7 percent) in private health insurance premiums, and the political information warns that most voters would be adversely affected by such a mandate. The message of the ad argues for reforming health care "one step at a time," a policy reference to traditional incrementalism, rather than the more comprehensive approach embodied in the Clinton plan. In this single advertisement, then, the Roundtable conveys policy and political information, with an empirical base and an appeal to values, all in the context of a traditional style of federal policy making.

Especially beneficial for the Business Roundtable in this advertisement is the group's ability to maintain complete control over its message. The price of such control is twofold—the literal expense (about $7,000) and the unknown (but real) costs of presenting the information in a paid format, which dilutes the power of the communication. Overall, however, with its clean style and clear message, the ad does not set off alarm bells of warning among readers, who may well retain the information without recalling its source. In addition, the Business Roundtable presented its mental health coverage message in various other contexts —including distributing copies of the study, having CEOs call their Capitol Hill friends, and obtaining publicity in news stories.

At the same time, the Business Roundtable did have to contend with alternative narratives. Among the most powerful were the highly personal pleas of fiscally conservative senators such as Pete Domenici (R-N.M.) and Alan Simpson (R-Wyo.), whose family experiences with mental illness became dramatic stories in support of federal mandates (see chapter 7).

Still, there are narratives and there are narratives. An extended, complex story spun out at length and in private for a congressional staffer would not work when presented to most average citizens. In these instances, narratives are ordinarily truncated, leaving little more than metaphors or symbolic appeals.[75] As Murray Edelman points out, "Unless their audience is receptive to the depiction of a condition as a problem, leaders and interest groups cannot use it to their advantage."[76] A complex, detailed narrative may, by definition, restrict the receptivity of a mass audience. What remains to be seen, then, is how various audiences are addressed in constructing problems and posing solutions. Indeed, individuals as disparate as independent presidential candidate Ross Perot and political scientist John Kingdon have pointed out that many proposed solutions, such as a balanced-budget amendment or a capital gains tax cut, have often existed long before the problems of the moment were defined.[77]

In hopes of shaping the policy thoughts and political considerations of elites, organized interests fashion their narratives to suit particular audiences. As the scope of the conflict broadens, narratives become less complex and their meaning more frequently is conveyed by metaphor and symbol. What this means is that different policy arenas, as framed by the scope of the conflict and the number of individuals ultimately affected by policy decisions, will encourage distinctive communication patterns. The details and facts of policy and political information conveyed by interests (among other actors) to multiple audiences varies greatly; at the same time, the overall themes of the messages remain at least roughly consistent.

In the symbolic and public confrontation arenas, for example, the audiences are extensive, although only occasionally would the great majority of all citizens be included within the audience (such as during the Great Depression or the Second World War) (see table 2.2). Still, for interests (and leaders) to influence these audiences, they must tap into well-developed societal myths.[78] As John Nelson observes, "political myth-making provides crucial requirements for the virtuous practice of mass persuasion."[79] But tapping into myths does not mean that they cannot be changed. In fact, constructing arguments around myths and metaphors may well encourage changes in their meaning.[80]

In the end, politicians usually employ metaphors that reinforce societal stereotypes, or those held by dominant interests within a policy community.[81] Audiences responded to Ronald Reagan's description of the Soviet Union as an "evil empire" and his desire to protect us with Star Wars technologies. Because of their ability to command the airwaves, presidents possess great advantages in employing such symbols and metaphors, when compared to legislators or lobbyists. On occasion, however, an individual legislator (such as Newt Gingrich on various issues and Bill Bradley on tax reform) can succeed in shaping the nature of a policy debate, as can an interest group (such as the Health Insurance Association of America [HIAA] on health care reform [see chapter 3] or the AFL-CIO on NAFTA), especially

TABLE 2.2 NARRATIVES, INTERESTS, AND THE SCOPE OF
CONFLICT

Number of people/ interests affected	Scope of conflict	
	Narrow	Broad
Few	Niche politics —detailed private narratives —sketchy public narratives —pure political "muscle"	Symbolic politics —truncated narratives —highly public reliance on symbol and myth
Many	Policy community politics —detailed narratives, available to public, but not widely spread —coalitions unified around agreed-upon narratives	Public confrontation politics —combination of detailed narratives (personal lobbying) and truncated narratives (public relations, ads) —highly visible coalitions

when the news media elevate alternative narratives into positions of prominence.

In the area of niche politics, one of the most aggressive players has been Archer Daniels Midland, the agribusiness conglomerate. The company pushes hard in the narrow area of agricultural policy making (such as ethanol subsidies), while also articulating highly public narratives and symbols (based on its "supermarket to the world" theme).

Their tactics stand in stark contrast to the other privately held grain companies, which assiduously avoid public presentations.[82] Some anti-abortion groups and environmental organizations incorporate few private narratives into their lobbying; their narratives remain public, in part because they may be distrusted by their own members if they are seen as offering stories in a context of negotiation.

Conclusion

To summarize our argument, we believe that interest groups use their power to define certain societal conditions as "problems" and particular policy proposals as "solutions." Many of these solutions have been kicking around for years.[83] Policy alternatives are floated, and in the end, a host of forces affect the decision that ultimately is made by Congress. In most analyses, the defining of issues and the shaping of agendas offer the greatest opportunities for interested narratives to affect policy making.[84] In the era of congressional committee government and closed policy subsystems that ran from the late 1930s into the 1960s, crucial decisions on specific alternatives and final passage of bills were often made far from the light of day.[85] Schattschneider, writing in 1960, could thus assume that expanding the scope of the conflict to bring the audience into the policy-making process ordinarily would benefit the mass of citizens at the expense of organized interests who labored with quiet success in the corridors of power.

Observing the policy-making process in the post-reform Congress of the 1980s and 1990s, however, we argue that Schattschneider's emphasis on expanding the scope of conflict, while still relevant, plays out in a very different way. *Conflict expansion does not necessarily redound to the benefit of the general public.* As budgetary concerns grow in significance, interests put forward highly public narratives that compete with each other to fashion future visions that can only be regarded as speculative. What will happen if NAFTA is adopted? What will be the upshot of a balanced budget? How can welfare reform usefully proceed? What will happen in the wake of telecommunications or electric utility deregulation? Even the best policy analysis can take us only a few steps down the road to answering these questions, yet all participants—legislators, executives, lobbyists, and journalists—want more complete articulations of future outcomes. In its myriad forms, narrative can satisfy our yearnings for certainty, even when we know that unanticipated (and unanticipatable) consequences will overtake the predictions and reassurances implicit in most story lines.

When the scope of the conflict is expanded, especially on high-stakes issues, well-financed interests are in the best position to tell their stories, over and over again, to a series of overlapping audiences. The old trusting relationship between lobbyist and legislator remains important, but so too is the overlay of public narratives—about medical savings accounts, the virtues of deregulation, or the importance (or danger) of free trade. Moneyed interests can tell their tales, through anecdotes, scientific studies, or symbolic appeals, again and again. Schattschneider's heavenly chorus has become more vocal, operates in more venues, and sings with more sophisticated harmony. As we demonstrate in the next few chapters, much of its influence rests upon the power of narrative to organize information in ways that ultimately serve some interests at the expense of others, even as the stories tell a tale of public benefit and a better future for all.

Chapter Three

═══════

The Heavenly Chorus Goes High-Tech

In 1992, a "pro-family" lobbying organization called the Christian Action Network (CAN) had become upset about the liberal drift of social policy in the United States. Led by activist Martin Mawyer, the group decided to take action. For too long, it thought, conservatives had sat on the sidelines while the country had gone downhill. What troubled group members the most was the "gay rights" political agenda that had emerged in preceding decades. A variety of organizations and individuals were devoting themselves to an agenda that, in the eyes of Mawyer, included: 1) creating job quotas for homosexuals; 2) providing special civil rights laws for homosexuals; and 3) allowing homosexuals in the U.S. Armed Forces. None of these were good policies, according to the advocacy organization.

Most galling, though, were the specific efforts Governor Bill Clinton, then the Democratic candidate for president, was making to appeal to gay men and lesbians. Convinced it was time to "take a stand," CAN decided to inform the voting public about Clinton's support for a gay rights agenda. The organization put together a television ad entitled "Clinton's Vision for a Better America," which was broadcast in the fall of 1992 at least 250 times in 24 major cities across the country. Along with direct mail letters, op-ed columns, and newspaper advertisements, this commercial condemned Clinton and his running mate Al Gore for supporting "radical" homosexual rights. Featuring images of the two Democratic candidates in sequence with pictures of young men wearing chains and leather marching in a Gay Pride parade, the ad concluded by asking, "Is this your vision for a better America?"

None of the group's $2 million in expenditures that year was publicly disclosed because the group did not register as a political action committee (PAC). Technically, CAN considered itself an educational organization, not an electioneering group that advocated the defeat of particular candidates. The extent of the "public education" campaign came to light only after the Federal Election Commission, the government agency charged with enforcing campaign finance laws, sued CAN for failure to register as a PAC. Subsequently, a federal court judge in Virginia threw out the case as an unconstitutional infringement on the First Amendment right to free speech.[1]

In adopting a public appeal approach, the Christian Action Network typifies group lobbying strategies that have become popular in recent years. The proliferation of communications options, including phone banks, desktop publishing, advertising, 800 numbers, and the Internet, has expanded the tactical possibilities available to organized interests. These technologies give groups much more sophisticated tools with which to control the content, focus, and timing of their messages. At the same time, because of their considerable expense, high-tech strategies are not equally available to all organizations. Simply put, some interests have greater access to sophisticated communications technologies than do others, and these differences can have profound consequences for the abilities of groups to generate narratives that play to their advantage in public debates.[2]

This chapter looks at the sophisticated, high-tech advocacy tactics that have been used extensively in the 1980s and 1990s, as structural changes in the political system and the development of communications technologies have dramatically expanded the lobbying options facing interest groups. Should they stay inside and lobby public officials directly? Should they expand the scope of conflict to involve a larger number of political players? Should they use outside strategies to leverage their inside game? In the current world of policy making, these decisions are critical. Timely choices by industry groups, for example, can make the difference between millions (even billions) saved or spent to satisfy new industry regulations. As noted earlier, with the costs of government mandates imposed on the private sector, it has become cheaper for many interests to spend large amounts of money on lobbying, broadly defined, than it would be to pay the costs imposed by government rules.

Public Relations

One time-honored method of playing the Washington influence game is to hire public relations consultants. A number of political firms specialize in image enhancement and framing policy options. These companies feature well-connected lawyers, publicists, and former White House staffers and members of Congress who can help open the right doors. If you need an entrée to key members of Congress, public relations companies offering "strategic planning" services can make the introduction. Or if you have an image problem, these organizations can use both time-honored and new communications technologies to develop favorable story lines for your company.

Former members of Congress are ideal public relations consultants because of their particular combination of legislative connections and expertise at how to frame arguments that will be persuasive with lawmakers. Former representatives understand how the legislative process works, know who the key players are, and realize what is the best way to influence current legislators. It is not surprising, given this situation, that a large number of former members—from House Speaker Thomas Foley to Senator Bob Packwood—have served either as registered or unregistered lobbyists after they left office.[3]

Burson Marsteller is an example of a well-known public relations firm specializing in insider political clout. It is a New York–based company whose clients are a who's who of private corporations and foreign governments. For one customer, the Argentine government, its mission was to make Argentina look stable politically so that foreign investors would put money into the country. As part of this effort, the company used "press kits, direct mailing, press/media tours of Argentina, visits with editors, lunches with business groups, and financial seminars." The fee for this successful promotion was $800,000.[4]

Private corporations also draw on this kind of expertise. Public relations firms help an organization set up interviews, place stories in leading newspapers, and develop mailing circulars. They put together ads designed to improve the organization's public image. This allows the company or trade group to attract favorable news coverage and get particular narratives out before the American public.

A classic illustration of successful image enhancement over a long period of time is the tobacco industry.[5] For years, tobacco companies have relied on well-connected agencies in order to sway reporters, run ads, sponsor sporting events, and underwrite cultural activities. Through its unique combination of public relations and philanthropy, tobacco has been more single-minded in its pursuit of public goodwill than perhaps any other industry. In 1997 alone, the top five tobacco companies spent an estimated $30 million on lobbying.[6] Even this sum, however, pales before the industry's public relations and litigation expenditures, which are tied directly to its lobbying efforts.

Philip Morris, for example, has sponsored a wide range of events including tennis tournaments and automobile races. The company has contributed generously to a range of philanthropic causes. It runs ads featuring company efforts to make the world a better place. It has been a leading underwriter of operas, museums, and theater productions. In 1995 alone, Philip Morris, Brown & Williamson, and R. J. Reynolds gave over $265,000 to the American Red Cross as part of tobacco's long-term goodwill campaign. Perhaps it was no accident that the head of the Red Cross was Elizabeth Dole, the wife of Senate Majority Leader Robert Dole, the front-runner for the 1996 Republican presidential nomination.

At the same time, Philip Morris and other industry groups engaged in traditional lobbying tactics. In 1997, tobacco companies were the top "soft money" contributors to the national parties, giving nearly $2 million to the Republican and Democratic national committees for party-building activities. Of this total, $1.6 million went to Republicans and around $400,000 was given to Democrats. Philip Morris led the pack, so to speak, among individual tobacco companies with party contributions of $794,500. The industry also contributed hundreds of thousands of dollars directly to congressional candidates around the country.

The results of these activities speak for themselves. Until the recent sea charges in tobacco politics, and despite overwhelming evidence about the health risks of smoking, government policy continued to protect tobacco interests on everything from farm subsidies to Food and Drug administration regulation. Philip Morris has combined campaign contributions to key legislators with philanthropy and public relations campaigns in order to maintain its advantages in the public policy area. Only in the last few years has "Big Tobacco," as the industry's largest players are known, begun to suffer regulatory setbacks.

Ironically, it was the defection of one of tobacco's own producers, Bennet LeBow of the Liggett Group, that allowed regulators dramatically to scale back tobacco advertising and philanthropy. According to a controversial 1997 agreement between the industry and 40 state attorneys general around the country, no longer would tobacco companies be allowed to advertise on television or to target young people in promotional campaigns, or be shielded from claims that tobacco is an addictive drug that causes heart disease and death. Even Joe Camel, the cherished marketing icon for Big Tobacco, would be retired based on the agreement.

Even with these new restrictions, tobacco remains among the most heavily subsidized sectors in American agriculture thanks to its longtime public relations efforts. Critics of the agreement received new ammunition when the 1997 balanced budget agreement incorporated language written by tobacco companies allowing them to deduct settlement costs associated with the agreement. "The industry wrote it and submitted it, and we just used their language," explained Kenneth Kies, staff director of the Joint Congressional Committee on Taxation.[7] If implemented, this clause could amount to as much as $140 billion in tax savings for the industry. Once brought to light, the deduction was eliminated from the legislation. Still, the creation of this special deduction provides compelling evidence that tobacco is not dead yet, and that future years will be busy ones indeed for industry lobbyists and their opponents.

Large-Scale Issue Advocacy Advertising

Another way to influence the public policy is through large-scale issue advocacy advertising. Issue advocacy is not a new phenomenon. More than eighty years ago, Senator Charles Thomas decried ads by the sugar lobby that appeared during congressional tariff deliberations.[8] In 1936, commercials run during *The Ford Sunday Evening Hour* bitterly protested Roosevelt's proposal to establish a Social Security system. In 1950, the American Medical Association fought against President Harry Truman's health care plan by placing ads in 10,000 newspapers, 30 national magazines, and on 1,000 radio stations.

More recently, Mobil attracted attention when it ran issue advocacy ads against President Carter's energy program.[9] Ten years ago, the nuclear power industry developed a $30 million television ad barrage against proposed restrictions. Beginning in 1992, several right-to-life organizations broadcast ads emphasizing an anti-abortion stance and nonabortion alternatives to unwanted pregnancies. The acrimonious 1993 debate over the ratification of the North America Free Trade Agreement (NAFTA) generated extensive advertising campaigns from competing forces.

What started as a trickle of ads over the past several decades has become a torrent on almost every topic. In the last few years, groups interested in health care, tort reform, term limits, global warming, and tobacco regulation, among other issues, have filled the airwaves with commercials promoting their point of view. Once the exception more than the rule, targeted television ads represent the latest escalation in public lobbying on policy issues.

One reason why issue advocacy has expanded is that interest groups have learned how to evade campaign finance disclosure laws. According to current Federal Election Commission rules and court decisions, unless a group runs ads or produces material that expressly advocates "vote for (or against) Representative Smith," it is not required to register as a political action committee. Emboldened by the failure of the FEC lawsuit brought against CAN, a wide variety of interests spanning the political spectrum have used the loophole of providing "public education" to influence the political dialogue without any disclosure of their efforts.

Recognizing that the post-Watergate system of campaign rules had been gutted, the AFL-CIO announced early in the 1996 presidential campaign that it would spend up to $35 million running ads in the districts of Republican members of Congress who opposed labor objectives. Even though these ads would be broadcast in the run-up to the election and would mention the names of the Republican representatives along with unfavorable commentary on their voting patterns, the AFL-CIO declared these expenditures as issue advocacy and therefore not subject to federal disclosure rules. In response, the Coalition, a consortium of 35 business groups including the U.S. Chamber of Commerce, National Restaurant Association, and National Association of Manufacturers, said it would raise $17 million for a pro-business advocacy campaign to defend these Republican incumbents. Although the group ultimately fell far short of its fund-raising target, its ads were not subject to federal campaign laws requiring detailed disclosure of contributors because the activity too fell under the guise of public education as opposed to electoral advocacy.

The chief virtue of public advocacy ads is that groups are able to frame policy battles and develop narratives in ways that advantage themselves. Unlike interview news and shows, which are journalist-controlled, ads are interest-controlled. Interest groups understand that ads are the most reliable means of conveying political messages because they control the content and timing of the message. Television appeals allow the presentation of unmediated messages directly to the viewing public.

Reliance on the news to fight symbolic policy battles is risky because reporters are professional skeptics who can not be counted on to convey a group's perspective. Authors from Thomas Patterson to James Fallows have noted how cynical journalists have become in the contemporary period and how this deeply rooted cynicism skews press coverage in a direction that exudes suspiciousness about any political organization.[10] In this situation, it makes more sense for interested groups to dictate their messages directly, rather than to communicate through the intermediary of news reporters.

The biggest problem of managing the news is that coverage does not always occur at the time necessary to further group objectives. Timing is everything in politics. Groups in the middle of political battles need to make strategic moves on the turn of a dime. Getting a reporter to write a favorable story a week too late will not advance group interests. Organizations require timeliness and repetition in their political messages for them to be most effective. News coverage consists of a one-shot occurrence, which often has modest impact. Paid advertising allows for repetition of a message, which enhances its effect and reduces the need for precise timing.

There are several possible ways for large-scale advocacy campaigns to be successful. The classic avenue is to influence citizens at the grassroots level.[11] If ordinary folks accept key points in the group message and act on those beliefs, grassroots mobilization allows groups to convey their viewpoint to elected officials via citizens. Traditional discussions of outsider campaigns indeed emphasize citizens as the key target of group influence.

But there are several other important audiences for grassroots campaigns. One is Washington officials, who develop their own impression about the policy under consideration. Even if citizens themselves are not swayed by grasssroots appeals, elites can perceive that there is a groundswell of support or opposition to particular proposals. For example, congressional adoption of Reagan's economic program of tax cuts and spending restrictions in 1981 arose because elites believed ordinary citizens supported Reaganomics, despite evidence that the programs were flawed.[12] Leadership actions that carry the force of law have a powerful impact even if they are based on lawmakers' misperceptions.

In addition, grassroots campaigns can be powerful if they

influence media reporters. Public policy making depends heavily on the way options are framed and particular story lines are generated. Although there has been little attention paid to the influential role of the media in constructing policy frames, news coverage plays a very important role in how policy debates get defined. Impressions of policy alternatives can be shifted substantially through coverage that invokes potent symbols or memorable narratives.

Despite—or because of—their proliferation, many policy advocacy campaigns do not succeed. In the abortion area, for example, the news coverage that ensued following the airing of pro-life commercials was neither extensive nor favorable to the groups running the ads. The press characterized the commercials as self-interested and politically suspect, both fatal flaws in shaping public opinion.

The general ineffectiveness of past advocacy advertising has led to the view that these types of ads never will be influential. Interest groups that run ads have clear partisan objectives and therefore are not seen as credible by reporters, legislators, or the public. Furthermore, policy advertising is tricky because of its multiple audiences—opinion leaders such as columnists, elected officials, grassroots activists, and the general public, each of which may be affected differently by the same ad. Few interest groups have sufficient financial resources to be taken seriously in advocacy advertising. In general, the amount of money spent on policy advertising pales in comparison to the $30 or $40 million per candidate spent on ads in recent presidential general elections or the $500 million IBM spends to market its products. Yet as we demonstrate later in this book, several recent advocacy campaigns on health care and telecommunications have yielded major victories for private sector groups. Equally important, perhaps, they have been *perceived* as highly successful.

Elite Advocacy Advertising

Not all advocacy campaigns are aimed at general-circulation outlets. Indeed, many are designed explicitly for the elite policy communities. For example, large corporations such as Lockheed and Boeing commit millions of advertising dollars to Washington publications, such as *Roll Call*, *National Journal*, or *CQ Weekly* even though few individual readers of these magazines are in the market for a "next generation airplane." That fact notwithstanding, these outlets attract major advertisers that run ads extolling policy positions because their readers are likely to include key journalists, members of Congress, influential committee staff members, and Washington bureaucrats.

A central point of elite advocacy advertising is that products are not directly pushed.[13] Rather, some public policy goal is presented that furthers the organization's long-term interests. For example, General Electric long has touted a strong defense as crucial to the country's well-being. This strategy is popular among well-heeled interests, such as corporations and trade associations. As shown in the next chapter, there was an increase in 1993 and 1994 in policy-related advertising expenditures on health care issues as groups sought to have their voices heard on the controversial Clinton reform package. More generally, interests have begun to advertise on specific policy decisions, such as granting "fast-track" trade negotiation authority to the president.

Committing substantial funds to advertise in elite outlets reflects several considerations. The most important is the number and type of readers. At first blush, readership numbers in these Washington publications cannot be very comforting to corporate ad directors. *CQ Weekly* has a subscription base of around 20,000, while the *National Journal* has a base of 6,714.[14] At one to two dollars per copy for each spot, ads in these publications are quite expensive. But each issue is passed around, to be read by several individuals (say, within a congressional office). The *National Journal* claims that each of its issues is perused by more than six readers, beyond the initial subscriber. In addition, both *CQ Weekly* and the *National Journal* report that their respective readerships spend more than an hour with each issue.

Advertising directors at these outlets perceive advertisers as being interested in developing a particular theme within their respective advocacy strategies. One example cited was the close connection between individual retirement accounts (IRAs) and ads run by Merrill Lynch. Former *CQ Weekly* ad director Bob Wallace stated that "IRAs as an issue was owned by Merrill Lynch." The policy niche helped the company push a specific idea while still publicizing Merrill Lynch's general virtues as an investment firm.

In this regard, Merrill Lynch illustrates the value of advocacy campaigns targeted to policy elites. Its Washington-based government relations staff has sought to deal with the changing Congress through a set of consistent, interpretative messages designed to get its point out to all members of Congress. Merrill Lynch is especially keen on conveying its pro-investment point of view to those legislator who have just arrived in the institution because those are the people who often are most open to new ideas.

A representative from the American Association of Retired Persons (AARP) noted that her organization considers advertising one tool among many. The problem is in deciding which tool to apply. Advertising, she states, "gives us some visibility and provides some talking points [arguments the group wants to stress].[15] At the same time, AARP's broad and varied membership keeps the organization from becoming a significant player in the advocacy

advertising game. Because of its heterogeneous membership, it sometimes is hard for AARP to take a strong lobbying stance.

The question remains why organizations advertise in
these types of elite publications. As the AARP representative put it, ads are only one tool among many available to
interest groups. John Kingdon's perspective on policy formation may offer one clue in explaining long-term issue
advertising. Kingdon views public policy making as composed of three distinct streams: political, policy, and problem streams.[16] According to his model, each stream runs
independently for the most part. As a result, solutions from
the policy stream often are not attached to particular issues
from the problem stream. For example, Merrill Lynch's
consistent backing of expanded IRAs helped keep that alternative alive, regardless of what the "problem stream"
produced. Merrill Lynch hoped to attach IRA legislation
to whatever issue floated down the stream, a hope that was
fulfilled in 1997 when the balanced budget agreement expanded IRA eligibility and developed a new retirement account called the Roth IRA, and therefore created new
business opportunities for the firm.

Adopting an advertising strategy should yield some type
of return, although the immediate impact may be nil or
impossible to assess. Given their modest circulation levels,
ads in *CQ Weekly* and *National Journal* are expensive. In
1997, *CQ Weekly* charged $11,000 for a single full-page,
four-color ad. The rate for a similar ad in the *National
Journal* was $9,500. Thirteen ads in either of these elite
journals would cost at least $130,000, the equivalent of
twenty-six $5,000 political action contributions or the an-
nual salary of a full-time lobbyist. But given the high stakes
of major policy decisions for their industry, elite journal
advertising is cheap for affluent interests.

A study of 898 advocacy ads run in the *National Journal*

and *CQ Weekly* from 1991 to 1993 revealed that the heavenly chorus of elite advertisers was tilted in a corporate, upper-class direction.[17] There was a complete void of public interest causes save for occasional ads from Planned Parenthood or anti-abortion groups. Most advertisements were run by corporate sponsors and were designed to influence specific policy decisions. Many of the advocacy ads were targeted at marketing specific products such as weapons systems. In addition, there was a substantial amount of advertising that simply attempted to enhance the image of the sponsoring organization. For example, Anheuser Busch purchased ads that spoke of its efforts to reduce underage drinking. In terms of specific industries, the most frequently run ads were placed by the defense and space industries (32 percent), the telecommunications industry (23 percent), and the finance and insurance industries (17 percent).

Various industries tend to use elite journals for different purposes. For example, the defense and space industry advertise primarily for the purpose of government marketing. Ninety percent of ads in this area fall within this general purpose, with many of the ads focusing on specific weapons systems such as the V-22 Osprey or the X-30 Space Plane. In contrast, the communication industry uses ads to promote private marketing strategies and to generate goodwill through public service advertisements. The finance and health industries focused more than 60 percent of their ads on specific legislation or general policy issues.

These results demonstrate two key points. At least in the realm of inside-the-beltway policy journals, pluralism is not the operational framework of issue advocacy. Rather, organized interests with the most resources are coming to the table. Put purely in investment terms, many corporate interests see a rich payoff in elite advertising. A million-dollar investment in a plant and equipment might produce an annual return of 10 or 15 percent, which is equal to $100,000 to $150,000. Alternatively, an investment in issue advocacy may net the company $10 million through a tax break, a subsidy, or an advantage in a competitive marketplace. Given these numbers, it is no surprise that companies such as Merrill Lynch and McDonnell-Douglas spend nearly $200,000 apiece annually on ads in Washington "trade journals" such as *Roll Call* or *CQ Weekly*.

Second, those interests employ ads as just one portion of an overall strategy that includes direct lobbying. Those industries that had the most advertisements also had the highest total number of Washington lobbyists. Regular advertisers in *National Journal* and *CQ Weekly* report that they often provide lobbyists with copies of their ads so that these materials can be given to staff and legislators in personal meetings. As Congress has become more decentralized, even fragmented, issue advocacy has become more common. One recent study concludes that structural changes in the legislature are "forcing groups to cast a wider net in order to interact with all legislators who wield some power over policy or relevance to the groups."[18] In the end, most affluent interests and their lobbyists use inside and outside techniques as complementary parts of an overall communications strategy.

Grassroots Organizing

According to Thomas Railback (R-Ill.), former-representative-turned-lobbyist, "the most effective lobby campaigns involve the local constituency. . . . If you get a letter from a constituent, you pay attention. He is not an outsider. He is somebody who votes for or against you."[19] Any number of Washington groups use tools such as direct mail, phone banks, and broadcast technologies to mobilize the grass roots and convey well-honed, if indirect, messages to legislators. The reason is simple. Constituents have a degree of credibility that no Washington lobbyist can match. They are not hired guns, they have not sold their soul for a special interest, and they reflect the concerns of ordinary citizens as opposed to Washington power brokers.

Many interests, such as the AFL-CIO, have aggressively employed grassroots tactics for decades. But since the 1980s, the number and sophistication of grassroots campaigns have grown markedly. Indeed, it is inevitable that interest groups will attempt to lobby indirectly through citizens. Some groups bring members to Washington to lobby Congress. For example, in 1993, more than a thousand travel agents went to the Capitol to fight proposed tax hikes.[20] In 1995, Nation of Islam organizer Louis Farrakan brought hundreds of thousands of African-American men to Washington for his "Million Man March." In 1997, nearly a million men active in the newly formed Promise Keepers movement converged on the Washington mall for a spiritual rally designed to bring men closer to Jesus Christ and their families. Every year, thousands of anti-abortion activists descend upon Capitol Hill.

For other interests, the rise of new information technologies such as phone banks, direct mail, toll-free 800 numbers, and the Internet has created alternative possibilities for grassroots mobilization. It is now commonplace—and relatively simple—for interest groups to attempt to mobilize ordinary citizens to call or write members of Congress. The National Rifle Association claims it is capable of "generating three million telegrams in seventy-two hours and blanketing Capitol Hill with so many phone calls that members cannot make outgoing calls." When Congress considered changes in Social Security cost-of-living adjustments, senior citizens groups "dumped up to fifteen million postcards on [former Speaker] Jim Wright in one day."[21] Not only was this an effective short-term tactic, it also resonated long after the immediate decision was made, as legislators sought to avoid another such onslaught.

A number of groups have created elaborate phone bank operations that can "patch" calls directly through to congressional offices. For example, the National Federation of Independent Businesses, a trade association representing small businesses, can contact its supporters and give them the option either of calling their representatives' offices directly or sending the legislator a personal mailgram. "Politics here in Washington have fundamentally changed," observed NFIB's chief lobbyist, Dan Danner, in 1998. "Instead of listening to the chairmen of their committees or the head of their party . . . what [legislators] listen to now are the grass roots—and that's what we're all about."[22]

Washington lobbyist Jack Bonner has established a D.C. firm that specializes in these types of campaigns. Formerly an aide to Senator John Heinz (R-Pa.), Bonner noticed that during meetings with constituent groups, "grassroots contact would stick to [Heinz's] ribs" more so than other types of communication.[23] Based on this experience, Bonner decided in 1984 to help corporations in America advocate their own perspectives on political issues through a show of grassroots support. Because his company can create an avalanche of calls and letters, Bonner often is accused of manufacturing "astroturf" rather than legitimate grassroots mobilization. Still, his track record is strong. In recent years, his firm has successfully protested funding for Northrop's stealth bomber, helped automakers defeat tougher fuel-mileage standards, and beat back attempts to reduce credit card interest rates.[24] These victories are all the more impressive given the fact that Bonner's agency has mailing lists but no members of its own.

Bonner's is not the only firm to engage in such tactics. Amy Fried reports how interest groups used the 1987 hearings on Iran-Contra to mobilize support for Oliver North.[25] Even though polls showed many Americans were critical of North's actions in the arms-for-hostages deal, interest groups orchestrated numerous letters and calls to congressional offices following North's testimony, which created the impression of a national outpouring of support for the Marine. The North case illustrates how in contemporary politics, power can flow from control of mailing lists and targeted phone directories, not just from large memberships.

Although astroturf campaigns often target political elites, especially members of Congress, they can also seek to influence the general public. One classic case of this came in 1993 during President Clinton's attempt to reduce the tax deduction for business meals.[26] The president's efforts were popular because "two-martini lunches" were seen as a "fatcat" issue for businesses and restaurants. In a textbook effort to reframe the issue in more sympathetic, politically advantageous terms, the National Restaurant Association put forward the story line of protecting restaurant employees who would lose their jobs if Congress cut the tax break. A waitress appeared in a television ad claiming that the tax change would cost 165,000 food service workers their jobs. The commercial concluded with a toll-free 800 number that patched calls directly through to U.S Senate offices. The tactic worked, and the deduction for business meals was saved.

Members of Congress place greater value on personal letters from their district than preprinted postcards from a central organization, or stimulated phone calls from uninformed citizens. The electoral imperative of the House and Senate encourages legislators to represent ordinary citizens. Well-paid influence peddlers from Washington seek to trade on the credibility of the "folks back home." The goal in mobilization campaigns is to make the outpouring of calls and letters look spontaneous to decision makers. As long as they perceive the calls as a genuine expression of citizen sentiment, members of Congress are likely to take them seriously. This boosts the persuasiveness of the grassroots campaign and enhances the effectiveness of the lobbying effort. But if representatives view the outpouring as manufactured, they place little stock in the credibility of the public sentiment and do not let it affect their decisions. The game for lobbyists, then, is to make their grassroots communications look authentic, so that the coordinated narratives get taken seriously by recipients.

Independent Expenditures and Issue Advocacy

The most notable recent attempt to influence the policymaking process is through so-called independent expenditures and issue advocacy during election campaigns. As implied by the name, independent expenditures are group or individual campaign activities on behalf of particular candidates that are not directly controlled by that candidate. This spending seeks to shape the political dialogue without officially joining forces with candidate organizations. The main requirement is that groups cannot coordinate their actions with candidates or engage in any type of consultation with the campaign staffs.

Issue advocacy refers to communications whose major purpose is to promote a set of ideas, not particular candidates. For example, the well-publicized 1996 AFL-CIO ads criticizing Republican legislators fell within the realm of issue advocacy because they were "public education" campaigns designed to publicize the voting record of members of Congress. So did the Christian Action Network ad decrying "radical" homosexual rights described earlier in this chapter. Issue advocacy commercials are careful not to cross the line demarked by the courts of directly exhorting to vote for or against a particular legislator. Nor, supposedly, should there be any consultation with parties or candidates' campaigns. In fact, advocacy messages do contain scarcely disguised appeals for votes, and implicit coordination of spending is rampant. As Elizabeth Drew observes, "on each side, the various participants swim in the same pond of pollsters, ad-makers, and consultants. They all had access to the same information . . . the [issue advocacy] ad buyers could simply check time availabilities . . . to find out who's doing what."[27] As former Republican House member Vin Weber concluded, "The kind of wall of separation that is envisioned here is not really possible in a free society."[28] In practice, free speech means the freedom to spend millions on dominating the political story line, be it in elections or within the policy process.

According to campaign finance experts, the amount of money spent by outside groups is rising. In 1996, the Federal Election Commission officially reported that more than $10.6 million was spent by independent groups in uncoordinated expenditures.[29] Although the actual spending undoubtedly was higher, this amount was double the independent expenditure total for 1992. Figures for issue advocacy are more difficult to estimate since there is no required public disclosure of such efforts owing to their official status as "noncampaign" activities. However, a thorough report by the Annenberg Public Policy Center of the University of Pennsylvania estimated that in 1995 and 1996, somewhere between $135 and $150 million was spent on issue advocacy advertising by at least 31 different groups, including the $35 million spent by labor. This was about one-third of the total of $400 million spent on advertising by candidates in federal races in that election cycle.[30]

Independent expenditures are not regulated in the same ways as direct contributions to candidates. There are no restrictions on how much independent groups can spend to influence the course of the campaign. The reason why independent expenditures are not limited is to allow unaffiliated groups to use their First Amendment right of free expression. Since campaign finance rules were set up in 1974, there have been two major court challenges on this subject. In 1980, the group Common Cause and the Federal Election Commission challenged the legality of independent expenditures.[31] After a number of conservative organizations said they were going to spend money promoting the candidacy of Ronald Reagan, the FEC sued them on grounds that unlimited spending would violate federal laws restricting political action committees from spending more than $1,000 on particular candidates. A federal judge rejected this claim as an unconstitutional restriction on the First Amendment right of free speech. An appeal to the Supreme Court failed; the high court voted 4–4 on the case, which left the former ruling in place and legalized independent spending.

The second major case came in 1985 when the Supreme Court, on a 7–2 decision, struck down a provision limiting the ability of political action committees to spend as much money as they wanted independent of candidate organizations. The case involved two organizations—the National Conservative Political Action Committee and the Fund for a Conservative Majority—which spent massive amounts of money on behalf of Reagan's 1984 presidential campaign. In all, $20 million was spent by independent groups in 1984, with $15.8 million devoted to supporting Reagan. In his opinion for the majority, Justice William Rehnquist de-

fended the decision on grounds that there was no compelling government interest that warranted a restriction of
First Amendment rights. Writing for the minority, Justice
Byron White dissented, saying that the First Amendment
allows the right to speak but not the right to spend.

In the 1980s, independent expenditures in presidential
campaigns advantaged Republicans more than Democrats.
According to unofficial estimates, in 1988, for example,
$13.7 million was spent on behalf of Republicans while
$2.8 million was spent to help Democrats. Much of the
Republican money was devoted to negative television ads
smearing the record of Democratic presidential candidate
Michael Dukakis. The most infamous expenditure was by
the Committee for the Presidency, comprised of a group
of Californians interested in promoting Bush's candidacy.
This organization spent $92,000 on a television ad featur-
ing the case of William Horton, a black felon who raped
a white woman while on furlough from a Massachusetts
prison, in order to make Dukakis look soft on crime.

Since that time, Democrats have become more sophisticated in their use of independent expenditures. Groups
such as the AFL-CIO have increased the amount of money
they have allocated to support candidates on their own. In
the 1992 and 1996 elections, for example, outside groups
spent almost as much money in support of Clinton as in
support of the Republican nominee. Candidates in both
parties have come to count on independent expenditures to
supplement their own activities.

In 1996, the big target for independent expenditures and
issue advocacy was not the presidential race, which seemed
a foregone conclusion, but congressional elections. Ninety
percent of the independent expenditures by outside groups
took place in House and Senate races. Across the country,
television ads broadcast by conservative interests attacked
Democratic candidates for raising taxes, opposing a bal-

anced budget, or not supporting welfare reform. On the liberal side, Republicans were blasted for cutting Medicare, education, and environmental programs. It was a classic case of an election pitting competing group narratives against one another.

One such ad, broadcast by the AFL-CIO against Congressman Frank Riggs (R-Calif.), showed an anxious woman sitting at her kitchen table talking about the high cost of a college education: "My husband and I both work. And next year, we'll have two children in college. And it will be very hard to put them through, even with two incomes. But Congressman Frank Riggs voted with Newt Gingrich to cut college loans while giving tax breaks to the wealthy."[32] Despite the broadside, Riggs won his reelection battle. Identical ads ran in thirty to forty other districts, but most incumbent Republicans likewise survived.

There are several reasons why groups increasingly are resorting to these kinds of spending. First, as pointed out earlier, such expenditures give organizations control of the timing and content of their messages. Both are crucial factors in the effectiveness of group efforts to frame contemporary policy debates. Second, these expenditures are visible both to members of Congress and group members at home. This visibility often gives groups greater clout in policy disputes. Third, these efforts illustrate how closely intertwined policy and electoral spending has become (despite election laws and court rulings that attempt to draw clear lines between them). Finally, such advertisements convey a powerful narrative to everyone in the district, namely, that Republicans are insensitive to the needy or that Democrats are tax-and-spend liberals. As illustrated in the next chapter on health care reform, this strategy helps interest groups "spin" the communications cycle in ways advantageous to their own cause.

Stealth Campaigns

Increasingly, direct advocacy campaigns are being supplemented by stealth campaigns in which direct disclosure of lobbying activities is masked from the public through "fronts" or alliances with other organizations. For example, Covington & Burling, the law firm representing the major tobacco companies (Philip Morris, R. J. Reynolds, Lorillard, and Brown & Williamson) privately spent one million dollars in Philip Morris money to finance an international magazine called *Healthy Buildings*, which used suspect science to promote the industry's claim that indoor smoking bans were unnecessary.[33] In 1996, the firm also commissioned a study arguing that proposed federal tobacco restrictions would cost the nation 92,000 jobs and $7.9 billion in lost sales.

Stealth campaigns have spread to election campaigns. Larry Sabato and Glenn Simpson report in their book, *Dirty Little Secrets*, how interests use secret means to plant negative information with voters.[34] One such technique has been so-called push polls, in which mock pollsters call thousands of voters to ask whether their vote would be altered if they knew something negative about the candidate. In a Wisconsin congressional district, for example, push polls secretly were employed to accuse a female candidate of being a lesbian.

These and other promotional activities illustrate the wide range of stealth campaigns being conducted today. Stealth lobbying can take many different forms, from event sponsorship to commissioned think tank research projects to public opinion polls that get leaked to the press. Some groups work with so-called 501(c)(3) tax-exempt organizations. These alliances offer the advantage of freedom from any required disclosure as well as tax deductibility of group contributions.[35] The particular form can vary, but the key in each of these efforts is that the actual sponsor is masked by front organizations that make it difficult for the public to see who really is funding the activity.

Stealth campaigns are consciously designed to fly under the radar of press and public oversight. Unpopular interests recognize that one of the most important aspects of effective communications is "source credibility." Individuals or groups that are seen by the public as being independent or unbiased are more persuasive than those which are not. Interests that lack source credibility hide their activities under innocuous-sounding alliances, such as the National Smokers Alliance or Citizens for a Sound Economy. The former is funded directly by Philip Morris, while the latter is a conservative group devoted to lessening government regulations of the private sector.

From the standpoint of the affected interest, these alliances can be extremely effective. Companies that run ads or sponsor activities addressing policy controversies do not have to reveal their direct support. Rather, the interest can hide behind the alliance and shield itself from public suspicions about its motives for staking out a particular policy stance. This enables the group to avoid whatever backlash arises when the public or the press realize who actually is sponsoring the event in question.

At the same time, such activities help private interests evade public disclosure rules governing lobbying and campaigning. According to federal rules and recent court decisions, groups that lobby Congress or contribute directly to candidates for office are required to disclose the date and amount of the contribution. This information is released periodically to the press and general public. If, however, the group labels its activities as public education, there is no required public disclosure of the contributors or expenditures. The group can spend millions of dollars influencing the public without there being any accountability for their efforts. For "pariah" interests or unpopular causes, such as logging companies or tobacco interests, it is the ideal form of political advocacy.

The High-Tech Lobbying Universe

Whatever the strategy, be it advocacy advertising, grassroots organizing, or stealth campaigns, interest groups today have many different ways they can convey their point of view. Interests can lobby legislators face-to-face, advertise in specialty publications, expand the conflict to the general public, hide behind coalition partners, or use some combination of the various approaches.

At times, the range of lobbying options is simply overwhelming. In a world of great complexity, high stakes, and considerable uncertainty, it rarely is clear in advance what the optimal mix of strategies should be. But as we shall see in cases from health care and devolution to telecommunications and medical reform, well-funded, well-organized interests have learned how to turn the challenges of the contemporary process to their own political advantage.

Part II

The Sound of Money: Four Songs

Chapter Four

Health Care
Reform Unravels

The unraveling of the Clinton health care package in 1993–94 provided one of the most dramatic stories of recent public policy. After decades of piecemeal reform in America, a newly elected Democratic president made universal health care coverage the centerpiece of his domestic agenda. President Clinton and his wife, Hillary Rodham Clinton, delivered speeches around the country extolling the virtues of their plan, organized town meetings to mobilize grassroots support, and even devoted a major part of a State of the Union address to the issue. With a Congress controlled by the Democratic party and early public opinion polls showing support for health care reform, the prospects appeared promising to extend health insurance to all Americans for the first time ever in the United States.

By mid-1994, this effort had failed miserably. Not only was the president unable to push his legislation through Congress, the public turned against reform. In a historic electoral repudiation linked in part to the failure of health care reform, in November 1994 Republicans gained complete control of Congress, and Democrats were relegated to minority status for the first time in forty years. The opportunity for universal health coverage appeared lost for at least another generation.

The explanations for the failure of the Clinton plan have been varied: the public's concern over the government role in health care, fears about the quality of medical care, opposition to loss of choice in health care providers, and worries about the cost of universal coverage, among other things. But where did these fears come from? In such a short period of time, how did foes so effectively mobilize opposition to the Clinton package? Why was the president utterly unable to build support for a historic policy change?

In this chapter, we argue that interest groups, and the attendant ads and news coverage that emanated from their activities, were instrumental in creating a set of negative narratives about the president's program; these centered on big government, high taxes, and limited choice. In contrast, Clinton failed to respond by enunciating a clear and persuasive story line in favor of reform.[1] Because of the large amount of money spent by opposition groups, the one-sided nature of the ad expenditures between competing forces (especially early in the debate), and the prominent and noncritical coverage of commercials by the news media, sophisticated group lobbying played a crucial role in defining the issue and stopping the adoption of comprehensive health care reform.

The Controversy Over Health Care

Health care represented a classic example of large-scale policy change. The financial stakes of the Clinton reform package were simply staggering. Former Health, Education, and Welfare Secretary Joseph Califano characterized health care reform as a "trillion-dollar pot of gold" with extraordinary implications for hospitals ($409 billion), doctors ($195 billion), nursing homes and home health care ($108 billion), pharmaceutical companies ($100 billion), insurers ($62 billion), and others such as dentist, podiatrists, optometrists, physical therapists, and pharmacists (more than $100 billion).[2] National associations representing drug and insurance companies, for example, argued that the very survival of their industries was at stake. The pharmaceuticals feared the Clinton cost controls would erode profits and eliminate their ability to bring new medical treatments to the marketplace, while insurers worried that mandatory purchasing alliances would put them out of business.

Both the extraordinary reach and high stakes of the proposed health care reforms generated an exceptional amount of political and media activity. The large-scale nature of the Clinton proposal, the fact that a president made the issue the centerpiece of his domestic agenda, and the enormous number of lobbying dollars pushed health care, normally a peripheral public concern, to the center of the national political debate. Ironically, the very visibility of this debate should have reduced group influence. According to some observers, the more visible the arena, the less likely are parochial groups to obtain public benefits for themselves.[3] Yet in the case of health care, media coverage and high-visibility lobbying amplified the messages of certain special-interest groups, such as insurers, making them extraordinarily influential in shaping the ensuing discussion.

The Political Environment

President Clinton began his term promising to bring health care before Congress during the first 100 days of his administration. The timetable soon slipped to May, June, and then the fall as other issues, such as deficit reduction, NAFTA, and character charges against the president took priority. The delay in the initial timetable and the sequence of ensuing events had unforeseen consequences for the health care reform effort.

Although Democrats controlled the presidency and both chambers of Congress, the sheer complexity of the health care system presented serious barriers to Clinton's plans. The initiative was so massive and detailed that few understood how it would work. In addition, there were numerous points in Congress where opponents could undermine reform. The legislation could be stopped in any of the committees involved in the overhaul, on either floor of the House or Senate, or in a conference committee between the two chambers if different versions of the bill were passed.[4]

In 1993, important interest groups announced initial support for parts of what became the Clinton program. For example, the Health Insurance Association of America (HIAA), which represented small to medium-sized insurance companies and eventually became a staunch critic of the president, testified in March 1993 before the only public hearing of the President's Taskforce on Health Care that it supported universal coverage, paid for by an employer mandate, and a federally defined benefits package. The main concerns centered on federally defined premium limits and federally defined spending limits. According to HIAA chief Willis Gradison, a former Republican member of Congress, "our initial hope was to sit down and try and work something out with the administration but they wouldn't do it. I never did get a chance to meet with the First Lady"[5] (although he did meet with other top administration officials a number of times, who conveyed his concerns to the First Lady). This inability soured the lobbyist on prospects for working with the Clinton White House.

Other groups, such as the National Federation of Independent Businesses (NFIB), announced their opposition as soon as it became clear the reforms would mandate employers to pay 80 percent of employee health premiums. Since both HIAA and NFIB represented large national organizations with well-organized grassroots constituencies such as insurance agents and small businesses, this opposition was a crucial development in the early rounds.

The inaction on the part of the White House throughout the spring and summer of 1993 tuned out to be a blessing for HIAA. According to Gradison, "We had lots of time to get geared up. It gave us a lot more time to refine our message, raise our money, do internal staffing changes, and have training sessions with members of our association as to what they could do with their hometowns and their editorial boards." Eventually, the group put together a sophisticated campaign based on advertisements, phone banks, direct mail, and letters and calls to members of Congress. It would become a classic example of public and constituent-based lobbying by a well-organized group.

The delay until the fall further complicated health care reform by pushing the issue directly into the middle of the contentious national debate over NAFTA. Since NAFTA was opposed by many labor unions and liberal organizations, Clinton's support for the treaty strained relations with the very groups that should have been the bedrock of support for health reform. According to an administration official, "Lane Kirkland [of the AFL-CIO] came to see us in August 1993 and basically said, 'we have $5 million to spend. We can either spend it supporting health care or fighting NAFTA.' The president wanted to support NAFTA. As a result the AFL-CIO spent their time and money that fall fighting NAFTA. Some of the consumer groups that were going to support us on health care did the same thing."[6] These interest-group decisions had devastating consequences for the president's ability to sell his program to Congress and the American public. The inaction on the health care front by groups opposing NAFTA would turn what might have been a well-balanced fight between competing ends of the political spectrum into a one-sided battle dominated by insurers, pharmaceutical companies, and small businesses.

The Media Environment

Against this backdrop of contentious politics, the president unveiled his program for health care reform to Congress and a national television audience on September 22, 1993. His elaborate 1,364-page plan, called the American Health Security Act, was one of the most comprehensive domestic policy proposals ever put forth by an American president. Key features of his program included a guarantee of health care coverage by 1998 for all Americans, the establishment of regional insurance purchasing alliances (from which people would be required to obtain coverage for employees in firms above a certain threshold size), an employer mandate requiring employers to pay about 80 percent of the costs of the average health insurance plan for a single person, subsidies for companies with 75 or fewer employees or individuals with average annual wages of less than $24,000, the creation of a national health board to establish national and regional spending limits and to limit increases in insurance premiums, and health insurance reforms that would prohibit benefit terminations and assure coverage of people with pre-existing conditions.[7]

The scale of the proposal was stunning. It included a basic benefits package covering prescription drugs; rehabilitation services; mental health and drug/alcohol abuse treatment; hospice, home health and extended nursing care services; and abortion services. Under the plan, almost every aspect of the health care system would change. For a president charged with ending gridlock in Washington, it was a bold move.[8] The dramatic program unleashed extensive coverage by the news media and encouraged massive spending by concerned interest groups, many of whom favored reform but opposed one or another part of the specific plan.

The sheer volume of health care news coverage was extraordinary. Between September 1 and November 30, 1993, alone, 2,000 newspaper, magazine, and television stories about health care were published or broadcast.[9] Part of this unusual media interest came from the massive stakes inherent in this issue. But monetary grants from leading foundations for news coverage, focus groups, public opinion polls, and academic studies about what was expected to be landmark legislation also guaranteed a running story on health care. For example, the Kaiser Family Foundation gave millions of dollars to news organizations for health care coverage as well as to academics for studies of this coverage. And the Robert Wood Johnson Foundation devoted several million dollars for research on health care and for an NBC prime-time special on the issue.

Ironically, the close media attention to health care did not receive positive evaluations from most citizens. An October 1993 national public opinion survey found that while 57 percent of citizens gave the news media excellent or good ratings on coverage of foreign affairs and 55 percent offered similar support on general government and public affairs, only 42 percent gave the media excellent or good ratings for coverage of health care reform.[10] Forty-eight percent said news coverage of health care was fair or poor. An August 1994 national poll undertaken for the Robert Wood Johnson Foundation revealed even worse numbers: 32 percent said the media had done an excellent or good job and 64 percent felt the coverage had been fair or poor.[11]

One reason for these low marks was the complex nature of health care. With press emphasis on personalities and the political game, many readers and viewers thought that reporters had not told them how health care reform would affect their personal lives. A comprehensive news monitoring project found that citizens believed that 31 percent of the stories focused on the political impact of health care, 21 percent dealt with the impact of reform on the health care system, and only 17 percent concerned the effect of reform on individuals and families.[12] The latter, of course, was the topic of prime interest to ordinary Americans.

From the standpoint of emerging narratives, the sheer complexity of the reform package allowed the story of health reform to remain up in the air. In the early days, it simply was not clear what was happening or how the proposal would affect average people. Many interest groups delayed the decision to support the plan, given the particulars they opposed. Early coalition groupings proved quite fluid. Confronted with these political uncertainties, a positive overall story line was very slow to develop. This gave opposition interest groups crucial time to organize lobbying strategies. The lead time proved even more valuable because the president failed to dictate the terms of the policy debates over health care.

The Center for Public Integrity, a Washington think tank devoted to money and politics, estimated that 650 organizations spent at least $100 million to influence the 1993–94 health policy debate.[13] This came as a windfall to many lobbyists. Almost 100 law and public relations firms were hired for lobbying purposes by dozens of interests. On top of this came campaign contributions. From 1993 to early 1994, over $25 million was given to members of Congress by health care interests, with top contributors including unions, trial lawyers, life underwriters, and health-related concerns. Nor did interests stop there. They provided more than 350 free trips for members of Congress, many from the American Medical Association, the American Cyanamid Company, and the Pharmaceutical Research and Manufacturers of America, to name a few. Still other groups, such as the NFIB and its 600,000 members, put their resources into grassroots mobilization via direct mail and phone banks.

Nevertheless, despite all these expenditures, the single largest share of total lobbying funds was spent on political advertising. An estimated $60 million, or more than half of the overall spending, was devoted to advertising.[14] Through a combination of news reports and personal interviews with officials in relevant groups, we developed estimates of the spending by top organizations on health care ads. By far the biggest advertisers on the issue were the Pharmaceutical Research and Manufacturers of America (PRMA), which represented leading drug companies, and the Health Insurance Association of America (HIAA), which represented small and medium-sized insurance companies. The PRMA spent approximately $20 million, while the HIAA spent roughly $14 million, much of it on a series of "Harry and Louise" ads that gained wide exposure in news stories and provoked counter-ads by reform supporters.

These groups devoted most of their money buying targeted ads in Washington or New York, although some of it was spent for ads aired either on national cable networks (mostly on CNN) or in the home states and districts of crucial members of Congress. Ben Goddard, president of Goddard*Claussen/First Tuesday and developer of the Harry and Louise ads for HIAA, said "Our media buys were targeted on involved Americans, people who were registered to vote, wrote letters to editors or public officials, attended meetings, and made political contributions. We bought time on CNN and Headline News, CNBC, Rush Limbaugh, and in New York, Washington, and Los Angeles. We wanted to get on the agenda of the national media. Those areas are where editors and reporters who decide the news live."[15] Groups opposed to the Clinton program outspent supporters by more than a 2-to-1 ratio, although the president did have the advantage of obtaining free publicity through his and the First Lady's statements and trips.[16]

Initially, the White House did not anticipate the scale of the paid advertising campaign. Former Clinton Domestic Policy Council analyst Christine Heenan noted, "In the Fall of 1993, it was not clear this was going to be a paid ad battle as opposed to one based on field organization. Our initial plan was to create teams of validators in local communities, such as doctors, pediatricians, and small business leaders. They would disseminate information at the local level. . . . The outside campaign would be in specific districts of needed members."[17]

Crucial weeks passed before the White House realized the scope of the HIAA campaign. HIAA president William Gradison described the specifically targeted nature of his group's ad campaign and its integration with a sophisticated phone bank and direct mail operation. "We moved our ads around, focused on the districts where key committee members were and also on key geographical areas. We felt the battleground would be the border states and Southern ones. That's where there were conservative Democratic members of Congress who we thought would be sympathetic to our message. [Given their minority status,] we didn't focus on Republicans because there weren't enough of them to do anything with."[18]

Every ad included a toll-free 800 number that people could call to obtain more information or register comments. According to Gradison, almost half a million people called the 800 number with comments and personal stories about health care. Because of the emerging narrative that the Clinton proposal would restrict health care choices for ordinary Americans and would create a big government bureaucracy, this information became a vital resource in dealing with members of Congress and the media. Indeed, many citizens could plug their own experiences into the general story lines provided by HIAA and other interest groups.

Gradison noted that all respondents "were filed by zip code and activated. We tried to get them to write letters or patch through phone calls to congressional offices. It was a highly integrated program." Out of the people who called the 800 number, Goddard said HIAA got "45,000 performing members of the coalition, [meaning] people who wrote letters or made calls on this issue. According to our research, those 45,000 people made over a quarter of a million contacts with the media and members of Congress. They were interested in public policy and understood the value of communicating with Congress."[19]

Each caller or letter writer became a grassroots lobbyist for HIAA with a personal story of fear or indignation to tell. Given the value accorded such communications by members of Congress, these individuals had an unusually high degree of source credibility. Every story became a part of the opposition narrative that health care reform would hurt ordinary Americans. And many legislators incorporated their own constituents' stories in the overarching narrative of "limits on choice."

At the same time, groups such as the NFIB were devoting several million dollars to mobilizing their members to contact elected officials. According to NFIB health lobbyist Mark Isakowitz, his group used direct mail and phone banks "to create a dynamic where when key decision makers on this issue went home, someone always would be coming up to them saying the employer mandate would be bad for their business and when they came back to Washington, their staff would tell them 'we're getting hundreds of phone calls and letters against the employer mandate.' . . . We tried to create a blanket effect. . . . If you get two hundred or three hundred members to call representatives, that creates a remarkable shock wave in congressional offices. That can tie up the phones for a couple of days."[20]

Groups supportive of the president's position on health care, such as the Democratic National Committee (DNC), were drastically outspent. An administration official attributed this to the NAFTA debate: "We had senior citizen groups like the AARP focusing on the final details of our plan and polling its members instead of being out there with its $5 million. They didn't spend their money until March or April [1994], which was too late."[21] In the health care debate, supporters were numerous but remained slow-moving and unfocused.

The net result of all this was that in the crucial period of October to December, 1993, opposition groups had the advertising field virtually to themselves. In fall 1993, HIAA and PRMA spent a total of approximately $17.5 million ($10.5 million by HIAA for television spots and $7 million by PRMA on print ads). During this same period, the DNC devoted just $150,000 to ads. According to an administration official, this imbalance "was true not just in the airwaves but in the newspapers too. Two-thirds of the headlines were negative towards us and Robert Pear [a highly influential health care reporter for the *New York Times*] was writing stories with virtually every headline being negative. . . . From October 1 to mid-December, instead of having four weeks to define our message, we had one presidential day. We didn't have the president out there the way we expected defining what we were trying to do. International events like Somalia and Haiti occurred. We had the opposition spending a ton of money."[22] And this money, effectively spent, purchased the set of messages that dominated the discourse.

When questioned about their expenditures, HIAA officials cited fear about the long-term survival of their industry as the primary reason for their spending.[23] President William Gradison felt that the Clinton Administration had singled out a few groups for political demonization: "In the first meeting [with White House health care advisor Ira Magaziner] he said to me, 'Bill, I'm not a politician but our pollsters at the White House tell us that it will help us sell our plan if we identify as enemies the pharmaceutical industry, the physicians, and the health insurers.' . . . It became clear that this was part of a plan on their part to demonize the industry."[24] Ira Magaziner, special advisor to the president for policy and a leading architect of health care reform, disputes this account of the meeting, saying that White House polls were indicating that attacking the insurance companies would be very popular with the public, but that he made clear to Gradison that that was not what the White House wanted nor intended to do.[25]

To counter the plan coming from the White House, one

group of ads sponsored by PRMA emphasized the positive contributions of pharmaceutical research to health care.[26] In some of these ads PRMA utilized a female announcer, which is atypical for political advertisements. But as Heenan pointed out, this made sense because polls were showing that "it was female decision makers who had to be targeted. Females make two-thirds of the health care decisons."[27]

One PRMA ad typified the positive approach: a person named Mike Quinlan says, "My dad has Alzheimer's. They have to continue the research they're doing." The ad then goes on to note: "To Mike Quinlan, and to all of America, we hear you. And we share your urgency. Right now, pharmaceutical companies have nineteen medicines in development to fight Alzheimer's. The fact is, more than ninety percent of all drug discoveries come from our research. So for the millions who are waiting, keep the hope." Similar personal story ads were run on AIDS (featuring HIV-positive patient Dan Gunnells), breast cancer (Claudia), cystic fibrosis (Ashley), ulcers (Mike), asthma (Katie), and strokes (Phyllis). Personal stories helped drug companies shape the policy narrative and focus attention on their contribution to the quality of health care.

PRMA ads appeared frequently on television as well as in elite journals published on Capitol Hill. Both *CQ Weekly* and *National Journal* contained full-page, four-color ads playing on the theme that pharmaceutical research was crucial to the future health care system. It was just the type of elite advocacy program that costs less than a handful of national television ads and allows interests to target influential members of the Washington establishment.

Unlike the PRMA ads, the HIAA spots directly challenged specific elements of the Clinton proposal. The

Harry and Louise commercials developed by the advertising firm of Goddard*Claussen/First Tuesday started running in September 1993. These ads were modeled on a very effective campaign HIAA had run against a 1992 California health reform initiative called Proposition 166. According to Gradison: "when this [opposition] effort began it looked like—based on polling data—that the initiative would prevail by a vote of about two to one. It was defeated by two to one and the [Goddard*Claussen] ads were really important."[28] In an interview, Gradison recalled that during the Proposition 166 campaign, "Goddard*Claussen had a gangbusters television commercial which showed a black female entrepreneur talking about how [health care reform] would damage if not destroy her small business. It was a powerful piece."[29]

Goddard described the Proposition 166 campaign as "a real-live laboratory test of how you communicate. It taught us how to talk with people. . . . What HIAA learned is that you could win these issues in a public debate. Winning a state campaign gave the health lobby confidence to fight on a broader scale."[30] The California initiative battle taught HIAA how to present their position: "The two significant things we learned were that you can't be against reform and the need to personalize issues so that people understood their personal stakes. Scare tactics with big global messages don't work. You need to bring it down to a level people understand and can relate to."[31] The proposition campaign thus became the blueprint for the subsequent Harry and Louise campaign.

In one early HIAA health care ad, a yuppie couple, played by Los Angeles actors Harry Johnson and Louise Clark, are sitting over breakfast.[32] He scans a newspaper, while she reads a printed version of the president's health care plan. Harry says, "I'm glad the president's doing something about health care reform." Louise: "He's right. We need it." Harry: "Some of these details." Louise: "Like a national limit on health care?" Harry: "Really." Louise: "The government caps how much the country can spend on all health care and says, 'That's it!' " Harry: "So, what if our health plan runs out of money?" Louise: "There's got to be a better way." Later ads by HIAA emphasized problems related to government bureaucracy, medical costs, and choice of doctors in the Clinton program.

Goddard described how these and other Harry and Louise ads were developed through twenty-six focus groups and two public opinion surveys conducted by Public Opinion Strategies: "The key thing in advertising is finding the right message and messenger. In putting together the materials, we tested as spokespersons high-profile celebrities, doctors, and academic experts. Bill Gradison then gave a speech and said, 'this issue is going to be decided around people's kitchen tables.' My first reaction was skepticism, but we tried it with a couple around a kitchen table and it was a huge success over other formats. People respond to a familiar environment. The kitchen is a symbol for family decisions. Our research told us that people would respond to the message and that they would like the messenger."[33]

The Harry and Louise spots generated extensive coverage from the news media.[34] Between January 15 and July 12, 324 seconds of actual air time on network evening news time were devoted to HIAA ads, compared to 122 seconds for those of the DNC in favor of reform.[35] Almost every leading newspaper and television network in the country ran stories about the ads, including one on the front page of the *New York Times* on October 21, 1993.[36] According to Goddard, the environment was ripe for news coverage of Harry and Louise: "Health care was the definitive program of the Clinton administration. The delay in introducing the bill heightened press interest in the issue. We worked the press corps very hard. We had a press conference every time a new ad was released. We had an editorial board program, we wrote op-ed pieces, we hit the talk shows all across the country. It was a combination which built press interest."[37]

This set of ads became so prominent that on November 1, First Lady Hillary Rodham Clinton lashed out at the health insurance industry, saying: "They have the gall to run TV ads that there is a better way, the very industry that has brought us to the brink of bankruptcy because of the way that they have financed health care."[38] This brought front-page headlines in the *New York Times* ("Hillary Clinton Accuses Insurers of Lying About Health Proposal: Says Industry Ads Mislead Public to Guard Profits")[39] and *Washington Post* ("First Lady Lambasts Health Insurers: Methods Have 'Brought Us to the Brink of Bankruptcy,' Clinton Says").[40] President Clinton joined his wife in these criticisms on November 3, blaming health insurers for "over-complicated, bureaucratic, burdensome, bureaucratic" requirements.[41] That same day, Richard Celeste, chairman of the DNC's National Health Care Campaign, crashed a HIAA news conference in Washington. According to a *Washington Post* account, this had the effect of "turning a dry, technical session into a newsworthy event."[42] According to Goddard, these attacks backfired: "when the White House attacked us, it helped us because the press loves a dogfight. That's what they like to cover."[43]

Though the media had been attentive to the accuracy of ads in the 1992 presidential campaign, there were almost no news stories assessing the accuracy of health care spots. In the period from fall 1993 to summer 1994, only four "Ad Watches," the "truth monitor" news features that criticize the accuracy of campaign ads, appeared in the *New*

York Times (on October 21, 1993, February 1, 1994, and two on July 17, 1994). This was well below the 44 "Ad Watches" run by the *New York Times* during the 1992 presidential campaign.[44] Few formal "Ad Watches" appeared in the *Washington Post, Los Angeles Times,* or *Wall Street Journal* during this time period. There were just two "Ad Watches" (or "Reality Checks," as they were called by some news organizations) on the ABC, NBC, and CBS evening news. Aside from "Ad Watches," there were a number of general news stories about health care ads. In looking at the number of national newspaper and network television stories about health care ads, peak coverage of health care commercials occurred in October/November 1993, February 1994, and July/August 1994.

The weakness of media ad oversight led University of Pennsylvania communications scholar Kathleen Hall Jamieson to complain to *Washington Post* columnist David Broder, who then wrote a February 23, 1994, column conceding that the news media had failed seriously to challenge the accuracy of health care advertisements.[45] Despite the public admonition, little changed after his column. By the end of July 1994, a University of Pennsylvania study reported that 28 percent of the print ads and 59 percent of the broadcast ads on either side were "unfair, misleading, or false."[46] The story line for health care reform was being dominated by industry ads that were incomplete at best, inaccurate at worst. Adding insult to injury, the mainstream media had magnified their impact with its less than skeptical coverage.

The Public Response

Early polls showed strong support for the Clinton health care initiative, although the public also was cautious and uncertain about the president's plan.[47] For example, a *Washington Post*/ABC News poll of adults nationwide conducted shortly after the Clinton program was announced in September 1993 revealed that 67 percent approved of the president's program and only 20 percent disapproved. By late February 1994, the same survey organization using an identical question found approval of Clinton's plan had declined 23 percentage points to 44 percent. Similar results were obtained in other national surveys. *USA Today*/CNN/Gallup national polls from September 26, 1993, to April 18, 1994, found an 18 percentage point drop in public support for the Clinton health care program—from 57 to 39 percent.[48] Other polls showed the percentage of people who believed they would be better off if the plan were enacted dropping sharply from 77 to 52 percent in the space of a few months.[49]

According to an administration official, White House polls right after the president's September 22 speech showed support of 58 to 23 percent in favor of the plan. By the end of December, though, this 35 percentage point margin had dropped to 17 percentage points.[50] The HIAA conducted a nightly national tracking poll following the president's speech. HIAA president Gradison said "support for the president's plan took off with that outstanding speech, but it went down ten days later. The turn occurred around October 2 and 3. I can't explain why, but it was measurable. Public support consistently drifted down thereafter."[51]

These results were suggestive of the problems faced by the Clinton program. But given the range of events taking place between the fall and spring, a much more detailed analysis of public opinion surveys is necessary to determine why public support dropped. We examined three national surveys that included questions both about health care ads and sentiments on health care reform.[52] This included surveys conducted by the Harvard School of Public Health/ Kaiser Foundation from September 30 to October 5, 1993, of 1,200 adults; by the *Washington Post*/ABC News from February 24 to 27, 1994, of 1,531 adults; and by the *New York Times*/CBS News on March 8 to 11, 1994, of 1,107 adults (which asked specifically about the Harry and Louise ads).

The surveys cover the crucial fall 1993 to spring 1994 time period when overall support for the Clinton program deteriorated. Beyond the analysis of public attitudes on health care over time, they also allow us to determine whether people who reported seeing health care ads had different views from those who did not.[53]

The Harvard poll is useful to examine early thinking on the Clinton program because the survey went into the field a week after Clinton announced his plan to a joint session of Congress and after the HIAA and PRMA started running some of their fall ads. In looking at the results of this survey, the poll's most notable finding is that few people overall felt they knew much about health care reform. Fully 42 percent said they knew nothing or only a little, 49 percent felt they knew a fair amount, and only 9 percent indicated they knew a great deal about the subject. In regard to the Clinton proposal in particular, 44 percent indicated that they did not understand the Clinton plan either very well or at all. This uncertainty reflected the fact that the plan was large, complex, and had been privately crafted.

There was widespread ignorance among the American public about some crucial features of the debate. For example, only 22 percent said they knew the meaning of consumer purchasing alliances, one of the cornerstones of the Clinton program. Only 20 percent expressed familiarity with the idea of managed competition. At the same time, almost 8 in 10 respondents (79 percent) were aware that

Clinton's plan would require employers to contribute to the cost of health insurance for their workers. In addition, 63 percent knew the Clinton plan guaranteed health coverage to all Americans, and 52 percent realized the president's program guaranteed that workers would not lose their benefits if they lost or quit their jobs.

When asked what they were most interested in learning about health care proposals, 79 percent of all respondents indicated it was the amount they would have to pay out of their own pocket for a doctor or hospital visit, 77 percent said it was the cost of their family's health insurance premiums, and 73 percent said it was the amount of taxes they would pay. Most people (72 percent) believed that under the president's proposal, they would personally pay either a great deal more or somewhat more in taxes; 43 percent worried that the Clinton plan would lead to rationing of health care; 39 percent believed that under the president's reform, the health care system would be run mainly by the government. In short, Clinton had delivered opponents a powerful set of negative health care symbols relating to high cost, limited choice, and big government.

The general absence of specific, positive information about the Clinton proposal and the substantial concern over the cost of reform and the impression that government was taking over the health care system created an opportunity for opponents to attach unfavorable narratives—on big government or reduction in choice—to the president's program. In 1991, Clinton had anticipated these criticisms and had explicitly rejected a single-payer system advocated by Yale professor Ted Marmor because the "proposition of Big Government and increased taxes was simply unacceptable."[54] Ironically, within days of the Clinton proposal's announcement, these very criticisms already had emerged full-blown in the public's mind.

The early stage of issue consideration is often when political communications are most influential. People are still searching for information and generally have not made up their minds how they feel.[55] According to the Harvard health survey, 65 percent indicated that in the past week they had seen a TV program, heard a radio program, or read a newspaper or magazine article having to do with health care reform. And 40 percent said they had watched, heard, or read about advertisements having to do with proposed changes in the health care system. All of these figures indicated a high degree of media exposure to health care messages on the part of the public.

The most immediate impact of ads and news coverage was in regard to knowledge about health care.[56] People who reported seeing ads or hearing news stories felt more knowledgeable about health care. They were more likely to understand the meaning of managed competition and health purchasing alliances and to say they were familiar with the Clinton reform plan. There were weaker ties in terms of knowing that the Clinton plan guaranteed coverage and had an employer mandate.

In terms of negative evaluations, there was no association between seeing ads and feeling there would be a big tax increase under the Clinton program. But there was a significant relationship between that tax impression and seeing the news. Those who said they relied on the news for information about health care reform also were likely to think there would be a tax increase and to report they were interested in the tax and cost dimensions of reform. The public relations strategy of reform opponents—aided by the mainstream press—was beginning to work.

As the debate moved from the fall to the spring, important changes started to take place in public opinion. The February 1994 Washington Post/ABC News poll showed that 58 percent of Americans said they had seen or heard advertisements either for or against the Clinton health care plan, up from 40 percent in October. This is comparable to the baseline of 58 percent of Americans who say they saw Clinton ads during the 1992 presidential nominating process, but far lower than the 82 percent of Americans who reported seeing Clinton ads in the presidential general election.[57] Of the people who saw ads, 39 percent claimed the spots made them less likely to support health care reform.[58]

Many individuals still felt they knew almost nothing (14 percent) or a little (62 percent) about Clinton's health care program. But 24 percent felt they knew a lot about it, up from 9 percent in October, and 73 percent said they supported a federal law requiring all employers to provide health insurance for their full-time employees. Still, 43 percent worried than the Clinton plan created too much government involvement in the nation's health care system. More importantly, seeing ads was becoming linked to fears that Clinton's reform created a bigger government and that employers would eliminate existing jobs as a result of the plan.[59] The health care story line was turning in favor of those opposing the president's plan.

The Case of Harry and Louise

Of all the advertisements run against health care reform, none achieved more infamy than HIAA's Harry and Louise commercials. Indeed, this set of ads may well be the best-known issue advocacy campaign in American history. As noted previously, these ads achieved particular prominence in Washington circles. Many news stories emphasized the commercials, and the ads even spawned counter-ads and attacks by the president and First Lady.

To look at the impact of the Harry and Louise ads, we studied a March 1994 *New York Times*/CBS News survey that asked specifically whether people had seen television ads showing a couple called Harry and Louise sitting in their living room criticizing the Clinton health care plan. To this close-ended question, 19 percent responded that they had seen the Harry and Louise ads. This compares favorably to the 6 percent in late October 1988 who named Bush's "Revolving Door" prison spot in an open-ended question asking them to name the ad that had the greatest impact on them in the fall presidential campaign.[60] It demonstrates the extraordinary reach of this series of health care commercials.

Yet a majority of viewers did not find these spots very accurate. Of those who saw the Harry and Louise spots, 32 percent believed the ad criticisms were completely accurate or more right than wrong and 52 percent felt the criticisms were either completely untrue or more wrong than right. This lack of credibility was significant given the general importance of source credibility in models of political persuasion. Information sources not viewed as credible are much less likely to be persuasive with the general public.

In addition, not everyone was able correctly to identify the source of the Harry and Louise ads. Of those who saw the ad, 38 percent correctly identified the source of the ads as the insurance industry, 50 percent had no idea who sponsored the spots, and 12 percent incorrectly attributed sponsorship to some other organization. Nearly two-thirds of respondents were unsure who was criticizing the Clinton program.

Taken together, these findings help to explain an interesting twist in the results of the Harry and Louise ads. Exposure to the Harry and Louise commercials was associated with reporting a good understanding of the Clinton program, but it was not related to most other impressions about the plan. For example, 64 percent of those who saw the ads believed the Clinton proposal would increase their health costs, while 60 percent of those who didn't see the spots felt costs would increase, a trivial difference. There were equally small differences in beliefs about the importance of universal coverage (a difference of only 1 percentage point), worry about the adequacy of medical care (a difference of 2 percentage points), and evaluations of the employer mandate (a difference of just 3 percentage points). There were no links at all to impressions of an employer mandate, the plan increasing paperwork, lowering the quality of care, or guaranteeing universal coverage.

The absence of many relationships between seeing the Harry and Louise ads and views about health care reform is noteworthy in light of the fact that these items were central to the advertising campaign against Clinton. Many of the HIAA spots specifically criticized Clinton's program for being costly and overly bureaucratic and for limiting patient choice. Contrary to the conventional wisdom, exposure to the Harry and Louise ads was not associated with negative impressions of the Clinton program. Elite views were being altered by the public relations campaign, but there is little evidence documenting a significant impact on the public at large beyond increased knowledge about the president's program.

Our survey evidence on the impact of Harry and Louise is consistent with focus group research reported by Jamieson.[61] In her research, Jamieson found that the Harry and Louise ads "had a negligible impact on the public." The problem, according to her analysis, was that the ads evoked little short-term recall of central themes and were considerably less memorable than other health care reform ads. Despite the sums spent by HIAA, most of the ads aired in Washington and New York or on CNN, where legislators would be sure to see them, but not a majority of the public.[62] There simply weren't enough broadcast repetitions over the twelve-month campaign to be persuasive with the American public. Harry and Louise were not, however, selling a policy position to the public at large. Their focus, as signalled by a modest advertising budget of $14 million, was on elite attitudes, not mass opinion.

Elite Responses

The analyses to this point suggest that the Harry and Louise ads did not have a consistent impact on many of the doubts citizens had about health care reform.[63] Contrary to the claims of its sponsors, this research shows that the public impact was in knowledge about the plan, more than the evaluation of its merits per se. The only negative impression attached by the public at large to the Clinton program associated with ad viewing was about the cost of the president's plan.

But this does not mean the anti-Clinton public relations campaign failed. Public relations campaigns can target audiences other than the general public, namely, news reporters and Washington elites. Effective grassroots campaigns can influence citizens directly or they can lead elites to conclude that a groundswell of support or opposition to specific policy proposals exists.

Misperception is created by targeting key decision makers and by holding highly visible events. The impression of a nationwide movement can be projected by tightly focusing the public policy campaign. As described by Goddard, his group's theory was "you go to the people and they go to Congress. [Former Senate Minority Leader] Everett Dirksen said when they feel the heat, they see the light."[64] In this campaign, the heat was very selectively applied. Isakowitz put it more bluntly: "You don't have to turn around public opinion as long as congressional offices are getting flooded with hundreds of calls."[65]

A survey of the attitudes of legislators as well as interviews we conducted with several leading figures in early 1995 reveal evidence that reporters, key members of Congress, and White House officials took the Harry and Louise commercials seriously and believed these ads were decisive in altering the national political debate on health care. In response to the legislator survey question "which interest groups had the greatest influence in the congressional debate and decisions on health care reform," the top group mentioned was the insurance industry and HIAA (mentioned by 29 percent), followed by small business and NFIB (22 percent) and health care providers (11 percent).[66]

In fact, the yuppie couple achieved enough prominence in Washington to reach the status of inside-the-beltway cultural icons, a notable achievement in and of itself. HIAA president Gradison described his group's ads as "like a soap opera. We started getting questions like what are their names, where do they work, do they have any children, [and] what kind of car do they drive?"[67]

The Harry and Louise ads became a virtual mini-series that spawned numerous headlines, counterresponses, spoofs, and cartoons. One national news organization (the *New York Times*/CBS News) even conducted a survey specifically to gauge the impact of Harry and Louise. Clinton friend Harry Thomason produced a spoof ad that began in a graveyard with church bells ringing in the background. The actor in the ad says: "You've probably seen a young yuppie couple named Harry and Louise on television recently, questioning the President's health care plan. I thought I'd bring you up to date. Harry lost his job and also his insurance. Louise owned a small and struggling company that could not afford group insurance, so she had always depended upon Harry's policy. Unfortunately, she had a pre-existing condition that prevented her from obtaining new coverage." Eventually, according to the ad, Louise died, Harry moved to another state where he got a job making coffee commercials, and his new company did not have an insurance plan. The ad closed with the actor saying, "Oh, by the way, if you see Harry, tell him to hang in there. The president's plan is just around the corner."[68]

This was followed by a spoof at the Gridirons Club in March featuring Bill and Hillary Clinton as Harry and Louise, sponsored by the "Coalition to Scare Your Pants Off." The befuddled first couple sat on a couch expressing bewilderment at their own health care plan, their words designed to poke fun at their critics. Hillary: "Some of these details sure scare the heck out of me." Bill: "Like what?" Hillary: "Like for example, it says here on page 3,764 that under the Clinton Health Security plan, we could get sick." Bill: "That's terrible." . . . Hillary: "It gets worse. . . . Eventually, we all are going to die." Bill: "Under the Clinton health plan? You mean after Bill and Hillary put all those new bureaucrats and taxes on us, we're still all going to die? . . . I've never been so frightened in all my life." Bill and Hillary in unison: "There's got to be a better way."[69] The crowd of journalists gave the Clintons a standing ovation.

Even cartoonists and other groups joined in the Harry and Louise spin-offs. A newspaper cartoon by Don Wright showed a couple watching television while the wife said to her husband, "All we know is that Harry and Louise, the insurance couple, have been shot and the cops are chasing Clinton round and round the beltway!"[70] Supporters of a Canadian-style, single-payer system ran an ad in May featuring the comedy team of Jerry Stiller and Anne Meara declaring: "Harry and Louise, there is a better way."[71]

Numerous officials blamed the HIAA spots for turning public opinion against the Clinton proposal and bemoaned their difficulty in countering the opposition message. White House health care advisor Magaziner said the HIAA ads "scared a lot of people by putting out misinformation. It was akin to a presidential campaign where one candidate has tens of millions to spend on ads and the other candidate can't spend any money on advertising."[72]

The fact that HIAA ads, phone banks, and direct mail were integrated gave the group unusual flexibility in targeting members of Congress. Gradison said, "we moved around our focus depending on what committee or subcommittee was considering a bill at a particular time. In that sense, it was highly focused. We tried to reach the swing members of those committees on a serial basis depending on when they would be taking things up."[73]

Magaziner pointed out that the combination of ads, phone banks, and direct mail "were effective at creating the impression of a grassroots campaign." Continuing, he said, "Every place I would go to a town hall meeting, a lot of people would have received letters or calls from these groups. They would ask questions like why are you taking over all the hospitals, which was not true. The same thing would happen on talk shows." He said the ads were particularly important in Washington. "They were all over the airwaves. I used to have a twenty-minute drive to work and they were frequently on the radio."[74]

Reporters were affected too, regularly crediting the Harry and Louise spots "with undermining public confidence" in the Clinton plan and doing "more than any single lobbying tactic to hobble Clinton's plan."[75] A June 20, 1994, network story by John Cochran of ABC News credited Harry and Louise with "creating real doubts" about the Clinton program among the general public. In fact, this story line emphasizing widespread doubts was becoming ingrained in many press reports about the controversy.

A study we conducted of national newspaper stories in the *New York Times, Washington Post, Los Angeles Times,* and *Wall Street Journal* found 55 articles about health care ads, many of which extolled the power of Harry and Louise. Of the stories, 51 percent had headlines mentioning television ads, 9 percent had headlines specifically mentioning Harry and Louise, and 13 percent had pictures of Harry and Louise. In terms of the news content of these stories, 36 percent had comments emphasizing the importance of ads to the health care debate and 22 percent had comments emphasizing the importance of the Harry and Louise ads to the discussion of health care. A parallel study we undertook of the television network evening news revealed 11 broadcast stories. Of these, 8 mentioned the Harry and Louise ads and most showed video from the HIAA spots. For a single set of advocacy ads, this was an extraordinary degree of exposure.

As a sign of the potency of the advertisements, the summer of 1994 featured the unprecedented spectacle of then House Ways and Means Committee chair Dan Rostenkowski (D-Ill) negotiating an agreement with HIAA. Rep. Rostenkowski agreed to changes in health care legislation *in exchange for an agreement that the HIAA would not run ads in particular states.*[76] HIAA president Gradison, a former Ways and Means member himself, recalled that "Rostenkowski referred to the [Harry and Louise] ads as the "Willie Horton" ads and said it was time to stop shouting at each other. . . . We just agreed to stop the ads during the markup after Rostenkowski agreed to a couple of substantive changes we had asked for." However, Gradison said, "nothing came of it so we went back on the air."[77]

Gradison conceded that this was "an unusual arrangement." In regard to the agreement, an administration official said "the idea was you let up on my committee members and we'll help you out on the legislation."[78] Remarkably, an interest group managed to cow the powerful chair of a powerful congressional committee through a series of television ads. Within weeks, though, this pact came unglued when a felony indictment forced Rostenkowski to relinquish his committee leadership.

In his interview with us, Gradison indicated that the Rostenkowski negotiations were not the first time such a deal had been offered by HIAA. The day of Clinton's national speech on September 22, 1993, Gradison said he had "called [Dick] Celeste [who was managing the field operation on health care] and said 'We know you guys are sore about the ads. I don't want them to stand in the way of our working together. We unilaterally and with no preconditions stopped the ads. We are going to watch very carefully tonight to see if you guys stop beating up on us.' I also told him we had a couple of new ads in the can which were being tested in focus groups." But the offer bore no fruit, Gradison said. "A couple of weeks went by and they hit us again, and that was our signal to start our ads again. Once it became very clear that things had not changed at their end, we went back on the air around October 10."[79]

By summer 1994, the anti-Clinton campaign was defining the policy debate. The Democratic National Committee began airing a new spot on July 10 called "Harry Takes a Fall." In the ad, "Harry and Louise are in bed. Harry is in a full body cast; his head is bandaged. Louise's arm is in a sling. She chides Harry for having been skeptical about proposals for universal health insurance coverage. Harry, it seems, has lost his job, his health insurance and most of his financial assets."[80] If imitation is indeed flattery, the HIAA ads had succeeded in defining the core issues of health care, at least inside the beltway.

Rolling the Elites

The anti–Clinton health reform effort was one of the most successful policy advertising campaigns in American history.[81] A newly elected Democratic president who had made health care reform the centerpiece of his domestic agenda was defeated without a definitive vote being taken on the floor of either house of the Democratically controlled Congress. By attaching an opposing narrative based on high cost and big government to the president's proposal, opponents effectively derailed Clinton's initiative. With media coverage reinforcing the message of interest group advertising, the electorate could not disentangle truth from falsehood, and policy-making elites found it easy to construct explanations for opposing the Clinton plan.

This case demonstrates several key points. There is little doubt that big financial resources made a difference in consideration of health care reform. HIAA alone spent $20 million overall, with $14 million devoted to producing and broadcasting ads. The heavenly chorus of interest group influence was instrumental in defining the terms of the ensuing public debate. And group influence was enhanced, not diminished by the highly visible policy debate.[82] Constructing a powerful set of stories and repeating them to selected elites allowed the interests opposing the Clinton plan to defeat the issue before it even got off the ground.

This research also suggests a new way for interest groups to be effective. Traditionally, group campaigns have been successful either through direct lobbying (the inside strategy) or by mobilizing the public, who then communicated group objections to Washington (the outside strategy). The health care experience demonstrates that outside strategies can work not just by targeting the public, but by altering the impressions of news reporters and Washington elites. As an administration official explained, "the lobbying effort scared the heck out of legislative members. . . . The effectiveness was all money-induced."[83] If elites can be persuaded that the public does not approve of a particular proposal, that campaign is successful even if it turns out elite views are based on misperceptions.[84] The big early spending by a few prominent interests created a major new dynamic in the policy debate. But the subsequent failure of the media to critically evaluate those interests' claims led to a widespread Washington view that credited a grassroots uprising with derailing Clinton's program, as opposed to a savvy media campaign by a few interest groups.

These problems were accentuated because the issues were complex, yet still salient to the American public. Although surveys indicated more people felt knowledgeable as the debate unfolded, most Americans did not have a good sense of what President Clinton was attempting. This allowed opponents to fill the void through advertising that was deceptive or misleading. For example, one group called the American Council for Health Care Reform ran a stealth campaign of direct mailings that accused the Clinton administration of advocating prison time for people who bought "extra care." The charge was blatantly false, but became part of the negative narrative surrounding health care reform.[85]

An administration official pointed out that all the personal attacks on Clinton's character in 1993 and 1994 hurt the health care effort as well. According to one such official, attitudes on public health care reform tracked "very closely with presidential popularity."[86] Another official (Heenan) added that "[Clinton pollster Stanley] Greenberg's early polls found that people's view of reform indicated a certain nervousness and lack of full understanding. It was going to come down to people's trust in the reformers."

The combined emergence of Whitewater and the Arkansas trooper situation hurt Clinton on this crucial trust dimension. Criticisms about the Clintons' investment in a failed savings and loan raised doubts about the president's basic trustworthiness. Meanwhile, trooper allegations that Clinton routinely used them to pick up women for him when he was governor of Arkansas reinforced public impressions that the president was utterly lacking in any moral fiber. Quoting Rush Limbaugh, Heenan noted, "Whitewater [was] about health care."[87] If the president could not be trusted on Whitewater and on his personal character, why should he be trusted on health care reform? It was a question President Clinton never managed to answer very convincingly. Moreover, the central counternarrative on reform, articulated by Harry and Louise, was that although some reform might be needed, this one—the Clinton plan—could not be trusted to solve the important problems. Rather, things would only get worse, and neither the public nor political elites would take that chance.

Chapter Five

===

Selling the Contract
with America

The demise of Clinton's health care reform proposal in 1994 dramatically altered the political environment facing organized interests of all stripes. The decision by Congress not to enact comprehensive health care reform was vivid testimony to the power of well-organized and well-financed interests. Powerful interest groups were able to use sophisticated lobbying strategies to mold media coverage and create narratives that undermined the very essence of the president's domestic agenda. When this lobbying victory was followed a few months later by the dramatic Republican takeover of the House and Senate, it was one of the most extraordinary reversals of recent American history.

The 1994 elections brought to power a new leader, Speaker Newt Gingrich, who had big ideas about American politics and the role outside interest groups could play in helping the new Republican majority.[1] Gingrich and his allies in the GOP moved quickly to exploit their historic opportunity. Progressive organizations were dispirited at their rout on health care, and many of the groups that had played such a crucial role in blocking comprehensive health care reform, such as insurers and small businesses, rallied behind the new Republican party manifesto known as the Contract with America.

The Contract was a bold effort to reshape the core of American public policy. Revolutionary in its scope, the Contract sought to downsize the federal government, devolve responsibility to state and local government, and create what proponents called an "opportunity society."[2] Much in the same way that Franklin Roosevelt used the New Deal to control the legislative agenda, keep divisive issues off the docket, and maintain party discipline, Speaker Newt Gingrich employed the Contract to keep his party focused on a clear set of objectives.

In the short term, the Contract was at best a partial political success. Although the House passed 9 of the 10 Contract planks in the first 100 days of the 104th Congress, the Senate approved parts of just 3 planks. The one major bill (tort reform) that passed both the House and Senate was vetoed by President Clinton in 1996. Although fiery in its rhetoric, the "Republican revolution" of 1995 produced far fewer legislative enactments than many of its proponents had hoped. However, Republicans held control of Congress in 1996 and soon produced an historic agreement with President Clinton to balance the budget. By 1997, major parts of the Contract had become law, which indicated that the Republicans may well have altered the terms of the debate on large chunks of public policy.

These particular ups and downs notwithstanding, the Contract represents a fascinating case of how dramatically the political agenda has changed in recent years.[3] The issues that have come to dominate public discourse are topics such as the devolution of federal authority, a balanced budget, tax cuts, toughening criminal penalties, and welfare reform, among others. Hopes of extending health care coverage to all Americans or developing new social programs remain a faded dream.

In looking at how the agenda shifted from universal health care to devolution and the Republican revolution, it is hard not to notice the crucial role played by interest groups supportive of the GOP. The Contract with America represents a telling illustration of how powerful organizations developed market-based narratives in order to further large-scale policy change. As seen with health care reform, large sums of money from outside groups were spent on research, ads, polls, direct mail, and phone banks to build support for Gingrich's program. With the rise of a new Republican majority in Congress, all-out pursuit of a business-oriented legislative agenda became a viable political strategy, as opposed to the uneasy alliance that had existed earlier between corporate interests and Democratic majorities in the House.[4] The Republican takeover of the House and Senate in 1994 gave business and conservative groups the means to move inside the legislative system, construct new narratives, and sell these notions to reporters and the general public.[5]

Developing the Contract

The initial idea for the Contract came in early meetings between House Representatives Gingrich, Richard Armey, Bill Paxon (then chairman of the National Republican Congressional Committee), Tom DeLay, and Robert Walker. All these men later would serve in the House leadership during the 104th Congress. Discussed first at a February 1994 conference of House Republicans held in Salisbury, Maryland, the Contract was refined in meetings throughout the summer and announced publicly that fall. After post-election interviews with key participants, *Washington Post* reporter Dan Balz found that the Contract "was the product of months of planning that included everything from polling and focus groups to consultation among Republican constituencies to analysis and scrubbing by GOP experts."[6]

This pretesting reflected the Republican recognition that their core ideas needed the general support of the American public. Since support often dwindles as policy controversies unfold, House Republicans sought to start their electoral and policy battles with substantial political capital in the bank. Poll-based approval ratings of 60 percent became the threshold level for inclusion of individual items in the Contract, according to Barry Jackson, director of the Contract with America office at the Republican National Committee and a former administrative assistant to Rep. John Boehner of Ohio.[7] "We wanted a unifying document. You couldn't use items that would divide people, such as abortion, school prayer, or gay rights."[8] Also recognizing the importance of language and code words in American politics, Republican pollster Ed Goeas conducted three focus groups for the House Republican Conference in June 1994 to try out various themes: "[We] tested verbiage and nuances on words to make sure there were no red flags we should worry about."[9]

Based on this research, the Contract planks took on carefully scripted names, such as the Personal Responsibility Act (welfare reform), the Taking Back Our Streets Act (crime), the American Dream Restoration Act (tax relief),

FIGURE 5.1 PLANKS OF THE CONTRACT WITH AMERICA:
LEGISLATION AS NARRATIVE

---

1. The Fiscal Responsibility Act
2. The Taking Back Our Streets Act
3. The Personal Responsibility Act
4. The Family Reinforcement Act
5. The American Dream Restoration Act
6. The National Security Restoration Act
7. The Senior Citizens Fairness Act
8. The Job Creation and Wage Enhancement Act
9. The Common Sense Legal Reforms Act
10. The Citizen Legislature Act

---

and the Common Sense Legal Reforms Act (tort reform), among others. Originally, there were "over eighty items" discussed as part of the Contract, but "through polls and discussions with Republican candidates, this was whittled down to ten issues."[10] In the end, the symbolism of the items became at least as important as their substance, as can be seen in the titles of the individual planks of the Contract (see figure 5.1). After all, the Contract was devised to help Republicans gain control of Congress in 1994; at the same time, it also set much of the legislative agenda in 1995–97.

Beyond the information gleaned from focus groups and public opinion polls, Republicans understood the importance of organized interests in determining the shape of legislative conflict. To make sure they had key players on board, Armey held a series of working sessions composed of legislators, staff members, and outside groups to develop specific language for each of the ten Contract planks. According to Jackson, "the working groups were crucial. They were mini-markup sessions. We held hearings, went to outsiders, and tried to develop the best possible ideas."[11]

The goal of these meetings was to produce a "user-friendly Contract. We wanted it to be a document where ordinary citizens could see the title, read a couple of bullets about it, and understand what we wanted to do."[12] This view was reiterated by Gingrich communications coordinator Leigh Ann Metzger. She said, "the task of education was the biggest hurdle we had, letting people know what was in the bill, [and] why they should be for or against it."[13]

Each plank had its own working group. Based on a model of restricted group access, ideological affinity with the goals of House leaders was paramount in every coalition. Consistent with this approach, David Mason, director of the U.S. Congress Assessment Project for the Heritage Foundation, which helped write the Contract, described the ideological litmus tests used in outside consultation. According to him, people consulted included "organizations that supported the political objectives of the House Republicans developing the Contract. That meant mostly conservative groups and think tanks like us and lobbying groups interested in selling the idea and getting it adopted on the Hill."[14]

Among the most important groups were "the Christian Coalition, Free Congress Foundation, Citizens for a Sound Economy, Americans for Tax Reform, Family Research Council, National Taxpayer Union, and U.S. Term Limits." Mason felt House Republicans "were very receptive to our suggestions. On staff cuts, they got advice they had not anticipated and ended up taking the advice. . . . In the tax area, the $500 child tax credit was our baby."[15]

All of this suggests that, in an era of limited resources, legislative leaders hoping to win a majority will try to keep group coalitions narrow so that they can target political beneficiaries. There are not enough resources for political minorities to build permeable issue networks involving lots of interests. Political alliances need to be kept tightly focused in order to use resources most effectively.

This view was echoed by Christie Carson, staff aide to Rep. John Boehner (R-Ohio) and previously to Gingrich, who helped coordinate the meetings with outside groups. According to her, "we had meetings with outside groups every week where we let them know what was going on and let them know what we were doing. Our natural allies were Citizens for a Sound Economy, Americans for Tax Reform, the Heritage Foundation, the NFIB [National Federation of Independent Businesses], and the Chamber of Commerce."[16]

When asked what the common thread was pulling these groups together, she responded, "they believe in American rights. . . . [T]hey believe in a smaller government and returning power to the state. That is a natural ally with the Republican party. The whole idea behind the Contract was getting the federal government out of people's lives. We wanted to give power back to the states and the people. That is a real big common thread with a lot of the members and [outside interest] groups."

Pollster Goeas described the outside groups this way: "we worked with the National Federation of Independent Businesses, American Medical Association, and anti-tax groups. The NFIB was the lead group. Our consultation was with groups we normally would work with on policy issues and in the campaign. They were our core support groups."[17] With 600,000 members, NFIB has a widely distributed and highly activist set of constituents around the country, which, as demonstrated on health care reform, makes it a very powerful interest group.

Metzger argued that "small business increasingly has become a base group within the Republican party, especially when you are talking about regulation and taxation."[18] Rep. DeLay (R-Texas) said House party leaders consulted with "mostly Republican groups." With a mixture of irony and sarcasm, DeLay added, "Ralph Nader was not there."[19]

On the tax plank, there were four meetings before the Contract was announced. The meetings involved "all the tax groups, like the National Taxpayers Union, the tax people from Heritage and Cato, just everyone who is a tax expert in town—who is pro-lower taxes," according to Grover Norquist, executive director of the anti-tax group Americans for Tax Reform and a key participant in the formulation of the Contract.[20] In these meetings, Norquist said, outside groups were asked, "What do you think is important? What do you think is more important and less important? What is important to your members? We had debates. I wanted to include the flat tax and they were correct in rejecting my advice. I was not thinking correctly that these were to be baby steps that we knew we could accomplish. We only promised what we thought we could win."[21]

Marketing the Contract

Figuring out how to market the Contract was a key part of early deliberations. In an era of many voices in the communications system and extensive uncertainty about political influence, planners understood it was not enough just to develop a Contract. Both legislators and lobbyists had to sell the idea to the press, the Washington establishment, and the general public. As discussed in chapter 2, the key marketing issues were simplicity, consistency, and repetition. The lesson of Clinton's failed effort at health care reform loomed over everyone like a bad hangover. The goal was to repeat a simple and consistent message over and over until the idea of government downsizing dominated political discourse.

To accomplish this task, the number of planks was set at ten, an easily understandable set of proposals. According to Mason, "the reason ten was chosen was that's a graspable, understandable number, from the Ten Commandments right on down to David Letterman's Top Ten List."[22]

The results of polls and focus groups were crucial in these discussions. After the Contract was developed, Republican pollster Frank Luntz conducted a survey and held focus groups to "test specific language." He showed focus groups four different versions of a national ad that then ran in *TV Guide* magazine at a cost of $250,000. *TV Guide* was picked because "the typical subscriber would open up the magazine repeatedly the week it was current," which was the week of October 22–28, 1994, right before the November midterm elections.[23]

The Contract was unveiled September 27, 1994, in a public signing ceremony with over 300 Republican congressional candidates. Organized with the precision of a major movie premiere, this ceremony marked the formal kick-off of the Contract's public-relations campaign. The date was chosen to capitalize on the final six weeks of the 1994 general election campaign, when both public and media interest would be at a peak. Republicans clearly hoped the Contract would focus national attention on their cause. According to Norquist, "the Contract was a political tool. It gave you a cohesive message nationwide. . . . Basically, we said there are two parties, one a conservative one and the other a liberal one. Vote for us."[24]

Initial reactions to the Contract were not positive. The

Contract was derided as a "Contract on America" by President Clinton. Jackson noted, "before the election, the Contract was belittled by the national media until the president attacked it. That gave it a lot of credibility and helped us."[25] Democratic pollster Stanley Greenberg noted that "hardly any Republican candidate around the country used the Contract in their ads."[26] The apparent electoral impact of the Contract was nil. Even Republican pollster Goeas said he "couldn't point to one 1994 election decided based on the Contract."[27] Indeed, national polls right after the election found that 60 percent of those who had voted in the election had not even heard of the Contract.[28]

Still, the Contract wasn't irrelevant. Rather, the lack of detailed public knowledge meant that in the upcoming congressonal debate, external forces such as interest groups and the media would play a crucial role in determining how the public evaluated the plan. If voters knew little about the Contract, it meant others would define for them what it was all about. After Republicans won control of Congress, Gingrich used the Contract to claim victory for a clear legislative mandate. It would become part of his personal story about leading a surprise policy revolution.

Passing the Contract

The unexpected Republican takeover of the House and Senate in the 1994 elections gave a new burst of energy to the Contract with America. Ironically, considering its marginal status during the campaign, the Contract became the dominant focus of news coverage. Newly elected Speaker Gingrich used the Contract to frame the national policy agenda for the first 100 days in the House of Representatives and determine the content of House legislative deliberations. The story line he consistently pushed with colleagues and reporters was that the Contract was central to the Republican victory, that the party had a clear mandate, and that Contract legislation was strongly favored by outside interests.

From a political standpoint, the group consultation model developed during the 1994 campaign became the organizing framework for legislative action and public relations in 1995. According to Barry Jackson, "we used working groups because we needed a structure which crossed committee lines. We couldn't do what we needed to do by working through the traditional committee structure. The working groups helped us manage the process."[29]

Congressional committees were considered weak by the new party leaders. Gingrich sought to centralize power over committee chairs. Friendly chairs were appointed, sometimes instead of other members with greater seniority. Much of the policy agenda was controlled by party leaders, not committee chairs.

To promote the Contract, outside groups and communications consultants played a major role, often through the vehicle of legislative working groups. Many of these groups had been aligned with House Republican leaders during the campaign and had strongly opposed the Clinton health care initiative. It therefore was natural for House leaders after the election to turn to these outside groups for research and publicity.

One of the first things Republicans did after taking over Congress was to let major interest groups know a new regime had taken over in Washington. Recalling past slights when they were in the minority, Republicans employed their new majority to "collect donations and change [donor] allegiances" from major groups to the GOP.[30] For example, many Republicans were "instructing schedulers to run what are essentially background checks on lobbyists who want meetings" to discover their political loyalties. Some groups were blackballed because of past associations with Democratic legislators or rebuffs of Republican initiatives. Political action committees were asked to retire the campaign debts of freshman legislators, the key support group for the Contract with America, and groups were asked to hire pro-Republican lobbyists.[31] Word was put out to lobbyists that they needed to help Republicans. Jack Abramoff, a Washington lobbyist who was close to Gingrich, said at the time: "Assistance for the freshmen is clearly the most important goal from the political contribution point of view. Perhaps even more important is whether they're being helpful to the conservative movement and the philosophical agenda."[32]

What was remarkable about these efforts was not just that Republicans rewarded their political friends, a time-honored tradition in American politics, but that the GOP made these moves with such vigor, passion, and visibility. It was a clear affirmation of the investment theory of interest groups. According to Republicans, lobbyists should give money in order to expect to receive policy benefits from the new majority.

Groups sympathetic to Contract goals were brought into the bill-writing process and given unprecedented access.[33] For each of the ten Contract planks, Republicans formed working groups composed of lobbyists and conservative interest groups designed to promote the Contract, similar to what had been done during the campaign. For example, the "Thursday group" (also known as the Coalition for America's Future) met every week to develop tax-cut strategies with Rep. John Boehner (R-Ohio), chair of the House Republican Conference, and Sen. Paul Coverdell of Georgia.

The coalition represented the same types of groups that had been consulted by House Republicans during the campaign. It was a "who's who of American industry, from the National Association of Home Builders to the Chamber of Commerce."[34] The Thursday group demonstrated that interests that had proved their loyalty when Republicans were on the outside now were given extraordinary inside lobbying access. It signaled the dramatic turnabout in conservative group influence.

According to Keith Apel, an outside media consultant for the Contract, "small business groups like the National Federation of Independent Businesses and the National Restaurant Association hooked up with the Christian Coalition and the Family Research Council to lobby to get [the Contract] passed."[35] Grover Norquist described the discussions as "weekly meetings Boehner held with business groups, taxpayer groups, and the Christian Coalition. We just sat down and said here is where the legislation is and who can help call their members in certain districts and get the word out on what is happening and help publicize the fight."[36]

In a sense, Republicans were devising the ultimate grassroots lobbying campaign. Interest groups were instructing legislators how to use their members around the country to put pressure on other legislators in order to get bills passed. It was a potent display of a coordinated inside and outside lobbying strategy.

According to participants, outside groups had unprecedented access to bill drafting. Democratic House member George Miller of California, for example, wrote in a *New York Times* column that "lobbyists [have been serving] as virtual staff members."[37] He reported that lobbyists had been seated on the dais with Republicans during formal hearings on issues of interest to their clients and that a lobbyist for Wholesale Distributors, a trade association, used a Capitol Hill office to work on strategy for the product liability bill.[38]

After bills were drafted based on Contract language, a variety of tactics were used to build support for the Contract. This included broadcasting ads, running phone banks, and sending direct mail, all under the slogan of "Saving Our Future." Each company and group involved in the working groups contributed money to pay for research, phone banks, ads, and direct mail. Rep. Peter Hoekstra (R-Mich.) was put in charge of promotion because of his marketing background. In daily meetings with Rep. Bob Franks of New Jersey and Rep. Susan Molinari of New York, five target groups were identified among the general public: "baby boomers nervous that Social Security will be broke when they retire; independent-minded Perot voters who want lawmakers to make tough decisions; blue-collar Reagan Democrats who favor welfare cuts but resent GOP tax cuts for the rich; seniors who worry that Social Security and Medicare benefits will be slashed; and young adults who fear growing national debt as a threat to their living standards."[39]

The Republican party organized training sessions to teach legislators and press secretaries how to use cable television, talk radio, computer networks, faxes, and town meetings to defend the party line.[40] The Republican television channel GOP-TV produced its own shows for about 2,000 cable systems, sent news clips to 750 local stations, and provided satellite technology for representatives to beam themselves back home.

Many of the activities used to promote the Contract were financed by outside groups that had participated in the formulation of the Contract. In an interview, Jackson explained, "so many things were moving quickly that we needed a way to manage the communications process. This is where outside groups helped."[41] Keith Apel set up the "Contract Information Center," which was completely funded by Republican contributor Fred Sacher, a real estate developer from California who was a long-time financial backer of Gingrich and other causes such as the Nicaraguan *contras*. According to Apel, "Fred Sacher hired us but we never would have done this without the blessing of Newt's office, Armey's office, and the RNC. They knew it was necessary to augment the communications approach from within the beltway."[42]

Because the public relations effort went through a private individual rather than the party or leadership offices, no disclosure of spending was required. The Contract Information Center never disclosed its total spending or the manner in which money was spent. This tactic was perfectly legal because the effort was privately financed and the Federal Election Commission only regulates political spending specifically related to election campaigns.[43] Once the first 100 days was past, the center was disbanded, and Apel's agency, Creative Response Concepts, was hired by the Republican National Committee to promote the GOP budget package.

Nearly all of this financial infrastructure for the Contract lay beneath the radar of the mainstream press. There were a few stories about the Contract Information Center and how it was financed by a single individual. But there was no massive coverage about the secrecy of the effort or the conflict of interest inherent in such an activity. It was a striking illustration of a successful stealth campaign by outside interests with almost no public oversight.

The Contract Information Center was designed, according to Apel, to be a "one-stop shop for the media which for many years has not had many Republican sources in their Rolodex because Democrats controlled Congress. . . . The media tend to skew leftward. They know who to go to in various liberal organizations to get quotes. They did not know who to go to on the conservative side. We made sure someone from a conservative or free-market organization got into those stories so that the coverage was more accurate and balanced."[44]

The center was part of a broad-based communications strategy put together by congressional Republicans and funded by outside interests. According to Carson, "a lot of these groups just took it upon themselves to run ads and do phone banks."[45] Specific pitches on behalf of the Contract were made through talk radio, television and radio commercials, videos aimed at grassroots activists, and direct mail to specific groups. Norquist said he personally did "three to four radio talk shows a day" during House consideration of Contract proposals in spring 1995.[46] Opinion leaders were wooed by sending lawmakers to meet with newspaper editorial boards. Polls and focus groups helped to fine-tune the merchandising of the final package.

One of the most active outside groups was the Christian Coalition. Using its 1.6 million members and $25 million annual budget, the Christian Coalition devoted one million dollars to promoting the Contract via phone banks, ads, and direct mail. Press accounts noted that "Coalition lobbyists sat among the select group of outsiders who met regularly in Newt Gingrich's suite to coordinate the campaign to pass the Contract with America."[47] Not only did the Christian Coalition help promote the Contract, it subordinated its own moralistic agenda against abortions and in favor of school prayer to the Contract objectives of downsizing government.

The anti-tax group Americans for Tax Reform ran targeted radio ads and sent mail into lawmakers' districts. According to Norquist, "on the balanced budget amendment, we targeted Nathan Deal [D-Georgia], who later switched to the Republican party; Fred Upton [R-Michigan], who voted with us; Dan Schaefer [R-Colorado], who didn't vote with us initially though he eventually did. We targeted Sherwood Boehlert [R-New York], who misbehaved" on a few votes of interest to Republicans.[48]

The subsequent level of party loyalty was remarkable. In 1995, the first year after Republicans seized control of the House, nearly all Republicans supported their party leadership on crucial Contract votes. Although Democratic party loyalty had risen steadily beteen 1981 and 1994, the Republican unity during the Contract votes was extraordinary. The Republican membership's general homogeneity and the leadership's careful framing of the issues made it possible for almost all House Republicans to be on the same page at the same time.

Beyond pushing for passage of the Contract with America, outside groups funded ads to proclaim the successful conclusion of the first 100 days in the House. The Republican National Committee broadcast an ad in April 1995 on CNN and in Washington, D.C., that bragged about the party's initial success: "The first Republican Congress in more than forty years began by forcing Congress to live by the same rules as anyone else. Not bad . . . for the first hundred days."[49] The ad was put together by Smith & Haroff of Alexandria, Virginia, at a cost of $300,000. Nine of the ten Contract planks were approved by the House by the end of the first 100 days. From his time in the political minority, Gingrich took the Contract, which was not a real success electorally in 1994, declared a mandate, and used a classic inside/outside lobbying strategy to push the legislation through the House.

The only thing Gingrich neglected in declaring victory

was that the House was not the end of the legislative process. Unfortunately for him, the Contract was not nearly as successful in the Senate. As its provisions generated controversy, opposition Senators were able to use procedural rules to delay and in many cases stop action. By the close of the 104th Congress, only three full planks had been passed by the Senate. The bill forcing Congress to abide by the same rules as the private sector was approved as were vague limits on unfunded liabilities for states and a comprehensive reform of tort law. But as the next section demonstrates, tort reform did not actually make it into law. After considerable agonizing, President Clinton vetoed the most comprehensive part of the Contract that passed both the House and Senate in 1995.

The Special Case of Tort Reform: The Limits of Narrative

Perhaps no plank of the Contract with America illustrates the sharp conflict on major legislation better than tort reform. Along with the tax cut, this policy area was the most sensitive plank of the Contract, and it reflected one of the most enduring political controversies in America. The topic was delicate politically for two reasons. First, the working group supporting tort reform felt strongly that "the legal system was out of control, that we needed to cap punitive damages, that it was too easy to sue, and that small businesses were being hurt by all these lawsuits."[50]

For years, businesses had complained about a "liability crisis" sweeping America. Individual anecdotes of extreme court decisions were publicized, such as a million dollar award (subsequently substantially reduced) for a woman who spilled searing hot McDonald's coffee on herself. It would become gospel in the tort reform narrative that lawsuits were ruining America and that Americans were overly eager to sue because of excessive jury awards. Because of these fears, the coalition in favor of tort reform was "a cohesive unit that worked together and put resources on the table."[51] Tort reform proponents spent $1.7 million on print and broadcast ads in the final week before the June 28, 1995, Senate vote.[52]

The second reason for the delicate nature of tort reform is that it involved a well-organized and well-financed opponent, namely, trial lawyers. "Trial lawyers had a humongous organization with a ton of money," according to Carson.[53] Metzger added, "trial lawyers are strong because of money, voice, and campaign contributions. If you look at trial lawyer contributions on the Hill, you'll find they have a great deal of influence."[54] Ultimately, a coalition of trial lawyers spent $1.5 million on a television advertising blitz in the ten days before the crucial vote in the Senate. The ads targeted twenty states with undecided Senators who had received campaign contributions from trial lawyers.[55]

As tort reform got under way, House Republicans realized that, among the Contract items, they would have the biggest problem in this area. The complex nature of the political conflict as well as the well-financed and well-organized nature of doctors, lawyers, and insurers meant that the battle would be intense. As a result, GOP lobbying efforts were "more structured and took on a clearer identity than on some of the other planks." House Republican leaders decided that on tort reform, "we were going to need to put all of our resources together."[56]

Because of the high stakes of the battle and the ability of both sides to marshal financial resources, it is no surprise that tort reform elicited the most spending by outside groups. Three planks within the Contract (tort reform, the balanced budget amendment, and term limits) generated television ad campaigns, which is the most expensive type of public lobbying. But it was tort reform that had the largest television advertising expenditure. According to Metzger, several outside groups "spent about $2 million" on television advertising concerning tort reform on the House side alone.[57] Still, this amount could scarcely affect mass opinions; elites remained the key target.

Ben Goddard, creator of the by now legendary Harry and Louise health care ads, was hired by an ad hoc coalition of small business groups, including the NFIB, the Chamber of Commerce, and Citizens for a Sound Economy, to develop ads to push legal reform. Later, that coalition joined with the Civil Justice Reform group and the media agency Apco Associates of Washington, D.C., to support the tort reform campaign. Apco had a long-standing relationship with the American Tort Reform Association, a national umbrella group of 400 different organizations representing small businesses, medical people, and nonprofit associations. Apco had done polling in more than twenty-five different states, according to its director, Neil Cowan, and "knew it was a popular issue" with the general public.[58]

One of the reasons ads were run on this issue was to counterbalance the political connections and financial resources of the bill's major opponents, trial lawyers. According to Metzger, "we had been told the trial lawyers were going to spend $20 million against us on tort reform."[59] For the most part, however, the trial lawyers played an inside game; increasing the visibility of high-dollar awards was scarcely in their interests, and their defense of the present system was complex and legalistic.

The first pro–tort reform ad featured a traditional icon of American society, "a field of Little League players who, one by one, vanish in mid-play as a narrator explains that liability insurance costs their teams more than 'bats, balls, and uniforms.' "[60] Another ad bemoaned the plight of small businesses facing nuisance lawsuits. About $2 million was spent on television ads in Washington in March 1995, the crucial time of consideration by the House of Representatives. Later, when members headed home for their spring recess, tort reform commercials ran on CNN, CNBC, Court TV, the Rush Limbaugh Show, and on selected local stations.

As the legislation moved to the Senate, targeted ads were directed at key senators, such as John Glenn of Ohio and Arlen Specter of Pennsylvania. Other than the specific persons named in the ads, Goddard said there weren't big differences in commercials run during House and Senate consideration of tort reform: "there were only minor tweaks in the language used in the Senate Little League ad because the message was pretty much the same as in the House."[61]

This tort reform ad originally was not scheduled to feature Little Leaguers. According to Goddard, "first we talked to the Girl Scouts, which was the one group we wanted to do. They said, 'no way, you can't use us. We won't play.' So we looked for another American icon and the Little League folks were supportive of what we were trying to do."[62] Little League officials arranged for filming of an actual game in Granada Hills, California, and made sure Little League coaches were on site. Beyond the importance of the messenger, focus groups and surveys conducted by the coalition revealed, according to Goddard, that the tort reform ad must "make clear you would protect the right to sue and that you couldn't win this argument just by bashing trial lawyers."[63]

Each of the two Little League ads (one with a female

and the other with a male announcer) listed a toll-free 800 number that allowed callers to be patched through to a member of Congress or to an operator telling them how to send a mailgram to Congress. According to Goddard, "unlike health care reform, where we actually recruited people to join our grassroots coalition, in this case it was just simply getting phone calls made."[64] In a later commercial on medical malpractice, there was no 800 number, merely a tag line giving the name and phone number of the U.S. Senator from the targeted state.

Initially, the issues of concern to Goddard's coalition were not represented in the Contract. According to Goddard, "one set of our clients [the Federation of American Health Systems, the American Hospital Association, and the American Medical Association] was interested in medical malpractice and the other [the American Council of Life Insurance and various amall business groups] was interested in punitive damage limits. . . . The only thing in the Contract was product liability reform. To some degree, particularly in the early days, we had a somewhat antagonistic relationship to the House leadership group because we were asking for the bill to be expanded beyond what the Contract called for."[65]

Expanding the Contract on tort reform was a big request on the part of outside groups. In fact, no other plank witnessed a significant broadening beyond its original formulation. The reason was clear. According to Gingrich aide Metzger, "we tried to stay narrower on many planks because we were cognizant of what you could actually do in a hundred days. The narrower the legislation, the better the chance you were going to stick to a schedule and get it done. You also were minimizing areas of controversy. People had signed the dotted line on what the Contract would do. Christmas-treeing it, or adding a lot of other things to it, would be bad."[66]

But in a development that reveals much about the power of rich interest groups, medical malpractice reform and punitive damage limits were folded into the legislation at the last minute and ultimately passed the House of Representatives. When asked why medical malpractice was initially omitted, only to be added later, House Republican advisor Jackson explained, "medical malpractice originally was not in the contract. The reason was we had to keep the scope narrow to make it doable. If we broadened the bill too much, it would be difficult to manage."[67] The reason for its subsequent addition was, "medical malpractice is the defining issue with trial lawyers. It is a battle which has been coming for years. When facing the resources of trial lawyers and a sense that Congress could act on tort reform, we brought in medical malpractice. It was not brought in until the very end of the process, literally the week before it was voted on at the floor."[68] Apco representative Neil Cowan claimed, "it was brought in at the end because the doctors and their supporters were able to convince the leadership to bring up an amendment and were able to convince leadership they had enough botes to win. . . . The punitive damage side and the medical malpractice side was done because there was enough support demonstrated and by showing it was an issue constituents wanted. We showed legislators it was a popular issue and that it would not hurt them to expand the bill."[69]

It also appears clear that the resources of outside groups was one of the reasons why medical malpractice was added to tort reform. To take on a strong and well-funded opponent without sufficient resources on one's own side would be political suicide. Metzger noted, "We had a strong coalition. It seemed a viable vehicle to do something that we all cared about, which was medical malpractice reform. . . . It was in the spirit of what we wanted to do."[70]

Reflecting the pragmatism of House Republican leaders,

Metzger noted that expanding the bill would bring access to much-needed outside resources: "There were people who would immediately benefit from the bill." By adding the medical malpractice issue to the Contract, Republican leaders would gain money for a television ad campaign. Walking a fine line on the legality of coordinating inside and outside lobbying campaigns, Metzger explained the outside groups that favored tort reform "didn't clear that sort of stuff with us because obviously that would be illegal. We weren't driving the outside effort. They would let us know this is what they cared about and this was their position on it and here is what they were going to be doing. They'd be doing telephone calls, visits, letters to the Hill, and targeted media to put some pressure on members."[71]

Nevertheless, Cowan of Apco, who organized television advertising and phone calls for the American Tort Reform Association in support of the Contract, claimed House leaders played a very active role. He recounted, "we wanted to make sure what we were doing was consistent with what the House Republican leadership wanted. We coordinated things to make sure if we were doing advertising, that we ran ads in areas that lobbyists and legislators thought were particularly important. You only have so much money so you spend it in an appropriate way. We targeted the areas where the legislators and lobbyists thought we needed additional support."[72]

Goddard also confirmed that there was close coordination between lobbyists and legislators. He said while he personally had no discussions with the House leadership, "some of the lobbyists for companies that were members of the Civil Justice Reform group were also part of the House task force." It was clear to him that after medical malpractice reform was added, his clients "were in sync with the Contract" and worked actively on its behalf.[73] Still, it was something of a surprise to the outside groups when House Republicans acceded to their request to expand tort reform. According to Goddard: "No one ever expected to get medical malpractice in the bill. We were surprised when it was in the House bill."[74]

After House passage of tort reform, action moved to the Senate. Because of the Senate's rules and virtually unlimited opportunities for filibusters and delays, the bill moved very slowly. Owing to opposition from trial lawyers and indications of a possible veto from President Clinton, medical malpractice provisions were stripped from the legislation. Nevertheless, as a watered-down product liability bill moved through the Senate, Sen. Joseph Lieberman of Connecticut characterized the fight between trial lawyers and business interests as "two Goliaths battling each other."[75] Trial lawyers were Clinton's largest contributors in 1992 and 94 percent of their contributions went to Democrats during the 1994 congressional elections. On the other side were a variety of businesses that had been big contributors to the Republican party.

The Senate bill capped jury awards in punitive damage product liability lawsuits at $250,000 or twice compensatory damages, although it allowed larger awards in cases of "egregious conduct." After prolonged debate, the bill passed the Senate, but it was vetoed by President Clinton on the grounds that it restricted consumer rights.[76] Even in the aftermath of the veto, outside groups attempted to gain an advantage. The National Association of Wholesaler-Distributors and other business groups spent $5 million on ads in Ohio, Michigan, and Illinois that blasted Clinton for being too close to "rich trial lawyers."[77]

Although the bill died, tort reform allowed Republicans to show their sympathy toward business interests upset at the growth of lawsuits directed at them and to link Democrats to the greedy trial lawyers. Each of these interest groups returned the favor in the 1996 elections, giving record amounts to Republican and Democratic candidates respectively. By drawing a clear line in the sand on this issue, each party reinforced its electoral base and reaped millions of dollars in contributions from worried doctors, lawyers, and insurance agents. And interests demonstrated that they could succeed in setting the government agenda.

Lessons of the Contract

On the surface, the deep group penetration into legislative policy making by conservative groups appears little different from what Democrats have done for years with unions, environmental advocacy organizations, and minority groups. There certainly is little question that while Democrats were in charge of Congress, these constituent groups had preferred access to the policy process and that they reaped government benefits in return just as an investment theory of politics would have predicted.

Even on the legislative battle over the Contract itself, outside groups aligned with the Democratic party engaged in the very activities employed by Republican groups. For example, the Democratically affiliated firm of Greer, Margolis, Mitchell, Burns & Associates of Washington, D.C., which had created Clinton's presidential advertising campaign in 1992, developed a $500,000 print and TV campaign for the AFL-CIO stressing the importance of health and safety issues to Contract discussions.

Hoping to build on this, environmental groups such as the Environmental Information Center and the Sierra Club announced on April 5, 1995, a $2 million television and radio ad campaign warning that the new Congress might set back environmentalism by twenty-five years.[78] The Democratic Congressional Campaign Committee ran spots during the spring in the districts of Republican Representatives Jay Dicky of Arkansas and Phil English of Pennsylvania accusing them of having "marched in lockstep with Newt Gingrich" to cut programs for the needy. Each ad ended with the representative's picture being "morphed" into an image of Gingrich. In fall 1995, the Democratic National Committee spent approximately $25 million on ads warning about the dangers of Republican extremism and extolling Clinton's crucial role in moderating Republican efforts. And, to advance its agenda, the AFL-CIO devoted $35 million in 1996 to an issue advocacy campaign of television ads in congressional districts held by vulnerable Republicans.

Overall, the set of relationships Democrats had with constituent groups during their time in power was more permeable and open to a diverse range of interests than was true in the case of the Republican Contract with America. Republicans consulted with a more narrow range of groups and access was largely determined based on affinity with the ideological goals of House leaders. During their time in the majority, Democrats, in contrast, worked not just with unions and environmentalists but with business, agricultural, and corporate organizations not ideologically in sync with traditional Democratic values.

As a further sign of the tightness of group access during the development and promotion of the Contract, Republicans even went so far as to exclude some interests who should have been natural allies of the Contract. Due to their attentiveness to small business interests, Republicans limited access to big business because they did not trust large corporations to be aggressive in supporting cuts of government regulations and tax rates. House Majority

Leader Armey commented, "small businesses tend to be more ideological and principled in what they expect from the Government." Big business executives were "prags . . . [who] go where the wind blows."[79] Moreover, as we shall see, major corporate interests could fend for themselves in framing key issues.

The Republican situation furthermore is different because the groups with whom they chose to work were among the best organized and financed in the country. Many of the traditionally active Democratic groups represent the downtrodden and disenfranchised. Even when these groups are large and well organized, they do not have access to large war chests. Conservative and business groups, on the other hand, have abundant resources and no longer need to fund a party in Congress with whom they differ on many fundamental issues. Instead, they are able to pursue an ambitious and avowedly pro-business political agenda in conjunction with the Republican party.

Speaking more generally, it is apparent that the interest groups that participated in the development and promotion of the Contract reaped a beneficial payout in the planks of the Contract with America. The investment theory of politics postulates that groups give money to politicians in hopes of a return on their contributions. Although many parts of the Contract were not enacted into law, a number of particular interests did win beneficial provisions, especially in 1996 and 1997, as partisanship often bowed to pragmatism.

So generous were some of the legislative provisions of the Contract with America that a *New York Times* headline described the first 100 days as "Dreams Come True for Lobbyists."[80] The House passed measures that had been on business wish lists for years, such as lowering business taxes, reining in government regulators, and limiting the scope of civil lawsuits. Jerry Jasinowski, president of the National Association of Manufacturers, exclaimed "Our members are amazed at how much the House has achieved in terms of dramatically changing policies that are important to manufacturing. Finally, someone is trying to turn the place on its head and move in the direction of radical change."[81]

Small business groups were even more favored by the Contract with America. Mark Isakowitz, lobbyist for the National Federation of Independent Businesses, described the first 100 days as "a big triumph for small businesses."[82] Press accounts noted that meetings House Republicans had with outside interests during 1994 pushed the Contract toward "tax and regulatory recommendations friendlier to Main Street than to Wall Street."[83] The *New York Times* went so far as to say the Republican party "now champions small business."

This strategy was reinforced when congressional discussions moved to the budget after 1995. According to Norquist, "the budget is a continuation of the Contract. The Contract promised a balanced budget by 2002 so the hundred-day Contract has been extended to seven years."[84] The groups involved in formulating and promoting the Contract merely shifted their focus to balancing the budget: "The working groups which developed around the Contract are all continuing, completely and totally. People didn't even stop to change and take a shower."[85]

Republican budget proposals produced clear winners and losers: "interest groups representing veterans, the elderly, farmers, mayors, children and the poor castigated the Republicans' proposals, [but] the budget plans received high marks from business lobbyists who believe they will lead to lower interest rates, and from the conservative Christian Coalition, which supports the House's $500-per child tax credit."[86] By 1997, many of these interests saw their pet causes favored by GOP members of Congress. One graphic example involved Graco Children's Products, owned by the Cone family of Pennsylvania. Five years earlier, this company was forced to recall a baby cradle that had been linked to the deaths of twelve infants and the near-suffocation of others. After Graco contributed large sums of money to Republican legislators and $1.8 million to a conservative consulting company known as Tried Management Services (which funneled money to the nonprofit groups Citizens for Reform and Citizens for the Republican Education Fund in support of ads attacking Democratic incumbents), Rep. Helen Chenoweth (R-Idaho) introduced legislation sharply limiting the liability of manufacturers whose products harmed consumers.[87]

It is no accident that many of the business groups that helped develop and promote the Contract (and later the balanced budget legislation) had major interests pending before government agencies.[88] Gingrich's fund-raising arm, the GOP Action Committee (also called GOPAC), raised more than $7 million over a five-year period from large donors. Gingrich, for example, broke with his party's own position on import quotas to align himself with textile magnate and major GOPAC contributor Roger Milliken (who gave GOPAC $255,000). Josh Nash, Milliken's Washington lobbyist, said: "We've known Newt for a long time and like him. Being a Southern congressman, he has been enormously helpful to the textile and fiber industry over the years."[89] Gingrich has fought to overhaul the Food and Drug Administration in order to ease government regulation of medical device manufacturing, whose companies were big GOPAC contributors.[90]

As shown earlier, Republican ability to deliver government benefits created a political environment in which well-organized and well-financed groups did quite well, just

FIGURE 5.2 THE CONTRACT WITH AMERICA IN PERSPECTIVE

Item	Signed into Law
Preface, Congressional Reform	1995
1. The Fiscal Responsibility Act	
—Balanced Budget Amendment	not passed
—line-item veto	1996
2. The Taking Back Our Streets Act	
—various crime bills	1996
3. The Personal Responsibility Act	
—welfare reform	1996
4. The Family Reinforcement Act	
—various items	1996
5. The American Dream Restoration Act	
—middle-class tax cut	1997
6. The National Security Restoration Act	
—various, including missile defense, no UN control of U.S. troops	not passed
7. The Senior Citizens Fairness Act	
—social security earnings limit increase	1997
—repeal of 1993 tax on benefits	not passed
8. The Job Creation and Wage Enhancement Act	
—capital gains cuts	1997
—reduction of unfunded mandates	1995
9. The Common Sense Legal Reforms Act	
—civil law and product liability reform	not passed
10. The Citizen Legislature Act	
—term limits	not passed

as had been the case when Democrats were in the majority. Conservative business interests joined forces with Republican legislators to develop a narrative featuring a clear agenda and definite beneficiaries. It was a political transaction that yielded tremendous advantages to the affected interest groups.

The cleavages that emerged from the Contract and balanced budget battles became a continuing part of the political story line. In fact, the ultimate success of the Contract as narrative resonated long after the adrenaline rush of the 1995 "100 days" had faded into a jumbled memory. The Contract's metanarrative of a government that was too big, too entrenched in bureaucracy, and too expensive moved the political discourse in the United States considerably to the right. Moreover, despite numerous delays and roadblocks, much of the Contract did ultimately become law (see figure 5.2). In the end, the Contract succeeded in both substance and symbol—not bad for an electoral initiative that had little impact on the 1994 election results.

Chapter Six

Telecommunications

Public Lobbying, Private Decisions

For two generations, communications policies were staid and predictable in the extreme. There was AT&T, Ma Bell to us all, which provided the dial tone for local and long-distance calls, and there were the three major television networks, which had evolved from their radio ancestry to offer a limited selection of mass entertainment and news. Nothing else mattered much: not cable television, which allowed isolated rural communities the possibility of obtaining clear reception; not the nascent computer industry; not local and independent telephone companies that operated in little niches throughout the country.[1]

Then came the 1980s, and everything changed; deregulation and competition became the order of the day. Federal Court Judge Harold Greene inserted himself as the most important force in telecommunications policy, as he oversaw the break-up of AT&T and the subsequent establishment of seven regional bell operating companies (RBOCs). Cable television companies from ESPN to CNN to Ted Turner's superstation WTBS grew to the point that they could challenge networks in producing programming and began to siphon off chunks of the mass audience. In quick succession, computer networking took off and the Internet became a major source of mass communication, commerce, and entertainment.

By the early 1990s, the only thing that had not changed drastically was congressional legislation overseeing the policy area. Despite the dramatic change in technology and industry organization, legislative policy was roughly the same as sixty years ago. The core legislation, the 1934 Communications Act, which served as the basis for federal policy governing telephones, television, and even the Internet, had been passed at a time when only a minority of American households had telephones, and the rest of the affected technology was more science fiction than reality.[2]

In 1996, Congress passed a comprehensive telecommunications bill. It was exactly the type of large-scale policy change that on the heels of the Clinton health care defeat seemed impossible to enact. Befitting legislation that would affect one-seventh of the U.S. economy (nearly one trillion dollars in all), the landmark legislation rewrote the sixty-year-old communications act, deregulated much of the industry, and allowed greater competition than previously had been the case. It also overturned a 1992 law that had reregulated cable television.

This chapter examines telecommunications deregulation, with an eye toward three questions: 1) How did Congress pass comprehensive reform on such a complex policy area? 2) What did contending groups do to gain particular advantages? and 3) Why did Congress tilt against cable television operators in 1992 but in favor of them in 1996? Like health care reform and devolution, telecommunications deregulation generated a tremendous amount of lobbying by many kinds of organized interests. As seen in the earlier case studies, many of these contending forces made energetic efforts to develop narratives supportive of industry positions. Groups saw this as a way to reduce the uncertainty of large-scale political change.

Unlike health care reform and the Contract with America, though, this high-stakes policy battle did not reach very deeply into the public consciousness. Competing antagonists were able to restrict the scope of conflict to major industry forces. Given a situation in which industry groups tuned in and the public tuned out, it is little surprise that the eventual legislation favored industry at the expense of consumer interests. In the end, Sen. John McCain (R-Ariz.) condemned the newly enacted bill as "fundamentally flawed." According to him, "it is protective of all the interests that are involved in the telecommunications business with the exception of the consumer. That's why we are seeing increasing phone rates, increasing cable rates, consolidations and mergers, and little if any increase in competition."[3]

Preparing for Battle:
The 1992 Cable Reregulation Bill

The contestants who battled on telecommunications had been circling one another for several years. The first round had come in 1992, when Congress passed a bill over President Bush's veto reregulating cable television. In 1984, cable companies had won deregulation of the industry. Their chief argument was freedom from government interference in the marketplace. The market was a more effective protector of consumer interests than the government, the industry claimed.

By 1992, however, these claims were ringing hollow. Service was poor, cable rates were rising well above the rate of inflation, and most cable companies had a monopoly in particular communities, thereby negating the entire logic of market competition. In this situation of widespread public dissatisfaction and a clear target for blame, the time was ripe for a move to impose new regulations on the cable industry.

To those who argue that campaign contributions buy political influence, the 1992 legislation offers a sobering rebuttal. Despite donations from cable companies between January 1991 and June 1992 of more than one million dollars, with the largest sums going to the majority members of key committees (House Energy and Commerce, Senate Commerce, and Senate Science and Transportation), cable interests failed to block a bill that sought to reduce their revenues and increase their costs. Beyond contributions, the lobbying from the cable and broadcast industries was intense. A Time Warner lobbyist called reregulation "the single most intensely lobbied piece of commercial legislation pending before the Congress."[4]

The problem for the industry was that cable companies found themselves caught in a two-front attack by consumers and by broadcasters, who took advantage of cable's weakness to press their own interests on provisions that would allow local stations to seek payments from cable companies to rebroadcast their signals.[5] On one level, the debate emphasized consumer interests that reflected a very

broad scope of conflict. Consumer lobbyist Gene Kimmelman argued, "When the issues are whether cable rates
are too high, is service poor, [or] should something be
done about monopoly control of the cable industry, no
amount of money can change that."[6] One cable spokes-
person graphically acknowledged the industry's problems
by pointing out, "You go into forty million homes, you're
going to drop some mud on the rugs."[7] Even with these
difficulties, however, the theme of cable reregulation may
not have been enough to move Congress to pass the legislation (or, more significantly, to override a presidential
veto).

Late in the 1992 battle, the cable industry engaged in
an extensive series of grassroots lobbying efforts to blunt
the pro-consumer themes of the reregulation forces and to
try to avoid a veto override. Industry representatives from
local communities across the country pleaded with legislators for help. But these calls and in-person appeals fell on
deaf ears. The television broadcasting industry combined
its inside clout with the consumer movement's populist appeal and won payments from the cable industry's revenues,
a much more complex and less visible outcome than the
modest reduction of cable rates. Consumer advocate Kimmelman concluded, "The only way you win on this kind
of issue is if you got enough muscle on your side. We had
the perfect combination of rural, urban, consumers, and
broadcasters. And it still wasn't easy."[8]

In the end, the necessary, if not sufficient, condition for
reregulation was the resonance of the consumer-based narrative that cable companies had raised their rates with little
restraint—56 percent on average between 1986 and 1991.[9]
One analysis concluded, "Lawmakers now realize that constituents feel the same way about television as they do
about roads, schools, and parks,"[10] although subsequent

politicking would soon put such a conclusion to the test. Still, Schattschneider's basic proposition that policy outcomes could be altered by broadening the scope of the conflict was borne out (see chapter 2). The cable industry had lost an important round to consumers, and cable leaders understood that their tactics and accompanying set of stories would have to change if federal regulations were to be eased.

Given the combined industry revenues of $45 billion, *CQ Weekly* rightfully could label the 1992 broadcasters versus cable tussle as a "Clash of Titans."[11] But in truth this conflict was just a preliminary bout leading up to the main event—the telecommunications reform free-for-all that ended with comprehensive 1996 legislation. Little was settled by the 1992 bill, in that both legislators and interests agreed that most basic issues of competition were still unresolved. In fact, narratives extolling the virtues of competition would soon push aside the story that consumers required regulatory protection from price-gouging cable companies.

The Bigger Battle: The 1996 Telecommunications Act

Decisions on telecommunications (or health care, devolution, or tort reform for that matter) do not quite fall into the "winner-take-all" category of many modern markets.[12] But the stakes of major policy decisions are both very high and perceived as such by most actors. Rep. Billy Tauzin (then D-La.) observed that much of the 1996 telecommunication fight was over "the big enchilada . . . the [long-distance business] is where the bucks are"—about $60 billion a year.[13] Still, long-distance competition was only one part of a bill whose reach extended to a trillion dollars.[14] In addition to telephones, the legislation affected everything from the size and concentration of television networks to cross-ownership rules for radio, television, and newspapers, as well as newly emerging technologies such as cellular phones, electronic mail, and the Internet.

Moreover, beyond the immense economic stakes, fundamental societal questions were at issue. Most highly publicized was the ultimately successful attempt to mandate that television manufacturers install "V-chips" in all their sets, thereby providing a technological tool for parental control of children's viewing choices. Some groups viewed this as opening the door to government censorship, but President Clinton and many others saw the V-chip as a way to reduce the impact of violence and sex on children.

Befitting such massive policy stakes, numerous groups from television networks, cable companies, and AT&T to the "Baby Bells" and Internet providers jumped into the debate. The overriding goal of interests was clear: to cut through the myriad voices in this complex controversy, reduce uncertainty, and secure some clear, if limited, advantage for their own particular priorities.

No listing of the interests involved in telecommunications politics is likely to be complete. Running down the roster of major players, however, presents little difficulty. Some minor actors did have their successes (most notably the burglar alarm industry), but a few groupings of substantial interests dominated attempts to influence the policy changes. These included:

- **the regional Bell operating companies (RBOCs)** that sought to enter the long-distance and manufacturing markets, as well as to solidify their previous court victories allowing them to offer cable TV.
- **the long-distance industry,** which sought to delay and

restrict the Bells' capacity to compete, as well as "to persuade lawmakers to require the RBOCs . . . to open their networks and face competition before being allowed into the long-distance market."[15]

- **the cable industry,** which was beaten in the 1992 regulatory legislation, to the point that it could not get Congress to sustain President Bush's veto of the bill. After 1992, the industry, despite some divisions, sought to rebuild its reputation and clout, in part by accepting the general trend toward deregulation.

- **broadcasters and media conglomerates,** who sought to be able to own larger numbers of outlets and larger shares both of national and local markets. The V-chip mandate was another concern, along a different policy dimension. These interests often combined concern over the production of content with the delivery of programming (such as the Disney–Capital Cities/ABC union).

- **consumer groups,** which saw media concentration and deregulation as leading to higher prices and the domination of content by a handful of large entities.

- **other public interest groups,** which took various positions on the V-chip and Internet censorship issues.

In almost every category listed above, there were differences on policy preferences either among the major interests (such as the RBOCs, who hung together despite some intense disagreements) or between major interests (AT&T) and minor players (the re-sellers of long-distance service).

The only thing that was definite as the legislative process lurched forward was that some type of bill was going to pass. Dissatisfaction with the sixty-year-old status quo was so widespread that even bitter rivals conceded a new law was necessary. Greg Simon, the top policy aide to Vice President Al Gore, noted how important this realization was on the part of affected groups: "There has been lots of people getting ready to do battle, but . . . it's because *they know there's going to be a bill*, not because they think there's not going to be a bill."[16]

With favorable prospects for the passage of a bill, hundreds of interests, often banding together in coalitions, sought to make sure that they would not come out as losers in the chaotic politics that surrounded this almost incomprehensible piece of legislation. They could not seek to defeat the entire bill. Support for change was too strong, and it emanated from too many quarters. The main questions were: what kind of bill would pass, which interests would benefit, and how long would particular advantages last? Those were the uncertainties that bedeviled organized interests from AT&T to Disney.[17]

The politics of this policy area offers a wonderful opportunity to examine how narrative can provide unifying themes as legislators and interests address complex issues. Highly visible public lobbying, advertising, and public relations activity proceeded inside the Washington beltway, largely to offer ways for members of Congress, their staff, and other key decision makers to consider the proposed policy changes—and to construct explanations for their own positions on various issues that would profoundly affect a host of interests and constituencies.[18]

In 1992, Schattschneider's classic logic was used by policy losers (consumers) and their allies successfully to expand the scope of the conflict to the general public against a single adversary—the cable industry. This relatively straight-forward confrontation contrasts markedly to the multifaceted, highly complex efforts to pass the comprehensive communications legislation in 1996. Much as the 1992 debate was dominated by the theme of escalating cable costs that harmed ordinary consumers, the 1994–96 discourse revolved largely, though not completely, around the narrative of competition. One would have to be dead to irony, however, not to note that a) the 1996 legislation essentially reversed the consumers' victory in 1992; b) the emphasis on competition obscured the rush toward both concentration and overlapping alliances within the telecommunications sector of the economy;[19] and c) the 1996 law, while ratifying changes driven by technology, worked to slow the pace of change of many powerful interests.

From Issue Networks to Narratives

As the telecommunications battle got under way, a host of interests stood ready to participate. Writing in 1994, political scientist Jeffrey Berry painted a picture of the telecommunications community as an issue network defined by "the large-scale integration of different companies into business alliances that provide a range of products and services to consumers."[20] The complexity of these alliances is staggering, and nothing that has occurred since, such as the Capital Cities/ABC-Disney merger, invalidates Berry's conclusion that consolidation will continue. Strangely enough, consolidation and integration within the industry means that "predictable lobbying fault lines are disappearing, leadership within the [policy] network is changing, and there is extreme uncertainty because of the movement toward full deregulation of telecommunicaitons"[21] (see figure 6.1).

Berry's analysis, while often on target, remains within the "issue network"—or policy community—framework. His snapshot, however, is blurred at best and barely takes note of the Internet or the central position of Microsoft. The logical question that remains is whether the issue net-

FIGURE 6.1 THE FULL MARKET INTEGRATION MODEL

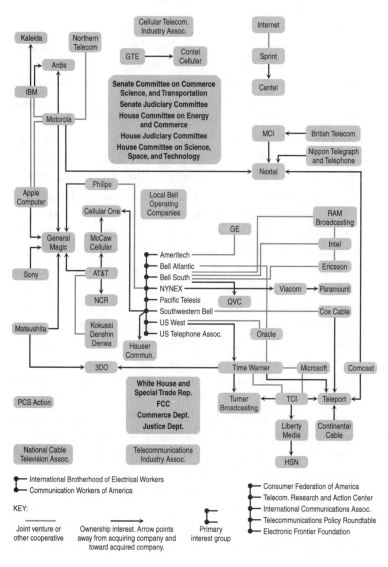

Source: Jeffery Berry, "Dynamic Qualities of Issue Networks," paper presented at American Political Science Association meetings, Chicago, Sept. 1–4, 1994.

work concept has much general worth given the dramatic changes in the industry.

In a similar vein, telecommunications policy analysts within the industry offered a depiction of the information sector, organized along two overlapping dimensions of products, services, and relationship to content[22] (see figure 6.2). As information-based corporations have merged, formed joint alliances, and entered new fields, the distinctions between the separate parts of the industry have rapidly disappeared, even as analysts were attempting to describe it as a whole. For example, the distinction between a product and a service began to vanish on the Internet, as information may be considered both. Likewise, merging computers with television sets, replete with interactive features, combines the medium with the message.

The numbing array of alliances, announced almost daily, and the continuing entry of new players (Internet companies such as Netscape, which went public in 1996) make any modeling of the issue network a frustrating, if not fruitless, task. Only if and when consolidation has occurred to the point that there are just a handful of major players will an accurate rendering of what Berry labels "full market integration" be possible. Given the difficulty of predicting beyond a few months in this field, such a condition can scarcely be foreseen. What remains is great uncertainty.[23]

In short, the issue network notion, while attractive as a description, may not serve as a coherent framework for understanding broad, diversified policy communities, at least until the largest market forces essentially complete their concentration. Even then, however, one would be brave, perhaps foolhardy, to predict some new stable equilibrium. We need some other concept to understand the politics of influence within such a complex environment having such a changeable set of alliances that result from mergers and

FIGURE 6.2 THE INFORMATION INDUSTRY DURING THE NEXT DECADE

Container/Medium	Transport	Translate	Transform	Present	Content/Message
Distribution	International long distance and local telephone services	ISDN	Cable networks and operators; National data highway		**Information Vendors** Information on demand
Telecom	Video conferencing Voice and video Electronic mail Digital and cellular telephones Telephones	Transaction processors Mainframes Minicomputers	Custom software Operating systems	Public kiosks Virtual reality	**Entertainment, Media, and Publishing** Videogame cartridges CD and videodisk Film, TV, and video Records and cassettes
Computers			Personal computers Information appliances	CD-ROM	
Consumer Electronics		HDTV Two-way TV	Electronic photography	Interactive entertainment and education	**Custom Publishing** Newspapers Newsletters Magazines and journals Books
Office Equipment	Copiers Printers Scanners Faxes	Video Printer		Interactive news	

Services — Products

Source: Apple Computer

acquisitions. As with health care reform and the Contract with America, focusing on the narratives of the various interests, the venues in which they articulate these narratives, and the extent that the stories are adopted (and adapted) by decision makers can illuminate the politics within a technologically driven policy community in which the number of interests and their relationships can change dramatically, almost on a day-to-day basis.

The Debate Unfolds

At the onset of discussion in the Democratically controlled 103rd Congress (1994) and the subsequent Republican 104th Congress (1995 and 1996), all the major interests desired significant policy changes. Yet none of the lobbyists could legitimately argue that they could understand what the consequences of the legislation would be, at least beyond a year or two into the future. With billions of dollars at stake, and in an environment of great complexity, overlapping interests, and tremendous uncertainty, groups turned to narratives that conveyed their messages to legislators in as much detail as they desired, but accompanied by simplified versions that allowed lawmakers to build the explanations they would offer their constituents.

Despite millions of dollars spent on advertising, grassroots lobbying, and public relations, the scope of the conflict only briefly expanded beyond the broad and admittedly ill-defined confines of the telecommunications policy community. With the limited exception of the public debate that swirled around the V-chip technology to facilitate greater parental control over television program content, the conflict over telecommunications proposals between

1994 and 1996 never became visible beyond the over-lapping policy communities with direct interests in the legislation. Even though all interests and observers acknowledged the sweeping impact of the telecommunications reform, the public was never drawn into the debate. Consumer lobbyists were active and sometimes influential, but this convoluted policy debate was not like Clinton's health care reform or Gingrich's Contract with America, both of which motivated citizens to contact members of Congress. The subject was technical and complex, and one that many consumers felt they could not effectively influence. Save for the involvement of some corporate headquarters and Hollywood interests, most conflict remained almost completely inside the beltway, even though the policy decisions would affect virtually every consumer and business across the country. Telecommunications politics during this period demonstrates that even when the number of individuals affected by legislation is vast, the scope of the conflict need not be expanded beyond the policy community of core interests. Of course, the limited scope of conflict was not neutral; to the extent it was restricted, consumers likely would come out losers.

Ironically, one limitation in the ability of the public to mobilize was that the very organizations on which it depended for unbiased information—local news stations—actively lobbied in favor of a provision giving broadcasters free use of a publically owned spectrum worth nearly $70 billion for new channels. According to a study by J. H. Snider and Benjamin Page, local station owners used control of the airwaves to pressure elected officials, thereby undermining the traditional oversight role of the media. Despite this extraordinary "gift" on the part of the public, television broadcasters in 1997 used their political clout to kill a popular campaign finance reform proposal—free television time for political ads—because it would cost the industry several million dollars.[24]

Constructing the Story of Competition: Academic Studies and Survey Research

The regional Bell companies—the RBOCs—spent substantial amounts on advertising and public relations that reiterated their message of competition, and they constructed their story systematically. At the start of the 104th Congress in 1995, their coalition (the Alliance for Competitive Communications, or ACC) sponsored two separate research projects that would provide the information from which their stories would be spun. First, they hired the WEFA Group (a firm formed by the merger of Wharton Econometric Forecasting Associates and Chase Econometrics) to expand on a previous study to demonstrate the economic virtues of deregulation. In a 200-page presentation, WEFA's econometric analyses provided statistical evidence, based on the analysts' assumptions, that the prohibitions placed upon the Bells had kept these companies from offering various advanced services. In turn, non-Bell providers were not required to compete aggressively, which cost the public billions of dollars per year.

In a more speculative vein, the WEFA report claimed that the U.S. economy was almost $113 billion worse off, *per year*, due to delays in new services that the industry could offer.[25] Moreover, the study argued that the structure of the long-distance industry (essentially an oligopoly of AT&T, MCI, and Sprint) was essentially noncompetitive in terms of pricing.[26] The WEFA report articulated the very narrative the RBOCs would repeat continually in 1995 and 1996: "The clear conclusion is that the long distance market for consumers and small businesses is not competitive. . . . AT&T is the price leader with MCI and Sprint faithfully following each AT&T price increase. . . . [C]ompetition, not regulation is the answer to this situation. Bell company participation in the long distance market would immediately lead to lower prices. . . ."[27]

Does such a study have any real impact on framing an important issue? Certainly the interests involved take such studies—the fodder for subsequent narratives—very seriously. For example, in the wake of the passage of the 1996 Telecommunications Act, AT&T apparently lobbied the American Enterprise Institute to blunt the impact of an AEI book (co-published with the MIT Press) by economist Paul MacAvoy that reached similar conclusions as the WEFA study.[28] MacAvoy received $200,000 from the RBOCs to develop computer analyses of phone data; a rebutting set of analyses, paid for by AT&T, was prepared by Peter Pitsch of the Hudson Institute, who commented, "The stakes in these things are very high," even if the studies themselves are read by just a handful of scholars.[29] The studies are important because they are the raw material for subsequent narratives that circulate within the extended policy community, including Capitol Hill.

Complementing the scholarly debates over telephone rates and a few other key issues, from violence on television to the concentration of media ownership, were other studies that teased out public opinion on these issues, even when the public had given only cursory attention to the subjects at hand. Again, the RBOCs paid handsomely to generate information from which they could develop their narrative of needed competition. Whereas the WEFA study produced policy-oriented information, the polling for the RBOCs conducted by Public Opinion Strategies and the Mellman Group generated data reflecting the political potency of competition-based presentations.[30] The most compelling arguments for allowing RBOCs into the long-distance market were, in order, to enhance consumer choice (rather than decrease costs), to create jobs, and to make shopping for services easier.

In the end, the RBOCs could draw on the findings of their sponsored survey and econometric studies to weave a narrative of competition that might well appeal to elites and consumers—with members of Congress reacting to the arguments both as policy elites and representatives of constituents. The story line of maintaining or increasing choice could convey, simultaneously, both policy and political information. Even if its impact could not easily be measured, the competition message was easily disseminated and easily understood. And with the stakes so high, the cost of creating this story line was well worth the investment by these well-heeled interests.

Competing Narratives

If consumers and small businesses did not become major players in this phase of policy making, their presumed well-being was central to the broad, inclusive narratives expressed by almost every interest that sought to influence the outcome. Everyone from former President George Bush to small cable companies to Hollywood entertainment tycoons expressed their agreement with the general principle of encouraging competition to guide the development of the telecommunications industry, ostensibly for the ultimate benefit of the consumer. More than any other set of interests, the RBOCs captured the essence of this narrative in their simple, consistent advertising message. The core message was straight-forward: competition equals lower prices. There were some nuances as well, for instance, the idea that this argument was being presented by "local phone companies," not the regional Bells, some of the largest corporations in the country. But nothing could have been seemingly more simple than the central concept of competition, endlessly repeated.

Basing their message on data from the March 1995 Mellman/Public Opinion Strategies survey research, the RBOCs "came up with an easily understood theme and stuck with it throughout."[31] One congressional aide noted that the RBOCs "embraced the notion of competition—not for them but for the long-distance industry. The Bells turned the debate upside-down and made it sound like a great injustice would occur unless they were permitted to offer long distance services immediately."[32]

With 75 percent of those polled agreeing that all markets should be open to competition, one RBOC consultant explained their strategy: "We created a bottom line message—that people want choice—and stuck with it."[33] Subsequently, the RBOCs, under the banner of the ACC, spent approximately $750,000 in advertising in the *Washington Post* and the *Washington Times*, as well as such Capitol Hill vehicles as *Roll Call*, *CQ Weekly*, and *National Journal*.

The RBOCs' chief adversary, the so-called Competitive Long Distance Coalition (largely funded by AT&T), spent a like amount on advertising, but its message was never as clear, at least as articulated through their advertising. The coalition also emphasized competition, but its theme— "Bell monopolies are the problem, competition is the answer"—could not match the appeal of the ACC's basic equation. For example, the CLDC reprinted bits of 16 editorials to support its position, but the point is obscured, lost in small print and the complexity of the visual presentation. As CLDC executive director John Tuck concluded, "our ads were too busy." More importantly, Tuck conceded that the RBOCs "co-opted our message. . . . We talked all about competition being the solution. . . . The Bells' theme was punchier and easier to understand."[34]

Such a discussion of marketing tactics almost sounds like it could come from advertising firms for giant consumer firms such as Colgate-Palmolive or McDonald's. Central to these campaigns, however, was the fact that these ads never ran beyond the capital area; their audience essentially was 535 legislators and their staffs, who already had access to vast amounts of highly detailed and technical information about the telecommunications bill. Advertising had the virtue of simplifying a numbingly complex issue. In addition, as part of high-stakes lobbying, the costs—at least for the Bells and AT&T/MCI/Sprint (and their minor coalition partners)—were insignificant in comparison to the potential benefits of favorably defining the problem of impending competition.

Strangely enough, in expensive public lobbying campaigns, it may be easier to identify failed tactics than to discover those that proved successful. In the telecommunications arena, the major stumble occurred when CLDC purchased—literally bought—through two lobbying firms, phone calls to 175,000 Americans who would then consent to attach their names to mailgrams bound for Capitol Hill in reaction to an August 1995 change in the legislation that the CLDC opposed.[35] Faced with failing to meet its quota to fulfill a $1.5 million contract, one firm began using an old list of supporters and sending mailgrams to legislators without gaining the consent of those whose names they signed. In the end, Rep. John Dingell (D-Mich.), former chair of the Energy and Commerce Committee, and four other members requested that the long distance coalition explain its actions. Even though astroturf lobbying is common, grassroots campaigns that do not look authentic are not taken seriously by members of Congress. The disclosure of the CLDC missteps meant that legislators could discount its alleged grassroots support.

In narrative terms, the story line of grassroots outrage, initially presented as a set of facts, was exposed as fiction. Not only was the interpretation itself discounted, but the sponsoring interests lost control of a possible counternarrative. The potential for a pro-AT&T story was weak in the first place—as one top legislative aide noted, the plea by AT&T for protection from the RBOCs was a difficult case to make. He concluded, "AT&T underestimated the anti-regulatory bias in the debate."[36] Basing its argument on the most artificial sort of astroturf support did nothing to help its case.

Nowhere was the long-distance carriers' misreading of the orientation—both symbolic and substantive—toward competition more striking than in a set of crucial House decisions in July 1995. The CLDC lobbying strategy had focused its attention on the House Commerce Committee and, in particular, its chair, Rep. Thomas Bliley (R-Va.). The coalition generally failed to link its message to the dominant theme of competition—both by running a relatively ineffective advertising campaign and by sponsoring a grassroots effort that was exposed as more astroturf than real. Perhaps most damaging to its case were not the instances of demonstrated falsification of grassroots communications, but the publicity surrounding the massive effort to construct the appearance of an extensive public outcry on an issue in which citizens had only a modest interest. In contrast to health care, which citizens consistently ranked among the most important problems facing the country, telecommunications issues have never been accorded much significance.[37]

In contrast to the ad wars conducted by the competing

telephone coalitions, the cable television industry benefited from a long-term strategy to resurrect its standing with Congress in the wake of its 1992 defeat over reregulation. Like the telephone interests, the largest cable trade association accepted, then apparently embraced, the idea of competition. National Cable Television Association (NCTA) president Decker Angstrom noted, "We made a key strategic decision . . . to say competition is coming, let's get back into the political process rather than being outside it."[38] At the same time, like the telephone interests, the cable industry sought to define competition on its own terms. By agreeing to the broad story line of a highly competitive communications industry, the cable interests could deliver their complementary policy and political messages, which emphasized local concerns and the need for rate relief so that competition would be fair. As with the NAFTA opponents, who embraced free trade in theory but qualified by the notion that it must be fair for all nations, competition in telecommunications was endorsed, but qualified by detailed requirements for implementation in ways that were fair to each particular interest.

The NCTA did not convey its message through an advertising campaign designed to promote its interests inside the beltway. Rather, it embarked upon an extended effort to win back allies on Capitol Hill, ranging from staffers to committee chairs; it was clear that the industry had learned its political lesson from 1992 and could at least mouth the mantra of competition. The NCTA also used to full advantage its considerable grassroots potential arising from having cable companies all across the country make locally oriented arguments about competition and rates to individual legislators. One cable lobbyist remarked that the "grassroots work was fantastic. State associations did much of the work, coordinated by Washington staff. They would come in at the drop of a hat. It was calls plus physical presence."[39]

In the end, much of the 1996 legislation followed the broad outlines of the debate, which often was determined by public relations, grassroots lobbying, advocacy research studies, and elite-oriented advertising. Moreover, as one Senate legislative assistant noted in a clear tribute to financial muscle, in high-stakes policy decisions involving many multi-billion-dollar corporations, "you can't impose legislation on any of the major industries." Within the general framework of competition and deregulation, tremendous amounts of inside lobbying took place. Much of this fleshed out the public narratives with particular examples, technical requests, and legislative horse trading on issues such as the date and conditions under which RBOCs could enter long-distance markets.

At the same time, inside lobbying did rely heavily on pure "muscle"—that is, the economic weight of major interests, ranging from AT&T to the individual RBOCs to many of the cable companies. For example, Telecommunications Inc. entered into dozens of alliances with various companies, such as Sprint, to increase its already substantial heft.[40] More than any other industry, even the oligopolistic long-distance carriers, the cable industry found itself believing its own narrative—that competition was inevitable, and the industry would need to embrace it.

The rhetoric of competition, while real, also had a symbolic dimension that obscured both the lingering distaste many interests had for deregulation, at least to the extent it produced unfettered competition, and the great probability that such competition would breed increased concentration within an industry that already was rapidly consolidating. In Murray Edelman's terms, the policy of competition might fail, but the words would succeed. Indeed, in the weeks following the passage of telecommunications reform, two RBOCs, SBC (formerly Southwestern Bell) and Pacific Telesis, forged a merger that seemed sure to pass antitrust scrutiny. And cable companies announced their largest rate increases since the industry's 1984 deregulation.[41] By 1997–98, cable rate increases were running far ahead of the rate of inflation.

The Telecommunications Bill Roars by, Quietly

As the telecommunications debate wound down in February 1996, Senator McCain commented, in a mind-numbing mix of metaphors: "It was clear . . . all along that it was the, quote, special interests that were driving this train. So when the special interests declared a cease-fire, then it certainly paved the way."[42] The convoluted nature of McCain's description aptly captures both the substance and symbolism of the telecommunications deal. For all the talk of competition, virtually every interest won something tangible and, more importantly, did not suffer a potentially disastrous loss. Even consumer advocates could find some modest victories, such as "at least the hope of greater competition and lower prices."[43] Trying to get a handle on lobbying when the stakes exceed a trillion dollars is difficult to do, especially when the public is profoundly uninterested in most of the initial results. Noticeable, long-term price increases might spark more interest and a more lively public debate, as well as a more thorough examination of the lobbying tactics and costs.

In 1994–96, however, the discourse was confined to the numerous interests within the telecommunications policy community, and consumer groups found it impossible to expand the scope of conflict and therefore literally bring the audience into the fray. Given archaic laws, a debilitating antitrust agreement, technological advances, and the trend toward consolidation, virtually all interests had to embrace competition and agree with the argument that consumers would be better off. At the same time, all parties agreed that their capacity to predict outcomes was severely limited. The narrative of competition proved resilient, as it helped to hold together the hundreds of separate negotiated settlements that made up the telecommunications law revisions and provided the symbolic cover for interests that sought as much certainty as possible in the policy making process, even as they moved on to new, unfamiliar technological ground.

The public and private narratives of lobbyists cannot alone explain the passage of this immense bill, which affected even more of the economy than health care reform would have. But narratives offer some coherence to a process that ultimately produced huge majorities in favor of passage in both legislative chambers as well as the support of all major interests. Not every twist and turn can be accounted for (such as the intervention by Gingrich to help the long distance coalition, or the capacity of Senator Hollings (D-S.C.) to rework the 1996 bill back toward the product that he crafted in 1994). Still, the solid construction of the competition narrative allowed for the less elegant, but workmanlike, story telling of an unwieldy, ungainly 1996 legislative package, even as all sides rushed to reopen those provisions that did not suit them. And new narratives, based on emerging alliances and increased concentrations of power, soon appeared both in the *Washington Post* and in private conversations. After cable rates rose 8.5 percent in 1997, four times higher than the rate of inflation, critics called for new regulation of the industry.[44]

The plea illustrated the never-ending nature of telecommunications skirmishes. Indeed, the long-distance and regional Bell alliances continued to fight over the pace of implementing competition in local and long-distance service. Before the FCC, in the courts, and on the pages of elite policy journals, these communications giants stepped up their arguments after 1996 about the conditions of competition. With the stakes so high, even a modest change in conditions or a slight delay can mean hundreds of millions in revenue gains or losses. The competition narrative remains one constant in the fluid politics of telecommunications.

Chapter Seven

Medical Reform Revisited

To publicize incremental changes in policy or in well-
being is to establish categories that conceal the
institutional context in which the problem is grounded.
This form of structuring of a problem always produces
symbolic or token gestures
—Murrary Edelman, *Political Language*, 1977

The Kennedy-Kassebaum bill . . . is utterly inoffensive to
both big corporations and small business. . . . Some refer
to the bill as "incrementalist," but "minimalist" would
be more apt.
—Health care scholar Paul Starr, 1996

After the passage of the telecommunications bill
in 1996, legislators sought ways to address other
policy problems. The Clinton health care debacle
made it clear that comprehensive, large-scale medical reform was impossible. The health care area was too complex
and the political difficulties too profound for substantial
action. Nevertheless, the earlier debate had revealed pockets of potential consensus in which small-scale action might
be possible. After a short hiatus, members of Congress

started to think again about medical reform on a piecemeal basis.

Although much of the politicking remained entrenched inside the health care policy community, two sets of issues won spots on the legislative agenda. First, Senators Edward Kennedy (D-Mass.) and Nancy Kassebaum (R-Kansas) put forward a modest proposal that addressed ways in which insurance could be made available to workers who wished to change jobs and to those whose prior health problems prevented them from obtaining coverage.[1] The Kennedy-Kassebaum bill, known as the "Health Insurance Portability and Accountability Act," reflected a bipartisan approach.[2]

Simultaneously, and more significantly, Republicans in the House called attention to the steady decline in the trust funds that supported Medicare, the government program that pays for health care for senior citizens. Using figures from the trust funds, officials declared a crisis that required major reforms to insure the system's solvency. The narrative that followed illustrated the archetypal "story of decline" in which there is a predictable account of how things were good for a long while, but that the situation has become more difficult and that a complete breakdown—a crisis—is looming in the near future.[3]

As opposed to the extensive lobbying that developed on the Clinton health care initiative, coalitions did not rise up to present their own versions of problems and solutions on the Kennedy-Kassebaum reforms. On Medicare, many interests did raise their voices, but the fact that the Medicare figures were not in widespread dispute meant that an agreed-upon problem did exist, and discussions could focus on proposed solutions. Still, in this relatively quiescent environment, interested narratives did come to play major roles in framing the politics and policy making of health care after the demise of Clinton's comprehensive reform.

These story lines led to several important outcomes: 1) the overwhelming adoption of the Kennedy-Kassebaum legislation; 2) the inclusion in that legislation of major policy changes that largely benefited a single company specializing in medical savings accounts; 3) the infusion of tremendous amounts of so-called independent expenditures into 1996 congressional campaigns, bolstering opposing claims that Republicans had sought to destroy or (alternatively) insure the survival of Medicare; and 4) the adoption in 1997 of a balanced budget agreement that included a ten-year fix of Medicare, along with the appointment of a commission to propose a long-term solution to its funding problems.

For organized interests, the great benefit of public lobbying, through advertising, public relations, and grassroots mobilization, is the ability to control the message. Not only can expensive issue-oriented campaigns affect the policy agenda, they also can shape the nature of deliberation among elites and the public at large.[4] This is true even when interests do not dominate the policy story lines, as with the Kennedy-Kassebaum and Medicare reforms. Indeed, self-interested narratives offer great opportunities for taking advantage of "politics-as-usual" incrementalism. In particular, the presentation of well-crafted information may replace any meaningful deliberation among legislators or groups. Let us first turn to the opportunities afforded by incremental policy making. Then we will examine how detailed deliberation may be thwarted by the construction of public narratives.

Public Narratives, Private Advantage

When large-scale issues such as comprehensive health care reform or telecommunications deregulation move onto the governmental agenda, the scope of the conflict is socialized to the point that a great deal of the debate takes place in the realms of "symbolic" and "public confrontation" politics (see chapter 2). Although many issues will be resolved in private deals, far from the light of public scrutiny, the defining elements of the legislation (such as universal health insurance coverage or long-distance competition) will roughly reflect the decisions discussed publicly through the narratives offered by competing interests. Elected officials must respect public discourse because interest groups can make threats that they can back up, or seem able to, as occurred in 1993–94 over comprehensive health care reform.

Only a handful of issues each year, though, possess the policy reach of the Clinton health care proposal or the complete overhaul of telecommunications policy. What, then, happens on significant issues that do not have such an extensive potential impact? Narratives are constructed, to be sure, and political information is conveyed, but the possibility for disconnecting public narratives from the private policy decisions will increase in the absence of clear, well-articulated positions by a variety of interests. This suggests that groups argue on behalf of the general good in public while pursuing their own particular advantages in private.

In the wake of the 1993–94 failure to reform health care, two major health care initiatives moved onto the governmental agenda in 1995: a Republican attempt to cut back future Medicare spending (as part of balancing the budget) and a bipartisan effort to address specific problems surrounding health insurance portability that penalized workers for changing jobs. But in neither of these efforts did the president or outside interest groups generate the defining narratives of the debate (unlike the situation with the

Clinton health care plan and telecommunications reform, in which interest groups were able to produce the dominant story lines of the policy debates). Rather, in the case of these medical care issues, both agenda items largely were defined by key legislators. Interest groups conducted most of their lobbying within their specialized policy communities. Rarely did they seek to expand the scope of the conflict to the public at large, although they did keep their own constituents informed (such as members of the American Association of Retired People). At the same time, the role of interested narratives remained central to understanding the nature of policy making on these issues, even when the audience was severely restricted and the story lines remained more private than public.

"Saving Medicare": Part of a Never-Ending Story

With unerring prescience, GOP pollster Bob Moore laid out the politics of Medicare in a 1995 internal memo: "Messages that work [for Republicans]: If we don't act today, the Medicare Trust Fund will be bankrupt. We cannot wait until the system goes bankrupt before we solve the problem." Continuing, he pointed out, "[the Democrats'] message on Medicare is effectively simple: 'Republicans are balancing the budget on the backs of seniors while cutting taxes for their rich friends.'" He closed his memo with prophetic political advice: "No poll has ever found that the American people are willing to cut Medicare to reduce the deficit, balance the budget or pay for tax cuts. . . . People support slowing the growth in Medicare for one reason only, to protect the system from bankruptcy."[5]

Moore's memo clearly summarized the two parties' competing narratives on Medicare. Republicans would present themselves as saving Medicare from certain disaster, while Democrats would argue they were protecting the needy from greedy Republicans. While the narratives obviously reflected long-standing story lines in the two parties, these competing images placed Speaker Newt Gingrich in direct conflict with President Bill Clinton. Although some interest groups reinforced the party messages, the groups could add relatively little that conveyed much valuable political or policy information. The basic positions of many groups were well-defined within mainstream partisan politics.

Still, by the time President Clinton signed the balanced budget legislation (including Medicare provisions) in August 1997, a host of organized interests, led by the AFL-CIO, had spent tens of millions of dollars hammering home the partisan points outlined in Moore's internal memo. Never before had interests sought so directly to use issue advocacy advertising to alter the outcome of congressional elections.[6] The 1996 elections clearly confirmed the new era of interest group activism that has emerged in the contemporary political process.

Despite the best attempts of the AFL-CIO, however, the anti-Republican Medicare narrative did not dominate the ensuing politics. The eventual changes to the program were incremental, not fundamental. In the end, Medicare reform became a single element of the 1997 balanced budget agreement. As shown in the following sections, the modest cuts stood as a first act within a large drama, one that would continue several years into the future.

SCENE I: THE REPUBLICANS STAKE OUT AN EARLY POSITION

In the beginning, Medicare reform reached the policy agenda as part of a firm Republican commitment to balance the budget. Although virtually all analysts agreed that growth in Medicare funding faced a reduction, Republican leaders had the task of creating a story line that would protect their majority—especially in the House—from the so-called third rail of American politics, a metaphor originally applied to Social Security, but subsequently extended to Medicare. If touched, the issue would produce almost certain political death.[7] Addressing Medicare reform thus represented a major gamble on the part of the GOP leadership.

The most remarkable accomplishment of the Republicans' narrative on Medicare was that they succeeded in placing this issue on the agenda without suffering the fatal consequence of losing control of the House. Such a fear was very real, given the history of the last two Republican majorities. Both in 1947–48 and 1953–54, GOP control of the House lasted just a single term, as slender margins allowed political bungling by the Republicans to return Democrats to power in the House.

Even more than the attempt to pass the Contract with America, the Republicans' Medicare strategy depended on how they crafted their message. The fate of the GOP majority hung in the balance. Still, this was no ideological crusade. Medicare was on the congressional agenda because, in the words of infamous bank robber Willie Sutton, "That's where the money is." Yet that was the GOP risk as well. Republicans worried that they would be regarded as no better than latter-day Suttons, robbing seniors of their access to affordable health care. Worse yet, as Moore's memo warned, Democrats and labor would accuse them of cutting Medicare funding to pay for tax cuts that would benefit the wealthy.

Throughout the spring of 1995, during and after the Contract votes, Gingrich sought to construct a Medicare explanation that would resonate with the public and hold up to the intense scrutiny by groups such as the AARP.[8] Building on extensive focus-group findings, polling consultant Linda DiVall observed that the Republican task was to replace its "revolutionary rhetoric" of change with "soothing words that evoked stability."[9]

As they struggled to forge a message, congressional Republicans received an extraordinary windfall. In early April, the Medicare Board of Trustees declared in its annual report that the system faced bankruptcy by 2002, absent remedial action. Although the report's findings differed only in details from previous cautions, Gingrich and other Republicans cast it as a "triggering event" that prompted them to "save Medicare" with a set of proposed changes.[10] Seeking to alter a popular program remained a dangerous course of action, but the threat of bankruptcy opened the door for Republicans to craft a message that would make future reductions in Medicare spending an acceptable and responsible, if not exactly popular, policy option.

Along with DiVall, Republican polling consultants Bill McInturff and Frank Luntz honed the Medicare message. Their job was to turn the "mind-numbing" complexity of budget/Medicare reform into something that was understandable.[11] Based on polling and focus groups, the Republicans in the House, Senate, and the national party organization articulated the litany to "protect, preserve, and strengthen" Medicare. At the same time, rhetoric notwithstanding, the facts of the matter were clear. The GOP was proposing to take $270 billion out of Medicare over a seven-year period. This allowed Clinton, congressional Democrats, and a host of outside groups to mount emotional, yet credible, attacks on the Republicans' proposed reductions in future benefits.

The debate raged fast and furious, and it illustrated the power of language—both symbols and narratives. Republicans argued that they merely were restricting the rate of future growth in the program. Democrats and their interest group allies continually called the changes cuts. Following this response, Republicans removed the word "cuts" from their vocabulary on Medicare, but not before some political damage had been suffered. After all, just as it was easy to characterize Democrats as tax-and-spend liberals, it was equally easy to portray Republicans as cold and heartless.

Despite these attacks, the Republican achievement of putting Medicare on the table should not be underemphasized. A June 1995 national survey reported that almost three of four respondents favored " 'reducing the rate of growth' in Medicare spending to avoid 'bankruptcy' in the program."[12] One of the reasons for this public reaction was that Republicans had succeeded in keeping the public discussion of Medicare at a very general level. Moreover, they held back any final form of their proposal until late in the 1995 session, thus combining marketing and timing strategies learned from the Clinton Administration's difficulties in defending a detailed proposal over an extended period of time.

Drew Altman, president of the health care research group the Kaiser Family Foundation, noted, "The more you expose yourself to debate about details, the less chance you have to push through sweeping change."[13] Republicans mastered this lesson and kept the most controversial details of the plan secret until near the conclusion of the House debate. In the end, the House leadership's Medicare package ran to more than 400 pages. As had been predicted, the devil—and the opportunity—was buried in the details.

To the extent that health industry interests did enter the public fray over Medicare bankruptcy (given the trustees' unambiguous report) and cost reductions (given that there would be up to $270 billion less in spending, regardless of what it was called), they often regarded the Medicare reform bill as a vehicle for their particular policy goals. A common narrative among health groups was that they needed changes in laws that were "originally adopted in response to abuses that prompted public outrage."[14] For example, reacting to a series of horror stories about misdiagnoses due to inaccurate medical tests, in 1988 Congress passed a law that set detailed standards for doctor's office labs. The Group Practice Management Association, representing group-based physicians, argued that the standards were needless and costly regulatory intrusions into private practice.[15] Their argument could be cast within the broad theme of protecting, preserving, and strengthening the system, even as it served the particular interests of doctors who owned their own highly profitable labs.

Likewise, numerous provisions that enhanced the profitability of private health plans were incorporated into the 1995 Medicare package. Although many of the final provisions won approval in private deals, groups often offered public narratives to justify their positions. For instance, when the American Medical Association advertised in *Roll Call* in support of physician-sponsored health plans, its narrative conveyed policy information (see figure 7.1). Conversely, a coalition of groups, including the AMA, took a political tack in constructing a narrative around how voters would view Medicare reform. Maintaining care within the community was portrayed as a wiser electoral choice than farming it out to "commercial managed care" (see figure 7.2).

For the most part, however, health care lobbyists plied their trade in the relatively private corners of policy community politics. That is, they devised arguments to push for their favored changes (or for maintenance of the status quo), but these were not public narratives. Even though

FIGURE 7.1

"Without physician-sponsored health plans designed by the physicians themselves and not by antitrust authorities, today's marketplace could easily fail to serve consumers well."

Clark C. Havighurst
Professor of Law, Duke University
Former consultant on antitrust
to the Federal Trade Commission
October 3, 1995

Those who fear competition don't want the truth to be known. Insurance companies don't deliver care, doctors do. HMO's don't manage care, doctors do. And now, Congress is considering reforms that will allow physicians to work together to assure quality care for their patients. PSO's are healthy competition.

It's a time of transition...

"The antitrust agencies seemed trapped in a time warp that keeps them fearful of physician conspiracies...Although the health care industry is undergoing a remarkable transformation, the one group of players that might develop the most efficient systems for delivering high-quality personal health care at reasonable cost are somewhat constrained in doing so by the way antitrust law is currently applied to their undertakings."

Clark C. Havighurst
October 3, 1995

It's time for more flexible antitrust legislation...

"Two additional policies that might explicitly encourage more organized/integrated delivery systems and networks are a more flexible application of antitrust legislation to facilitate the formation of various alliances, consolidations, and mergers; and policies to encourage the formation of physician group practices."

Stephen M. Shortell
Professor, Northwestern University
Kellogg School of Management
Health Affairs, Winter, 1994

It's time to eliminate fear of legal repercussions...

"But I agree that there must be some changes in the antitrust law so you [physicians] can clearly get together without fear of legal repercussions. Otherwise, you are consigned to dealing with a middleman that will only add to the cost of you providing your services and undermine the choice that the consumer gets."

President Bill Clinton
March 23, 1994

It's time to put patients first, not shareholders. Pass reforms in Congress for provider-sponsored health care organizations.

American Medical Association
Physicians dedicated to the health of America

FIGURE 7.2

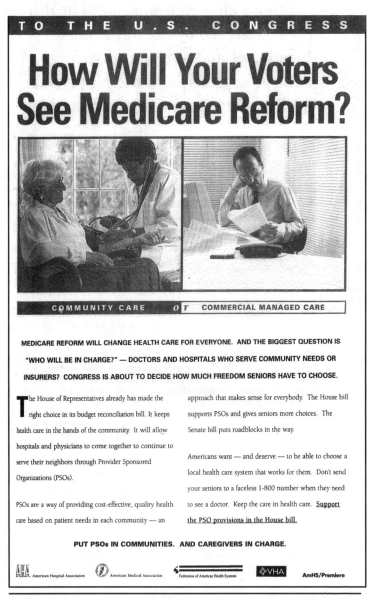

Source: *Roll Call*, November 2, 1995, p. 9. Reprinted with permission of the American Hospital Association, copyright © 1995. Courtesy of VHA Inc. Reprinted with permission of the American Medical Association. Courtesy of Premier Inc. Courtesy of the Federation of American Health Systems.

the reach of many changes, such as incentives for the elderly to join health maintenance organizations (HMOs) reflected high-stakes decisions, the scope of the conflict remained narrow. Rather, the dominant narratives were partisan, delivered ad infinitum by the Republicans (preserve, protect, and strengthen Medicare) and by their Democratic opponents (higher Medicare costs were helping fund a Republican tax cut for the wealthy). By August 1995, the parties had honed their Medicare messages and had begun some modest advertising in a few legislators' districts.[16]

By September, both *Time* and *Newsweek* had run cover stories on reforming Medicare, detailing both the politics and general policy implications of the Republican legislation, even though the specific proposals remained in flux as leaders sought to assure themselves of support from key organized interests. Indeed, beneath the "air wars" of press conferences and advertising, which sought to define the issue for the public, was the hand-to-hand combat of insider lobbying in Congress. Untouched by the rhetorical charges and countercharges about so-called cuts in the program, key interests such as the American Medical Association and the American Hospital Association agreed to support the legislation and, in turn, received favorable treatment from Republicans in protecting their members' financial interests.[17]

The October 19, 1995, passage of Medicare reform in the House of Representatives demonstrated that Speaker Newt Gingrich controlled both the substance and message of the legislative package, at least within the House. As *CQ Weekly* concluded, "Gingrich's efforts to mollify provider groups, seniors' organizations and worried Republicans had made passage possible."[18] Mollifying these groups combined rhetorical reassurances ("a serious solution to a very real Medicare crisis") and a series of specific, complex deals with rural providers, physicians, and managed care interests, among others.[19]

Despite early warnings that the Medicare bill would be decided by lobbying and public relations campaigns outside of Washington, House passage of the bill largely was determined by Republican leaders. The GOP leadership succeeded in two key respects: 1) crafting a palatable message for many if not all audiences, while responding to the entreaties of major interests that were articulated either privately or within the Washington policy community; and 2) cleverly controlling the timing of the legislation, thereby giving Democrats and their allied interests only a minimum window of opportunity in which to take shots at the bill.

Still, as with many other issues in the 104th Congress, House passage did not presage ultimate legislative success. The Senate refused to pass the House bill. What remained on the table were several Medicare proposals and a lot of partisan rhetoric—which grew increasingly nasty as the congressional campaigns heated up and after Medicare trustees issued a forecast for the program's finances that indicated a shortfall in hospital insurance by 2001, a year earlier than the 1995 report.

The 104th Congress adjourned in October 1996 leaving Medicare's problems unresolved. With both presidential candidates agreeing to the general need for a short-term fix and the appointment of a bipartisan commission to deal with long-term problems, Medicare remained a hot issue only for congressional campaigns, mostly in the House. With more heat than light, parties and their allies made changes in Medicare one of the cornerstone issues of the campaign.

SCENE II: MEDICARE AS A 1996 ELECTION ISSUE

Although the labor movement consistently declined as a force in American politics from the 1950s to the early 1990s, until 1994 unions could comfort themselves with the knowledge that, year in and year out, Democrats controlled the House of Representatives. Coupled with the Republican capture of the Senate, the unexpected triumph of House Republicans in November 1994 meant that labor lost its crucial access to the committee leadership on Capitol Hill.

In the wake of the 1994 election, organized labor sought to regain control of the House (the Senate seemed beyond recapture). On top of their traditional support for Democratic congressional candidates (Democrats received 95 percent of labor's $42.3 million in contributions in 1994), the AFL-CIO committed itself to a $35 million public education campaign, with at least $22 million going to "issues-oriented" radio and television advertising.[20] AFL-CIO political director Steve Rosenthal concluded that just funneling funds to congressional candidates would be inadequate: "We firmly believe we can't move our members around *candidates*. We can move our members around *issues*."[21]

More than any other issue-based initiative in the history of congressional campaigns, the AFL-CIO ads used a policy message to score points against incumbent Republicans, mostly first-termers, and all from highly competitive seats.[22] The comprehensive October 25, 1995, budget reconciliation vote gave Democratic candidates and their labor allies several major targets, including a $270 billion reduction in the growth of Medicare spending.[23] Republican incumbents, through their own well-financed campaigns and assisted by soft money infusions from the Republican National Committee and issue advertising from the business-financed Coalition and other, less well-publicized sources, constructed a consistent, two-part counternarrative on Medicare. First, both the candidates and the Coalition claimed that Republican representatives "voted to increase Medicare to stay ahead of inflation"; second, the ads shifted the argument to question the legitimacy of attacks from "Out-of-state organized labor leaders . . . using their members' dues, $35 million, to force their agenda through Congress."[24]

So it went; throughout the congressional campaign, these competing narratives (and those on other subjects) were repeated, ad nauseum, in thirty-two to forty-four targeted labor districts, most represented by first-term Republicans (the exact number of districts varied during the course of the campaign). Both labor and business claims were factual, but neither told the complete story. As health policy scholar Uwe Reinhart concluded in the waning days of the campaign, "No candidates can afford to tell the American people the truth about Medicare. . . . When Republicans are in opposition, they will use Medicare to demagogue the ruling powers, and, as we saw this year, when the Democrats are in opposition [at least in the Congress], they will use it to demagogue the ruling power."[25]

Very little changed in the opposing Medicare stories spun by Republican and Democratic congressional candidates—and their interest-group allies—as the campaigns continued through the fall. Regardless of their nominal source—the candidates, independent issue-based expenditures by interest groups (such as the AFL-CIO or the Coalition), or national party soft money advertisements, the Medicare narratives made no meaningful contribution to any substantive debate. Rather, each side turned up the volume, repeated vacuous slogans, increased the frequency with which it repeated its message, and hoped that the election would reward it with control of the U.S. House, the only significant prize of the 1996 elections that remained in doubt as the campaign drew to a close.

SCENE III: THE AFTERMATH OF AN "EPIC DRAMA"

A scant 10,000 votes scattered across a dozen congressional districts allowed Republicans to retain control of the House of Representatives in 1996. Aggressive, highly partisan initiatives were unlikely to get far in the 105th Congress, given that handfuls of Republican members—conservative freshmen from the 104th Congress or moderates from the Northeast—could stop the House majority dead in its tracks. At the same time, the roughly even partisan division within the House (227 Republicans, 207 Democrats, and one Independent) meant that some cross-party majorities would be essential to pass most legislation, even before it could win approval from the Senate and the president.[26]

All elections produce a host of self-congratulations for winners and rationalizations from losers. The 1996 contests proved no exception.[27] However the AFL-CIO might spin the results, the hard fact remained that Republicans retained control of the House, a condition that likely would continue in 1998, given the historical tendency of the president's party to lose congressional seats in the sixth year of a president's term.[28] Beyond celebrating their victory, though, House Republicans likewise had to confront the hard fact that their 1996 results did not open any real opportunity for passing a well-defined Republican agenda. But they had survived the Democratic and labor onslaught over Medicare, among other issues. Despite the pain of so-called Medigoguery, GOP explanations of preserving Medicare had worked. Republicans remained in the majority and found themselves—as the 105th Congress began—within shouting distance of President Clinton's budget position on Medicare funding.

Many Democratic and Republican legislators returned to Capitol Hill after the election chastened politically and ready to embrace the pragmatism of bipartisan politics in the 105th Congress. The realities of divided government and narrow congressional majorities encouraged compromise, especially among House Republicans, many of whom had come to understand their constituents' willingness to embrace reforms, but not large-scale changes in popular programs.

SCENE IV: REACHING AN AGREEMENT—
WHAT'S A FEW BILLION DOLLARS AMONG FRIENDS?

Medicare reform first made the Republican agenda because the program was too expensive to be ignored. Indeed, if the budget was to be balanced and taxes were to be cut, Medicare and other entitlement programs faced reductions in future growth. Like an uninvited guest, the Medicare issue hung around because no one could make it go away. In 1997, however, the budgetary forces that initially had opened the front door to Medicare reform were able to usher the problem out the back door, at least for a few years.

If the "triggering event" that pushed Medicare onto the congressional agenda was the 1995 Medicare trustees' report, the final nudge out the back door came from the Congressional Budget Office's last-minute recalculation of $225 billion in extra revenue for the 1998 through 2002 fiscal years. As *CQ Weekly*'s George Hager observed, "this windfall allowed for difficult choices to remain unresolved. . . . Gone was a controversial cap on Medicare spending that had infuriated liberal Democrats and governors of both parties."[29]

Balancing the budget became the dominant story line of national politics in the months following the 1996 elections. By August 1997, a landmark agreement had been reached that was quickly ratified by both congressional chambers and the president. In addition to balancing the overall budget, the agreement included a ten-year plan for Medicare and the establishment of a commission that would investigate the program's long-term funding difficulties.

Reaching this balance was scarcely painless, but $100 billion in reduced payments to hospitals and other providers, along with $15 billion in higher costs to beneficiaries, did not represent large-scale changes. Still, interested narratives proved important to the resolution of immediate Medicare problems and the deferral of profound, long-term challenges to the fiscal soundness of the system. Two distinct, sometimes complementary story lines proved important. First, various interests and experts sought to counter the new conventional wisdom about Medicare— that the only courageous politicians were those who would take on such a huge entitlement program.[30] Second, particular organized interests could present their specific arguments for protection outside the glare of publicity, thus privatizing the conflict and restricting the playing field to the health care community.

The strong CBO numbers allowed the critics of the "Medicare crisis" scenario to present a counternarrative that helped legislators adopt a politically advantageous, temporary fix that kept policy changes to a minimum. An article in the AARP monthly newsletter clearly articulated this perspective, drawing extensively on sympathetic sources from academia and the Social Security/Medicare policy community. The AARP's narrative, presented to its 33 million members, told its own tale of a national press adopting a "highly personalized approach" to Medicare reform that views issues "in terms of good guys and bad guys," which "eliminates the nuances and subtleties" of the debate.[31] "It's high drama," noted Urban Institute economist Marilyn Moon, one of a dozen media and social policy experts cited in the story, and "that is what the media are rewarding, because high drama is a lot easier to write about than careful analysis."[32]

Although the AARP's counternarrative surely did reflect one important substantive line of argument on Medicare changes, equally noteworthy is that this interest group, however great its political muscle, provided a ready-made political explanation to any lawmaker who needed to answer the charge that he or she had missed a great opportunity to restructure a system in crisis. Following Murray Edelman's textbook description of symbolic language, the Medicare crisis was first identified, and then, after a suitable period of hand-wringing, followed by a reassuring story that no major changes were necessary, at least in the short term.[33] More generally, as part of the budget deal, incremental adjustments might well "defang the Medicare attacks that worked . . . against Republicans in 1996. . . ."[34] Almost all visible factions—save, perhaps, for highly committed liberal Democrats and frothing-at-the-mouth antigovernment conservatives[35]—appeared satisfied with the budget agreement's ten-year Medicare fix.

At the same time that Medicare reform played out in highly symbolic ways, a host of interests made their cases more privately, far from the spotlight of public attention. Within the Medicare policy community, many interests needed to make arguments to retain their portions of the Medicare pie, which was open to being resliced. In the end, incrementalism meant modest changes, as teaching hospitals and managed care plans pleaded their case successfully in the detail legislation that emerged.

In addition, medical savings accounts—introduced on an experimental basis in the 1996 Kennedy-Kassebaum legislation (see below)—again won approval as a pilot project for Medicare recipients within the budget agreement. The bill approved 390,000 additional MSAs, which allowed those participating in the program to set aside money for medical expenses in a tax-free account modeled after individual retirement accounts (IRAs). The amendment also added a mandate that seniors purchase a high-deductible private insurance policy designed to protect against catastrophic illnesses. These complemented the 750,000 MSAs allowed a year earlier in the Kennedy-Kassebaum bill. That the MSA concept had been accepted was demonstrated by the absence of advertising and publicity on its behalf in 1997; the medical savings account story was familiar and well understood, both in policy and political terms. For the time being, the MSA narrative articulated a viable alternative market model, one that potentially redounded mainly to the benefit of a particular insurance company that had invested so much in making it an acceptable political option.

Passing Kennedy-Kassebaum: Sticking to the Story, Passing Out the Goodies

Tom Meredith died June 17 [1995] at age 55. The cause was cancer, but his wife Jean believes his difficulty maintaining health insurance shortened his life as well.

The Merediths had health insurance for 10 years through their small business. But when Tom's medical bills began piling up in 1990, their insurer canceled the policy, telling Tom he was no longer a profitable enrollee. He found a new insurer eventually, but the delay forced him to put off needed surgery for a year—which Jean believes contributed to his death. "I feel like the reason my husband is not here today is because of the delay."

—opening paragraphs from *CQ Weekly* story on Kennedy-Kassebaum bill

Even *CQ Weekly*, with its prototypical "just-the-facts" approach to legislative reporting, found it useful to begin one extensive article on the Kennedy-Kassebaum bill with an exemplary story. This was legislation with a clear narrative. Indeed, its narrative obscured the very issue of whether or not it would work, to say nothing of who would benefit most from its provisions.

If the competing stories on Medicare were dramatic, often well-publicized, and highly partisan, those surrounding the Kennedy-Kassebaum bill were somber, nonpartisan tales of frustration with inequities promoted by the current health care system. In the best tradition of problem-oriented, incremental lawmaking, Senators Kennedy and Kassebaum sought to address specific ills with limited remedies. The core of their bill provided that 1) insurers guarantee continued coverage for workers who changed jobs (portability) and 2) exclusions from coverage for pre-existing medical conditions be limited sharply. In the wake of the 1993–94 debate over comprehensive health reform, almost all interests agreed that such changes were advisable, both in terms of increasing coverage of the uninsured and, more importantly, reducing the impact of "job lock"—the unwillingness of employees to pursue more attractive jobs because they might lose insurance coverage.[36]

Most members of Congress found it easy to embrace the basic ideas addressed by the portability and pre-existing conditions provisions, and the Kennedy-Kassebaum bill won unanimous support in an April 1966 Senate vote. The modest intent of the bill, its convincing logic, and its bipartisan backing (sixty-two co-sponsors) seemed to give the measure "irresistible political momentum."[37] Ironically, the very attractiveness of the bill, with its palatable solutions to well-recognized problems, made it a target for legislators and special interests who wished to take advantage of the legislation's seemingly irresistible attraction by tacking on their own provisions. In particular, several senators, led by Budget Committee chair Pete Domenici (R-N.M.), sought to expand coverage for mental health illnesses, and a variety of Republican House members, in league with an aggressive insurance company, fought to include savings accounts in the final bill.

Even though the senators who worked for expanded mental health coverage failed to win such a concession, the fact that they got as far as they did reflected the potential impact of powerful narratives presented by major institutional figures. Conservative Senators Domenici and Alan Simpson (R-Wyo.) recounted personal, family-based stories of mental illness and argued energetically in favor of covering this kind of sickness in the same way as any physical ailment. In the end, however, the potential cost of covering mental illness prompted the business community to oppose the provision, placing the entire piece of legislation in jeopardy.[38] Although the mental health community did offer its support and sought to stake out a Capitol Hill position (most publicly in a *Roll Call* advertisement) in favor of the mental health provisions, it was the series of stories presented by individual senators that gave this potentially expensive agenda item any life at all. Indeed, the fact that it was Budget Committee chairman Domenici, a long-standing deficit hawk, who made the argument gave it particular power; he was not a profligate senator who increased federal spending without good reason.

Still, when push came to shove on the Senate floor, the poignant stories of a few senators were not enough to overcome the bottom-line logic that worked against adding any new entitlements to federal obligations. Moreover, Kennedy and Kassebaum laid out a "no amendments" strategy in an attempt to keep the bill clean, noncontroversial, and free from the possibility of a presidential veto. Such a strategy proved viable for initial passage in the Senate, but Majority Leader Dole and most Senate Republicans anticipated that one significant change—the establishment of tax-exempt medical savings accounts—would be incorporated in the House and subsequently stand a good chance of winning Senate approval in a conference committee report. The Republican leadership was willing to risk a veto to include an MSA provision in the final version of the bill. Why? Largely because of the persistence, persuasiveness, and political largesse of J. Patrick Rooney and the Golden Rule Insurance Company.

Rooney's company long had proselytized on behalf of medical savings accounts. Consistent with market-based reforms favored by the new congressional majority, this idea aimed to help people save money for their own medical expenses through the vehicle of a tax-deferred savings account. Not surprisingly, Rooney and Golden Rule employees were big Republican donors, contributing more than $480,000 in 1996 alone.[39] Indeed, Golden Rule had been an early, major donor to Gingrich's political organization, GOPAC.

As presented by its congressional and interest group advocates, the basic MSA story line was simple and beguiling; in the words of a briefing from the National Center for Policy Analysis (partially funded by Rooney's contributions): "MSAs give people the opportunity to move from a traditional low-deductible health plan to one with a high deductible (say $2,000 to $3,000) and to deposit the premium savings in a personal savings account. They use the account to pay for routine and preventative medical care, and the high-deductible policy pays for major expenses. If they have money left in the MSA at the end of the year, they can withdraw it or roll it over to grow with interest."[40]

Although Speaker Gingrich (R-Ga.) and Rep. Bill Archer (R-Tex.), chair of the Ways and Means Committee, had fervently advocated MSAs, the case for this initiative was crafted and articulated most consistently by Rooney and Golden Rule.[41] Golden Rule's policy narrative emphasized consumer choice and prospective refunds for healthy enrollees. Coupling advertisements, sponsored think-tank studies, substantial campaign contributions, and old-fashioned inside lobbying, Golden Rule moved MSAs onto the governmental agenda, helped shape the alternative passed by the Republican House in early 1996, and exercised enough influence to save at least an experimental MSA program within the final version of the Kennedy-Kassebaum bill. Golden Rule invested millions of dollars in its campaign for MSAs, which ordinarily are sold in tandem with high-deductible catastrophic illness policies—a major source of income for the company. In 1997, nearly 19,000 medical savings accounts were sold by Golden Rule. Overall, industry reports indicated that 100,000 such accounts had been opened nationwide.

The MSA policy initiative did not reflect a "high-stakes" policy decision such as those on comprehensive health care or telecommunications deregulation. Indeed, it was sold—like many other initiatives—as a "pilot program." Still, for Golden Rule, its implementation might well determine the company's future success, given that its revenues, after several years of growth, had remained stagnant in 1993–94.[42]

Within the health care community, strong and often

persuasive counternarratives developed in response to the MSA concept. The basic opposing story lines constructed an alternative future in which: 1) MSAs would draw disproportionately from the young, the healthy, and the wealthy, thus leaving traditional health plans to deal with less healthy, more expensive populations, which would require substantial rate increases; and 2) MSAs would "elevate the autonomy of the individual patient" as consumer, who would be encouraged to skimp on preventive care and to ignore early warning signs of potentially serious conditions.[43]

Although Senators Kassebaum and Kennedy fought to keep their insurance bill free of significant amendments, first Kassebaum and then Kennedy (after a long period of protestation) compromised on MSAs—allowing a four-year experiment to proceed. Golden Rule had lobbied in conventional ways and made more than a million dollars in individual campaign contributions, soft-money donations to the Republican Party, and gifts to GOPAC. It also produced a consistent story line that gave its key audience—Republican legislators—an adequate explanation for their actions. Most economic and health care research found little value in MSAs (and lots of risk), but the straightforward Golden Rule–sponsored narrative (with its own supporting studies) proved strong enough to withstand opposition efforts to expand the conflict through a fairly technical argument.

In the end, broad, interested public narratives did not affect the Kennedy-Kassebaum bill. To the extent that there were such narratives, they were articulated by politicians eager to do something, however symbolic, about problems that had been clearly defined within the context of the Clinton health care initiative. Even though the scope of conflict was fairly broad, the number of people ultimately affected was minimal; more than a year after the passage of Kennedy-Kassebaum, many insurance companies had found ways to avoid writing insurance policies on those seeking coverage under the law.[44] At the same time, Golden Rule did articulate a consistent message, both within Republican circles and inside the health policy community. In a sense, Patrick Rooney had won a double victory. Not only did the Kennedy-Kassebaum bill allow for 750,000 MSAs in a pilot program, but the basic concept had become institutionalized as existing policy, so that a year later 390,000 MSAs—another pilot program—were authorized under the Medicare provisions of the balanced budget legislation.[45] Strangely enough, in neither the Kennedy-Kassebaum experience nor in the balanced budget agreement was there much substantive deliberation over the merits of MSAs. Rather, legislative packages won passage based on compromises that allowed modest changes within an incremental framework.

Narratives and the Possibility of Public Deliberation

> Calvin: Doesn't it seem like everybody just shouts at each other nowadays?
>
> Hobbes: I think it's because conflict is drama, drama is entertaining, and entertainment is marketable.
>
> Calvin: Finding consensus and common ground is *dull*! Nobody wants to watch a civilized discussion that acknowledges ambiguity and complexity. We want to see fireworks. . . . Talk show hosts, political candidates, new programs, special-interest groups—they all become successful by reducing debates to the level of shouted rage. Nothing gets solved, but we're all entertained.
>
> Hobbes: Hmm, you may be right.
>
> (silence)
>
> Calvin: What a boring day *this* turned out to be!

As usual, Calvin and Hobbes (before their early retirement) had gotten it right. Debates over issues often end up as shouting matches, with little value save entertainment. Still, hope springs eternal. Political scientist Benjamin Page argues that professional communicators, such as reporters, writers, commentators, pundits, and experts from academia and think tanks, can facilitate public deliberation; their job is to assist policy experts to communicate with each other, and to "assemble, explain, debate, and disseminate the best available information and ideas about public policy, in ways that are accessible to large audiences of ordinary citizens."[46] In several case studies, Page finds that public deliberation is highly mediated by visible communicators; despite some biases and an occasional tendency to be out of touch, he concludes that "the marketplace of ideas actually works reasonably well, most of the time, so long as there is sufficient competition and diversity in the information system."[47]

Examining recent public discussion on major issues scarcely makes one sanguine over the possibility that public communicators can effectively deliberate through press releases, talk shows, op-ed pieces, and the like. For example, if the stakes of a decision are high and the level of understanding of the policy choices, even among elites, is relatively low, can we hope that public deliberation will be of much assistance? Moreover, will anyone seek to move the debate toward a reasonable approximation of the public interest? Thus, in the fight over telecommunications reform, the only time the public weighed in at all was early on, when the debate focused narrowly on the price of cable service. In the aftermath of the 1992 reregulation of the cable industry, the policy debate shifted to either a highly symbolic plane—more choice for consumers—or to arcane, often incomprehensible topics of market penetration, accessibility to spectrum, and the particulars of competition. As we saw in chapter 6, all of the major players did, however, hold a clear vision of what short-term gains they wanted to obtain from the complex legislative package. For example, the regional Bell companies desired rapid approval of their bids to provide long-distance service. Their contribution to the public discourse was to bombard elites with highly simplified narratives about offering increased choices to consumers; the Competitive Long Distance Coalition of At&T and its allies produced a seemingly similar public message, but its short-term goal was to keep regional Bells at bay as long as possible. Other elites contributed only marginally to the public discourse on the competition issue, and the important and highly complex set of decisions that made up the Telecommunications Act of 1996 was finally passed with a minimum of serious public deliberation.

Conversely, the Clinton health reform package seemingly enjoyed a great deal of public deliberation. Its demise has been interpreted by a host of journalists and scholars; despite various differences in their emphases and conclusions, their findings scarcely offer much hope for public deliberation contributing to a reasoned policy decision. In particular, the evidence is strong that it was the so-called professional communicators, not the public at large, who were unduly affected by the HIAA's Harry and Louise advertising campaign (see chapter 4). To make matters worse, "Media coverage reinforced the messages of interest group advertising, and thus an electorate poorly informed about a complex policy area found it difficult to disentangle truth from falsehood."[48]

In the end, the simplifying narratives of Harry and Louise and the apparent simplicity of the Canadian-style system (along with dozens of other specific stories put forth by dozens of interests) did little to move elites or the public toward some set of reasoned health care decisions. The very scale of the decisions surely worked against the possibility of adopting an integrated package of reforms, as many groups could support a story that called for health care reform, but not *this* one. What happens, then, when only one component (or a few parts) of the health care system is targeted for change? Might the convergence of several narratives produce a reasoned discussion and the possibility of public deliberation?

The very uncertainty of many high-stakes outcomes (and how to influence them) may well lead to an increased reliance on narratives among the interested parties. Narratives provide some comforting coherence in highly uncertain situations, in which large numbers of interests and complex issues combine to render incomplete any firm understanding of either policy substance or political linkages. As cozy triangles give way to loose, ill-defined policy communities, all kinds of relevant information (policy, political, and process) grows in importance, both to members of Congress and to those who would influence those legislators.[49] This lack of structure opens up the possibility for narratives to provide coherence in a messy and uncertain policy-making process, in that a narrative requires both a speaker and an audience. In the end, stories may seem concrete, but their very construction and interpretation derive from the intangible relationship between narratives and audiences. Stories remain open to change and reinterpretation.

Anyone who has spent time with legislators or lobbyists will appreciate that they communicate through stories much of the time. Although data and related analyses are plentiful and important, anecdotes often provide both lobbyists and legislators with a way to blend both policy and political information as well as combining empirical and normative approaches to a problem. In private settings among political veterans, narratives surely can convey clear, agreed-upon meanings that can serve as the basis for meaningful deliberation. But when interests "go public" with their stories, nuance often is lost, as with the Harry and Louise interpretation of the Clinton health care plan. Likewise, interests enjoy less policy and political flexibility when their positions are well-publicized. The opportunities for deliberation and an exchange of ideas decline, and confrontation becomes more likely. If a compromise does emerge, it may simply reflect a carefully constructed position that can win majority support, not the result of a deliberative process.

Compromise Without Deliberation

In his book *Revolt of the Elites*, Christopher Lasch writes: "The role of the press, as [Walter] Lippmann saw it, was to circulate information, not to encourage argument. . . . His point was that information precluded argument, made argument unnecessary. Arguments were what took place in the absence of reliable information."[50]

As interests craft their messages for given audience—congressional staffers, op-ed readers, or constituents of a committee chair—they are much more likely to try to convey information than engage in an argument. Even when there seems to be a real debate, messages ordinarily do not address the meat of opponents' positions. After all, as Lasch notes, *"Argument is risky and unpredictable, therefore educational."* Indeed, he points out that argument "carries the risk . . . that we may adopt [our opponents'] point of view."[51]

When interests convey information, they ordinarily do not engage in deliberation or argument. Rather, they are marshaling their own evidence. Compromise may occur, as with the initial four-year experiment on medical savings accounts, but that does not imply that any deliberation took place. The legislative result was purely opportunistic—a political deal, virtually unrelated to the substance of the policy at hand. For example, although President Clinton promised to veto any bill that contained a full-blown MSA program, he indicated that he would sign legislation with a "demonstration project."[52]

In conveying information, the interest-group universe scarcely offers equal representation. Schattschneider emphasized this most forcefully (see chapter 2), but Page also notes that there are inequalities and biases in the mediated marketplace of ideas. In particular, "large, dispersed groups of citizens" are disadvantaged in the information they convey relative to the "political knowledge and/or propaganda bought by businesses and other concentrated interests."[53] In particular, consumers as a large and diverse group encounter great difficulty in having their interests effectively represented.[54] Despite conceding that the information produced by private sources "may be quite important," Page observes that direct information about possible "anti-democratic biases" in interest group communication is difficult to come by.[55] Yet it is precisely those biases that stifle an effective exchange of ideas and encourage the development of self-contained policy narratives.

Jane Mansbridge, conversely, incorporates interested narratives into her notion of deliberation. Although not endorsing a corporatist model, she argues, "[e]mpirical research on the deliberative aspects of interest representation should begin to describe and model existing mechanisms both for deliberation among rank-and-file members and for interchange between members and their formal and informal representatives."[56] Mansbridge wants to transcend competitive frameworks for communication among interests, but she offers few hints as to how interests may move from conveying information to engaging in argument.

Looking back at "saving Medicare" and ensuring insurance portability, to say nothing of the comprehensive Clinton health care package, one can find precious little deliberation or argument. Rather, interests sought out particular audiences and crafted narratives that suited their policy and political ends. Even when there was general agreement on a goal, as with increased portability, many observers concluded that the interests and the decision makers shied away from many difficult and perhaps intractable issues in order to win a symbolic victory.[57] As for MSAs, there was merely the expedient politics of compromise, with one set of interests and elites seeking to limit the possible harm of the experiment, while another set sought to move tax-deductible MSAs further into the web of existing health care choices. In the end, a series of narratives—especially the most expensive ones—conveyed different packages of information, each neatly bundled for a given audience.

Part III

The Heavenly Chorus Redux

Chapter Eight

Many Singers, Whose Song?

G iven the cacophony of voices that participate in the policy process, it sometimes is difficult to determine whose song gets heard. Our review of lobbying on health care, the Contract with America, telecommunications, and Medicare demonstrates how the sound of money has become both loud and nuanced, often simultaneously. The debate over the Clintons' health care reform generated a very public display of lobbying on the part of insurers, pharmaceuticals, doctors, nurses, unions, senior citizens, and small businesses, among others. More than $100 million was spent by at least 650 organizations in an attempt to influence the course of the contentious debate.

Republican efforts to devolve responsibility to the states and reform the legal system through the Contract with America generated large expenditures on research, ads, polls, direct mail, and phone banks to build support for the GOP agenda of downsizing government. The telecommunications debate never managed to engage the public in the same manner health care and the Contract with America did. But the struggles among policy elites with a direct stake in the deregulation debate generated huge expenditures that directed interested information at Washington decisionmakers, from legislators and staff members to opinion leaders and pundits. Medicare featured intense debate among affected interest groups, with the electorate watching how members of Congress handled this political hot potato.

Traditionally, the large number of countervailing forces present in American politics have been believed to limit the power of particular interests and their lobbying efforts. Narrow interest groups can be outvoted at election time by the general public. Political parties, social movements, and public interest groups can arguably speak for larger segments of society than do particularistic groups. Journalists and legislators have sometimes checked the influence of private interests through their distinctive oversight activities.

Given our perspective and observations, it is time to re-examine the efficacy of voters, political parties, social movements, journalists, and government officials in limiting the power of well-organized and well-financed interests, especially as these interests have become more and more skillful at shaping the presentation of their favored issues. If moneyed interests can convey their messages ad nauseam, in any number of ways, many forces that historically have protected general interests may have lost their impact. To investigate this possibility, we look at who speaks in American policy debates, and to what effect.

Why Have Certain Interest Groups Become So Powerful?

Strong organization and control of financial resources have allowed many interest groups to exercise substantial—even disproportionate—influence in American politics. From the Health Insurance Association of America and the Sierra Club to the National Federation of Independent Businesses, Citizens for a Sound Economy, and trial lawyers, particular groups and organizations have carved out considerable power for themselves. Their phone calls gets returned promptly by decision makers, they have access to the mass media, and they are effective in shaping issues that emerge on governmental agendas.

To be sure, campaign contributions and political action committees are important. Out four case studies demonstrate, however, that it is not just raw economic power that translates into political effectiveness. Beyond money and organization, successful interest groups require: 1) an understanding of the political opportunities that are available to them given the institutional situation they confront, and 2) effective communications strategies that get their voices heard above the din of many contemporary debates.

Money determines the staying power of groups in policy debates because of the importance of resources in being able to change venues and control narratives. For example, in several of our cases, when groups confronted problems in a particular venue such as a difficult congressional committee or an intransigent bureaucratic agency, they used their clout to move the debate into another arena. On health care, congressional leaders had considerable flexibility in assigning various provisions of the comprehensive Clinton proposal to different committees. This allowed leaders and outside groups to control the institutional venue in which deliberations took place. The same was true for the Contract with America, telecommunications, and medical reform.

Beyond finding a supportive venue, be it a House committee, an executive agency, or a Senate committee, groups must construct effective narratives and communicate their point of view. Perhaps the greatest challenge facing interest groups in an age of information overload is message control. There are four key issues in political communications: content, timing, repetition, and clarity. Controlling message content means making sure in the midst of conflicting arguments that one's own perspective continues to come through. Message timing can be the essence of politics, emphasizing as it does the delivery of the message at the right time for effective political action. But timing is difficult to judge, so message repetition is necessary; most people pay scant attention to politics and most elites are overwhelmed with information. Clarity in one's message means making sure that given the range of policy participants and the competition of political voices one's own message communicates what is intended.

Most organized interests represent small and parochial slices of society. By their very nature, interest groups are narrow and self-interested. Save for self-proclaimed public interest groups, they cannot claim to speak for general social concerns. Given these conditions, organized interests begin with modest credibility when participating in the public dialogue or asking for benefits from the public treasury. On the crucial dimension of source credibility, most interest groups rank pretty low with the American public. Few citizens would attribute much altruism to insurers, pharmaceutical corporations, or the regional Bell operating companies.

So what allows these and other groups to overcome natural suspicion about their role in American politics? Many groups have learned that a good way to overcome credibility problems is to work through other organizations that have much higher credibility. This involves stealth campaigns with other organizations, alliances under positive-sounding names such as Citizens for Reform, or sponsorship of research studies or public opinion polls through independent organizations such as think tanks.

In each of these ways, interest groups can compensate for their own self-interested status and sound more credible to reporters and the public. They use this newfound credibility to construct narratives and story lines that allow both elites and citizens the chance to view complex policy issues in apparently straightforward terms. They also can use their clout to broaden conflict and to shape the debate. Dollar power often means that public narratives can be dominated by those who can afford to communicate most effectively.

Can Voters Fight Interest Groups?

The ultimate countervailing force in American democracy is the electorate. Voters are more numerous and more diverse than the membership of any specialized interest. Even the largest interest group in America (the AARP, with 33 million members) includes only a modest percentage of the overall electorate. Labor unions as a whole represent about 14 percent of the workforce. This proportion pales in comparison to the percentage of American citizens (half, in 1996) who vote in presidential elections.

Because they are taxpayers and members of multiple groups, voters as a whole are more likely than interest groups to represent collective interests. Voters pay the cost of government programs and they foot the bill for special tax breaks or subsidies granted to interest groups. The fact that group success in taxing the public till comes at the expense of the broad electorate gives voters clear incentives to serve as a check on group power.

If special interests ask too much of government or win too many public benefits, according to classical group theorists as well as our nation's founders such as James Madison, this will threaten the interests of the general public and mobilize citizens to prevent greedy raids on the federal treasury. In *The Governmental Process*, David Truman argued that the dynamics of interest group mobilization limit the demands private organizations place on government[1]. An inordinate amount of success on the part of some groups inevitably fosters a countermobilization by other organizations. When excessive group demands lead to burgeoning government spending, antispending groups appear to fight for taxpayer rights. In other words, the liberal coalition of labor, cities, education, and minorities begets such groups as Citizens for Tax Reform and the Concord Coalition.

According to Truman's theory, group demands also are limited by the fact that citizens have multiple ties to interests. The divided, overlapping nature of public loyalties prevents group conflict from getting out of hand. Leaders can move their organizations only within the parameters set by their membership. This creates an internal check on group demands and helps to insure an equitable level of political competition between groups.

As with the textbook lobbying model, it is not clear that the large mass of unorganized voters can counter well-organized special interests. The costs of organizing typically outweigh the diffuse social benefits that are gained.[2] As a general entity, the public is notoriously difficult to organize. People have diverse interests and many do not care about politics. In an era of massive public cynicism about politicians, it is difficult for the public to get outraged about particular pieces of legislation. Sweetheart deals are just more of the same for many ordinary people.

It is easy for individual citizens to let others act for them. This is what Olson described as the free rider problem. Short of selective benefits such as slick magazines, insurance, or discounted travel, there is little reason for individuals to pay the costs of organizing when they can piggyback on the efforts of others who act in their name. It is simpler to let others do the work in gaining collective benefits and then cash in on these benefits when they are made available to everyone.

Public interest groups occasionally do organize when there is a particularly visible problem such as government corruption or environmental disasters. But the challenge such groups face is staying power. Typically, after the original galvanizing event takes place, public outrage dissipates, membership falls off, and fund-raising slows dramatically. This was the case with Common Cause, an organization whose membership peaked in the mid-1970s around the time of Watergate but then dropped after Congress passed new campaign finance rules that appeared to address the money and politics problem.

For these reasons, it is nearly impossible to persuade voters that the cost of organization will produce significant individual benefits to them. Between the free rider problem and the mammoth task of organizing the general public, there are inherent limits to voters acting as a counterbalance to the demands of powerful interest groups. Voters have difficulty representing their self-interest due to the cost of information and the lags in information flow to the general public.

On controversial matters of public policy, such as health care reform and the Contract with America, there invariably are conflicting cues from political elites. This makes it tricky for citizens to determine how they feel about the issue. Health care reform was so complicated that voters never really figured out what Clinton's package would do for them personally. This complexity made it possible for private interest groups to attach criticisms such as big government and loss of consumer choice to the president's plan. Most voters had no idea what specifics were contained in the Contract with America. And on telecommunications reform, even though the consequences for ordinary citizens were enormous, the public scarcely noticed the policy battle at all.

In the absence of a clear consensus on social action, voters must search out information and decide which course of action best protects them. Public opinion polls create an opportunity for citizens to express their views in the policy-making process, but only on questions phrased by pollsters. In general, the problems citizens have in gathering information relevant to their self-interest restricts the public's ability to win out over smaller, but better organized interests. The result is that citizens have lost some of their power to protect their overall interests and restrain the power of parochial interest groups.

How Effective Are the Political Parties?

Because of the difficulty of organizing the general public, political parties historically have been seen as the most effective way for broad coalitions of interests to counteract the power of special-interest groups. The broad-based nature of political parties and the fact that they must compete for government seats before the general public gives parties special advantages in terms of political mobilization.[3]

First, parties are permanent organizations that monitor political developments with the frenzy of an army of ants. Citizens vary dramatically in terms of their attentiveness to public affairs. Grazing is an apt metaphor for public involvement. Sometimes voters pay close attention to politics, such as right before major national elections. At other times they are much more interested in the travails of nonpolitical activities such as their jobs and families. The public's fluctuating attention span limits its ability to check interest groups.

In contrast, parties are an institutionalized apparatus for contesting matters of public policy. Through their control of nominating contests, parties act as gatekeepers of the election process. In most cases, candidates do not end up on the ballot for voter decisions unless they have won their party's nomination.

Parties also act as the major organizing institution for government. Control of Congress is granted to majority and minority leaders of political parties. Congressional committees perform the bill drafting and consensus building that are key to legislative action. They, of course, are organized along party lines.

Due to their influential role in policy making, parties have an advantage over the citizenry in shaping the public dialogue. Simply by dint of their more broad-based coalitions, parties force interest groups to negotiate their differences. The need to win victories in which voters have a direct say encourages parties to restrain group demands. This moderates the demands placed by groups in order not to hurt the party at election time.

Parties simplify the choices placed before the electorate because they campaign on substantive platforms. This helps the public hold leaders accountable even when voters are not paying close attention to the details of policy making. At election time, the public knows that in choosing a Democrat or a Republican, they are choosing substantive platforms as well. For inattentive voters, this provides a natural countervailing force to the narrow appeals of groups.

But parties have difficulty representing general social interests. The traditional argument that the breadth of party coalitions restrains factions within the party is undermined by contemporary realities. Labor unions and trial lawyers have been particularly powerful in the Democratic party, while small businesses, fundamentalists, and corporations are well-represented in the Republican party. This fragmentation of party coalitions has generated fear that parties have been captured by special interests. If parties are dependent of private money to finance elections and issue advocacy campaigns, their ability to contravene specialized interests is reduced. Since the costs of electioneering have risen much faster than overall inflation, parties have intensified their fund-raising efforts. The 1997 congressional hearings into campaign finance abuses publicized dozens of ways in which moneyed interests curry favor with political parties through financial contributions. Financial imperatives have limited the ability of parties to stand above specialized interests and, in the eyes of some, have undermined the historic role of parties in countering interest groups.

There certainly is evidence in each of our case studies that well-financed interests exercised a lot of clout over political parties in the policy-making process. In the case of health care, pharmaceuticals and insurers funded much of the successful effort against Clinton's reform package. On tort reform, trial lawyers financed Democratic opposition to the Contract with America, while the small business community aided Republican efforts, and the AARP has long contributed to Democratic thinking on Medicare. The industry giants of telecommunications devoted millions to elite advocacy advertising. In none of these cases were parties effective agents of political change. They were not able to limit group demands very effectively nor overcome the power of specialized interests.

Traditional arguments that party voting cues simplify citizen choices also have been weakened by changes in party platforms. As Republicans have moved to the right in their political appeals and Democrats have mimicked GOP positions on welfare reform, crime, and budget balancing, these changes have undermined the ability of parties to provide clear choices to voters. Eras of party transition or outright partisan dealignment blur the meaning of party labels for voters who need guidance from leaders about what is going on during the government's official proceedings.

What Happened to Social Movements?

Parties represent the views of those who are active politically, but who represents the disenfranchised? One problem for any political system is how to represent those who lack resources and do not participate politically. This was especially apparent during health care deliberations, when the millions of Americans who lacked health care insurance were not well organized and hence not well represented. And in the 1996 telecommunications legislation, the interests of consumers were clearly subordinated to the views of well-financed lobbyists for the television networks, cable industry, and phone companies.

By the nature of electoral imperatives, politicians are especially attuned to the interests of those who directly control their fate. In democratic elections in which large sums of cash are required for electioneering activities, this means voters and contributors. But since voters are not well organized and half of them do not even bother to vote, legislators may pay closer attention to their contributors than their constituents. From a systemic standpoint, this produces a situation in which large numbers of citizens feel their interests are not well represented, because politicians pay far less attention to the politically weak and disadvantaged. These segments of society are not well organized and they vote less frequently than those of higher income and education levels. They also are less likely to care about politics and feel that an act of participation will make a difference in their daily lives.

In addition, parties have a way of losing touch with ordinary people. The longer parties are in power, the more they lose touch with the people they are supposed to be representing. Numerous examples exist of parties and politicians booted out of power because it was felt they had lost touch with ordinary voters: congressional Democrats in 1994, President Bush in 1992, and President Carter in 1980, among others.

Voter alienation from major parties creates the seeds of social movements that mobilize those who are underrepresented.[4] As parties grow distant from the electorate and party leaders pay excessive attention to the well-to-do and politically active, grassroots discontent rises. Citizens feel that leaders are not paying attention to them and are not representing their point of view. American history is replete with grassroots uprisings, from the Populists and the Progressives in the last century to Ross Perot's supporters in the 1990s (encouraged, of course with millions in Perot's own funds).

It used to be that with modest resources, social movements could win influence through rallies, protests, and demonstrations. Each of these strategies of mobilization required a considerable amount of time and effort, but not too much in the way of financial resources. Community organizers would merely spend time pointing out to people how their interests were being abused and over the course of time build a movement out of the disenfranchised.

The civil rights movement in the 1950s and 1960s is a vintage example of mass mobilization. Out of the hard work of clergy and local activists around the country, a movement was built that fought for civil rights legislation. Over a long period of time, this movement broke down legal barriers to political participation. In the process, the opposition of powerful interest groups was broken and new laws were passed to protect minority interests.

Another example is the pro-life movement. Organizations active in this area typically have been low-budget agencies committed to stopping abortions. Relying heavily on volunteers and a few staff members, this movement mushroomed into a major political force after the 1973 *Roe v. Wade* Supreme Court decision. It now has become a powerful wing within the Republican party. Because of the strength of the Christian Coalition and right-to-life organizations, Republican nominees now potentially face a litmus test regarding their abortion views.

The militia movement, similarly, was formed by those who felt alienated from mainstream politics. Since its adherents believe the major parties do not take their views very seriously, they use their weekend jaunts in the countryside to form political organizations. In some states, these units hold regular meetings, develop newsletters and videos, and have begun to participate in the political process. This has made them a formidable movement in some Western states.

But political protest in a high-tech era is much more problematic. As more tools of advocacy require access to financial resources, it is more difficult to mobilize and represent the disenfranchised. Minority groups, citizens associations, and public interest organizations do not have money for television ads, direct mail, phone banks, or Internet sites. This puts them at a serious disadvantage when lobbying requires access to resources. Even Ross Perot, who has invested nearly $100 million of his own money in support of his populist cause, has, with the partial exception of deficit reduction, made little impact on the national political landscape.

During several of the policy cases profiled in this book, certain segments of the debate had difficulty getting their voices heard. Those without health insurance did not run ads on television during health care deliberations. They did not conduct focus groups, commission polls, or run direct mail and phone bank campaigns.

The same was true during the debates on the Contract with America. Low-income groups whose members would be seriously hurt by proposed changes were silent. They received little news coverage and did not have the financial resources to publicize narratives favorable to their cause. For these reasons, the poor were not seen as a serious factor in congressional deliberations.

In regard to the telecommunications bill, less attention was paid to consumer interests than those of the affected industries. Elite advertising campaigns were waged by AT&T, Sprint, MCI, the regional Bells, the cable industry, and the television networks, but few ads were placed by phone users or cable television viewers upset with poor service or faced with higher prices. Not surprisingly, in the wake of telecommunications reform, cables rates have risen sharply and industry mergers have continued apace.

As lobbying has come to center on expensive political communications technologies, the voices of the disadvantaged and unorganized have become even less a part of the policy discourse. It requires money and organization to participate in contemporary political battles. This skews political mobilization away from community activists to media consultants, public relations experts, and direct mail specialists. Indeed, in an era with few genuine, clear-cut crises, social movements have become the missing element of American politics. And when we see what appears to be real citizen concern, it's as likely to be highly stimulated grassroots lobbying as authentic, broadly based public worry.

Journalistic Oversight: Fact or Fiction?

Changes in the political process over the last few decades have changed the balance of power in the policy-making process to the point that new countervailing forces have emerged. Among the most important new actors are journalists. Once ridiculed as ambulance chasers in the play *The Front Page*, reporters have become power brokers in their own right. Print and electronic media journalists provide most of the information we receive about campaigns and policy making. Journalists inform us about politicians' views, personalities, strategies, and goals. When a controversy unfolds, the press becomes a crucial agent in interpreting what is happening.

News coverage has major consequences for how people understand political events. By their manner of covering political events and their decisions on who to interview, journalists emphasize certain narratives and frame the political dialogue. Reporters rightfully see their mission as informing the public about important developments and describing how events have taken place, which puts them in the middle of the political communications process.

For years, politics has been seen as conflict over the mobilization of various interests.[5] In many respects, the most important political battles are fights regarding the terms of debate. The argument over abortion, for example, long has centered on the competing symbolism of choice versus life. Opinion polls have revealed sharp fluctuations in public support for abortion depending on which symbolic frame is most central at the time.

Health care was a clear case of a struggle over competing constructions of political reality. National polls showed that the public desired several conflicting goals in health care reform: the preservation of quality care, choice of health care providers, reasonable cost of coverage, security from lost coverage, and a system free of excessive bureaucracy. Whether it be a single-payer system, managed competition, or a hybrid based on an employer or individual mandate, no plan secured every principle. As preceding chapters have shown, these competing conceptions of health care led to vigorous conflict over the framing of this policy debate, well before any legislative decisions came to closure.

In a situation in which the policy frame dramatically shapes the nature of the discussion, reporters are key participants in interest-group battles. In cases in which the public is not organized or community groups lack resources for political protest, journalists provide oversight of the legislative process. This certainly was the case for telecommunications and tort reform. Since these were specialized policy areas far removed from the daily lives of most citizens, journalists were the key information providers. And that information often came packaged in a story line, directly prepared for citizen consumption.

In other areas, journalists have carved out a niche for themselves as investigative reporters. These types of stories have exposed rip-offs in military procurement, lying by public officials, and favors performed for legislative contracts. Investigative reports can have dramatic consequences for policy making. As reporters in recent years have taken on the obligation to protect the public's right to know and to point out abuses in group competition for government benefits, they have become a powerful force in the legislative process.

Reporters are often well suited for government oversight. For one, they are seen as independent of political parties and interest groups, which gives their reporting extensive credibility with the general public. Perhaps no other group of political actors has the source credibility that reporters have. Public opinion polls regularly show that citizens trust reporters more than government officials and that reporters are seen as above the partisan political process.

At the same time, reporters have excellent access to public officials. Because of their control over air time and newspaper space, reporters can demand and receive answers from officials about matters of public controversy. This gives them the means to hold leaders accountable for decisions that are made and the discretion to report on injustices they see in the political process. Many reporters see themselves as acting on behalf of ordinary citizens, which indirectly incorporates a grassroots perspective into government deliberations.

But there are problems with journalistic oversight of policy making. As journalists have become celebrities in their own right, especially through television, they have become another elite group in the political process. In addition, the media business has become highly corporate and thoroughly centralized. During the telecommunications bill debates, for example, local news stations across the country used their control of the airwaves to lobby for free use of a broadcast spectrum worth almost $70 billion. Equally troubling, how does ABC News, as part of the Disney empire, maintain distance and objectivity in covering entertainment issues? How can NBC, which is owned by GE, effectively cover nuclear power issues?

Moreover, journalistic oversight is limited because reporters are dependent on sources for news tips. In the Washington journalism community, this is a particular problem. The need for access to a few high-placed sources is paramount in the capital city. The relatively few number of top sources and the large number of enterprising reporters interested in breaking news stories alters the balance of power between journalists and officials. The symbiotic needs of reporters and powerful sources can create a cooperative relationship that undermines a reporter's ability to provide effective oversight. If reporters need sources more than sources need a particular reporter, public officials can gain dominance by playing reporters off one another. In this situation, it is tempting for reporters to go easy on high government officials because of the reliance on them for news tips.

Changes in the media industry, furthermore, have complicated the ability of journalists to conduct effective oversight. Competitive pressures within the media have increased the economic squeeze on news organizations. It is difficult to devote the time necessary for investigative journalism when the pressure to scoop the competition is so intense. Increasing competition clearly has raised the pressure on news budgets.

There is little doubt that budget pressures weaken the effectiveness of news organizations. If reporters are unable to provide in-depth reporting, this makes it difficult for reporters to serve as a countervailing force to interest groups. It compromises the historic independence of the so-called fourth branch of government. Reporters can be effective overseers only when they have adequate resources to perform their job.

On the Autonomy of Government Officials

In addition to reporters, government officials can act as a check on the power of interest groups. According to Raymond Bauer, Ithiel de Sola Pool, and Lewis Dexter, public officials have controlled the political dialogue with interest groups. In their path-breaking research on foreign trade lobbying thirty years ago, these authors found that groups served as service bureaus for government officials.[6] Rather than being pressure groups, as described by Schattschneider (see chapter 2), they provided valuable information and expertise for officials. Because of the number of competing groups, Bauer, Pool, and Dexter wrote, legislators can play groups off each other. By using information from a variety of different sources, legislators can avoid being used by any particular group in the political process. For those who worry about excessive domination of the policy-making process by interest groups, this historic model is reassuring. Instead of reinforcing negative stereotypes about interest groups, these authors found that groups had an educational impact on the system. Their key resource was information, not financial power. Instead of misleading and corrupting members of Congress, group representatives were seen as making a positive contribution to the political system.

This interpretation is consistent with evidence from other areas. Theodore Lowi has argued that legislators

avoid controversy by delegating the details of policy decisions to bureaucrats.[7] This frees them from having to make
unpopular decisions and insulates them from interest-
group pressures. But such a revisionist perspective ignores
contemporary political realities. Government officials have
become so dependent on outside money to promote their
agenda that it has limited their independence. Groups provide campaign contributions. They give members trips to
exotic locations. Most important, from our perspective,
much of the information used to make important decisions
is interested—that is, it flows through organized interests.
This makes it difficult for representatives to serve as a
countervailing force in public policy making, even if they
want to. The policy alternatives have already been framed
by outside interests.

In the health care debate, for example, interest groups
used contributions, trips, and speaking fees as lobbying
tools as well as flooding decision makers with expensive
messages. On the Contract with America debates, interest
groups financed much of the political communications
strategy of the House leadership. Campaign contributions
were a key strategic resource for the telecommunications
bill and Medicare reform, but group money also paid for
the airing of major alternatives, such as medical savings
accounts and opposition to mental health benefits.

Some interest groups accumulate political power by developing specialized knowledge that other groups lack. For
example, the Health Insurance Association of America became one of the chief information sources on issues relating
to health insurance and Medicare. The National Federation of Independent Businesses specializes in issues affecting the small business community, and NFIB's grassroots
lobbying conveys a powerful set of policy and political messages.

Strategic placement within a policy community strengthens groups and gives them considerable ability to control the political dialogue. Legislators count on the AARP for expertise on issues related to senior citizens. The Center for Responsive Politics has become a leading depository for information on campaign finance. Citizens for a Sound Economy has become an authority on tax cuts and business regulation. Information on automotive safety comes from Consumer Products. The NFIB communicates positions that are widely regarded as reflecting small business views. All these groups increase the legislature's dependence on them for vital information. Some private groups dominate their policy niche so well that they have reached a point at which they have better information at their disposal than do public officials. This weakens the power of government officials and clearly reduces their ability to check the influence of interest groups. If groups control the information flow in key areas (such as tobacco, historically), it undermines interpretations suggesting legislators can play organizations off each other. Indeed, it demonstrates that legislators are not as autonomous as previous research would suggest.

The Age of Big Interests

The greatest restraint upon large interests today is the impact of other large interests. Neither voters, political parties, social movements, journalists, nor government officials can effectively check the power of well-funded and well-organized groups. By mastering the communications process and focusing on persuasive narratives, moneyed interests have carved out considerable power for themselves by their ability to define problems and acceptable solutions, as well as to lobby key policy makers.

As shown by our cases, there have been many examples

in recent years of powerful groups dominating public policy making. On health care reform, insurers and small businesses combined with other groups to defeat the centerpiece of the president's agenda. On tort reform, one of the key planks of the Contract with America, trial lawyers played a key role in defining narratives that torpedoed the bill. A number of telecommunications companies negotiated differences affecting millions of consumers who went essentially unrepresented in the Telecommunications Act of 1996. On Kennedy-Kassebaum, a small insurance company was able to expand medical savings accounts to thousands of new customers without any detailed congressional deliberation.

Each of these cases demonstrates the nature of fundamental change in American politics over the past three decades. Thirty years ago, social movements and investigative journalists were powerful forces. From the civil rights coalition to the consumer safety movement, there were demonstrated cases in which broadly defined societal interests demonstrated their ability to alter public policy. Today, the dominant forces are large, usually corporate interests. The power to convey convincing narratives requires money and favors those who already are well-organized politically. Such an emphasis on moneyed interests weakens American democracy and threatens the very foundations of representative government.

Chapter Nine:

The Paradox of the New Heavenly Chorus

Thirty-five years ago, democratic theorist E. E. Schattschneider concluded that "the definition of the alternatives is the supreme instrument of power." He directed this argument at those writers who viewed politics as a relatively benign competition among sets of interests. Schattschneider countered with the oft-quoted observation, "The flaw in the pluralist heaven is that the heavenly chorus sings with a strong upper-class accent."[1]

In this book, we extend Schattschneider's observation to the new heavenly chorus. Simply put, we argue that is a world of information overload, moneyed interests will be able to construct narratives more clearly and effectively than other groups or organizations. To be sure, political parties, populist voices, and public-interest groups all work to convey their perspectives. All continue to have some real success in shaping the policy agenda. In the end, however, none of these voices can sing with the specificity, direction, and forcefulness of private interests that purchase a clear, coherent, and often-repeated message.

Virtually all scholars and observers agree that there has been an explosion of organized interests in American politics over the past thirty years, an increase fueled in part by the growth of governmental programs and regulations. Corporate and business interests, largely unchallenged in the American politics of the 1950s, have become highly sophisticated in policy matters in response to challenges form government regulators and public-interest groups. Moreover, through the 1980s the techniques of influence changed only modestly. As recently as the mid-1980s, two leading scholars catalogued lobbying methods and concluded that organized interests were simply doing "more of the same" in their attempts to affect government decisions.[2]

Policy making in the 1990s, however, belies this conclusion in a context that increasingly emphasizes the public fashioning of key policy ideas. For example, President Clinton lost control of the health care reform issue to opposing voices, who lobbied as effectively on the airwaves as on Capitol Hill. In Schattschneider's terms, Clinton's many opponents "expanded the scope of the conflict" in order to bring the audience of middle-class health care consumers into the fray and beat back the president's plan.

Historically, interests have expanded the scope of conflict in order to defeat unpopular policies. In the 1980s, for example, bills requiring banks to withhold taxes from customer interest payments and mandating the adoption of catastrophic health care were defeated by mobilizing the public. But these actions occurred only *after* Congress had either shaped (bank withholding) or actually passed (catastrophic health care) specific legislation. And the crucial constituencies—depositors and the elderly—were mobilized directly by the banking industry and a mix of senior lobbies, respectively.

What is new in the 1990s are the various, sophisticated means that some interests, often assisted by communications professionals, have employed in affecting national policy debates, especially as high-stakes issues come to a head. This is not to say that the use of new communications strategies has rendered incorrect or obsolete earlier notions of influence. Rather, traditional textbook notions of inside lobbying are incomplete. Groups simply have more options of influence available to them. Moreover, the actions of large numbers of organized interests have contributed to a growing level of uncertainty over each group's ability to influence important policies, to say nothing of the inherent complexity of issues such as telecommunications or health care. Thus, with high policy stakes and great uncertainty, many organizations have opted for a lobbying mix that relies heavily on paid media, public relations, and targeted communications, as well as more customary techniques, such as one-on-one contacts and testimony at hearings.

It is in the expense of these lobbying techniques that the problems for democracy are most serious. The most powerful advocacy tools, such as large-scale advertising, public relations campaigns, astroturf lobbying, and independent expenditures on behalf of candidates for office, while theoretically available to all interests, are just not affordable to the vast majority of American organizations. Generating a clear message and getting it across requires substantial funds. The paradox of the contemporary period is that

Schattschneider's heavenly chorus sings with more of an upper-class accent than ever before. Large, well-funded interests are crowding out consumer groups, public-interest groups, political parties, and even broad-based social movements. This is a dramatic change from the last three decades of policy making. As we discuss in the remainder of this chapter, it raises a host of issues for our political system.

Money and Messages

The biggest problem of the contemporary system is the dominant role money plays in creating narratives and story lines that are instrumental in policy making. It is not exactly new that big-money interests do well politically. Pundits often have referred to the Golden Rule, which is "he who has the gold makes the rules." As early as the 18th century, George Washington was accused of using rum and whiskey to buy votes at election time. Since that time, money scandals have bedeviled politicians from Warren Harding to Lyndon Johnson.[3]

More recently, the problems of campaign finance during the 1996 elections have been well chronicled. According to testimony before the Senate hearing chaired by Fred Thompson (R-Tenn.), large donors were solicited directly in the White House. The Lincoln bedroom was rented out to large contributors. Money was raised illegally from foreign sources. And congressional campaign spending, from all sources, reached record levels in 1996.

What many people have not realized in the growing concern over money is how closely connected the cash trail has become in governing as well as campaigns. Interest groups use campaign contributions to buttress their lobbying activities. Money given during elections buys access to public officials once they are in office. And the same consultants who work for candidates increasingly create issue ads throughout the electoral cycle.

In each of our cases, from health care and the Contract with America to telecommunications and Medicare, lobbyists constructed narratives through a combination of inside lobbying, large campaign contributions, personal visits, and outside lobbying (such as developing a grassroots campaign or running print or television ads). The most sophisticated groups, such as the Sierra Club, Citizens for a Sound Economy, and the National Federation of Independent Businesses, today routinely combine inside and outside lobbying approaches in order to take full advantage of the respective strengths inherent in each technique.

The dilemma for democracy is that not everyone has equal access to the financial resources necessary for these often elaborate efforts. If there were rough equity among various interests, money would not be so problematic. However, when a few interests have large amounts of money and many have little, democracy is threatened, especially if institutions such as political parties are weak. Our study demonstrates that large, well-organized interests fare disproportionately well in a policy-making process dominated by cash. Those who have the gold are in a much stronger position to make the rules by spinning stories that shape the political dialogue. In fact, their public narratives may foreclose deliberation on substance, as occurred with medical savings accounts.

This creates serious problems in terms of representation. To the extent that elected officials listen more to or are influenced by those who are wealthy and well organized, it skews our representational system in favor of the haves over the have-nots. With the expense of new communications technologies, this gap is growing wider and wider every day.

"Hidden in Plain View": The Rise of Stealth Campaigns

In studying interest-group lobbying, scholars traditionally have distinguished inside from outside strategies. However, our case studies suggest a third route to influence: stealth lobbying campaigns. Given favorable court rulings and the development of new technologies, an increasing amount of lobbying expenditures remain undisclosed, often embedded in corporate budgets or funneled through nonprofit groups that need not list their contributors. Such stealth campaigns are ideal for interests that are unpopular or seen in negative terms such as the tobacco industry (see chapter 3). In addition, with a focus on issues and not specific candidates, such interests can easily move from election campaigns to off-year advocacy. In 1996, for example, Triad Management Services coordinated millions of dollars in issue ads for various conservative Republican candidates; in 1997, Triad spent $500,000 to oppose the use of union dues for political campaigns.[4]

In our case studies, stealth campaigns were used to evade oversight by the press and public. A number of groups active in the 1993–94 health care debate secretly conducted misinformation campaigns designed to frightened people. For example, the American Council for Health Care Reform sent mailings claiming the Clinton plan would imprison people who purchased "extra care." By hiding behind innocuous-sounding organizations, opponents effectively shielded themselves from media scrutiny and made it impossible, at least in the short term, for anyone to figure out who was financing the mailings.

During Medicare and the Contract with America debates, liberals returned the favor by scaring people into believing that Republican reforms would deprive the elderly of much-needed medical assistance—that Medicare would be "cut." The campaign, conducted through mailings, phone calls, and radio ads by a number of different groups, complemented labor's televised advertising and achieved the intended effect. Many seniors came to believe Republicans were not to be trusted and would destroy Medicare if given the opportunity. These fears helped Clinton retain the White House in 1996 and led to some congressional defeats for Republicans that year.

For fear of undermining the First Amendment right to free speech, court rulings in recent years have made it nearly impossible to identify which organizations are sponsoring ads or financing smear campaigns. At the same time, their efforts are highly visible due to their influence and deep pockets. Groups can hide behind alliances such as the conservative Citizens for Reform that reveal nothing about sponsors or expenditures. Or they can label their efforts as public education as opposed to electoral advocacy, in which case there is no required disclosure of how they raised or spent their money.

In a world in which the power of narratives depends almost entirely on the personal credibility of the individual or organization making particular claims, stealth campaigns have become a vital new tactic in contesting public policy. Conceived in secret, such efforts generate little oversight by the press, yet they have the potential to frame issues and alter the terms of the policy discourse, given their targeted audience of elites and key constituents.

The problem of stealth campaigns is that they rob the

public of the information necessary to evaluate group claims. Since source credibility is so crucial to persuasive communications, this type of secrecy protects groups from undesired scrutiny while allowing them to participate in the public dialogue. When citizens do not know who is funding particular communications, they cannot fairly evaluate the narratives and story lines being presented.

The Technology Gap, or Why the Internet Will Not Revive Democracy

Some newly emerging technologies, such as the Internet, seem to offer hope of democratizing our interest-group system. Today, even the smallest group can open a website, set up a toll-free 800 number, or publish newsletters through desktop publishing programs. Much in the same way that transistor radios and Walkmans broadened entertainment options, the Internet has the potential to bring mass communications within the reach of groups with modest, even minimal resources.

There is good reason, though, to be cautious about this movement toward cyberdemocracy. In a study of Internet sites, Richard Davis found a major technology gap among interest groups. Well-to-do groups were able to "advertise more heavily, produce more technically advanced sites, and offer a greater wealth of relevant content" than poorer organizations.[5] If anything, the cost of promoting an Internet site may have widened the resource gap among interest groups in the United States. Moreover, sites focusing on money and politics tend to emphasize campaign funding. Stealth activities on policy matters continue to fly under the radar screen of scrutiny.

Technology is not a panacea for democracy, rather, it

can aggravate inequities that already exist in the system. If this technology gap continues, the on-line heavenly chorus also will sing with a strong upper-class accent. The Internet will not revive democracy as much as it will increase the disparities between rich and poor sets of interests. What is crucial is not getting on-line, but effectively cutting through all the information—or "data smog"—that is out there.[6]

The problem with technology is that it takes money to raise money. Groups that have large staffs, abundant resources, or strong organization are in a much stronger position to use new technologies to promote their objectives. Such groups can conduct polls or commission studies that help them develop narratives that both shape and respond to public wishes. In the end, this allows them to spin stories that politicians can incorporate in their explanations to their constituents. In fact, public relations and advertising professionals often judge the success of high-tech communications efforts by the elite's public use of the terms that have been privately crafted.

How Reporters Are Dropping the Ball on Group Advocacy

In large-scale advocacy campaigns, lobbyists and image merchants constantly seek to spin the press. If groups can get reporters to amplify the message of their television ads, direct mail, and private communications, it dramatically expands the power of the message. On health care, as Jamieson has pointed out, reporters often were not very rigorous in overseeing the claims of self-interest groups.[7] Issue ads were not subjected to as much scrutiny as has become the norm with campaign commercials. Commissioned research studies were not probed as intensely as they should have been. We recognize that the cost of effective coverage here is high, and that is the point. In any number of ways, money interests can and do raise the ante, allowing their narratives to dominate.

This lack of scrutiny increasingly has become the dominant pattern of press coverage in the advocacy area. Trevor Thrall, a communications scholar at the University of Michigan, recently examined news stories in fourteen major newspapers, three televisions networks, and two national news magazines. He found that news coverage concentrated on a small number of groups and that large, well-organized, and well-funded interests received the lion's share of media coverage.[8] Or to put it differently, not only is the interest-group system tilted in an upper-class direction, but so is the media system, regardless of the so-called liberal bent of many reporters.

Undoubtedly, these findings reflect trends we observed in our study. Groups that have the resources to develop clever narratives and compelling story lines ("good copy," in Thrall's terminology) attracted more attention than those that did not. In cases ranging from health care to telecommunications, big corporate interests garnered more press coverage than that accorded to consumer groups and public-interest organizations. This skewed the information even more dramatically in favor of vested interests. In terms of media coverage, the rich got richer.

For this reason, reporters need to exercise greater vigilance in their traditional oversight role. Journalists seem more aware of the danger of being spun by candidates than by interest groups, to say nothing of amorphous entities established largely to put out a story. Such organizations are able to commission polls and research studies and to develop themes that promote group objectives. Reporters should not take group claims uncritically but should subject them to the same scrutiny that they would a politician's rhetoric. While this is costly and time consuming, it is vital to safeguard public discourse.

Not only must journalists oversee and evaluate group activities, they must be careful not to follow a purely incremental model of press coverage. In his study, Thrall found that the biggest predictor of future coverage was past coverage. Groups receiving a lot of attention in the past tended to attract new coverage as well. He concluded, "the media seem to help the big get bigger while making it difficult for new or smaller groups to grow."[9] Reporters must actively resist this tendency. If anything, journalists should practice a kind of affirmative action for small organizations lacking abundant financial resources so that public-policy battles will reflect a wide range of informed opinion.

What's to Be Done?

There are three major options for dealing with the problems of money in politics: doing nothing, broadening disclosure, or increasing regulation. Each approach diagnoses the problem differently and calls for different kinds of remedies. Let us review the logic behind each in turn.

1. *Do Nothing*: One prominent line of thinking—blending the approach of Sen. Mitch McConnell (R-Ky.) with that of the American Civil Liberties Union—assumes that nothing seriously is broken in American politics and that therefore no dramatic fix is needed. Among the advocates for this view are some surprising allies, such as the Republican National Committee and the Sierra Club. Uniting these organizations is the view that the First Amendment right to freedom of speech trumps all attempts at regulation and most ambitious efforts at disclosure.

In the court case *Federal Election Commission v. Christian*

Action Network, Inc., and Martin Mawyer, which dealt with issue-advocacy advertising in the 1992 presidential campaign, the ACLU of Virginia took a near absolutist line on federal regulation of public education campaigns. Even though the Christian Action Network had run a television ad just before the 1992 general election featuring pictures of candidates Clinton and Gore and attacking their stance in favor of homosexual rights, the ACLU urged District Judge James C. Turk in an amicus curiae brief not to interpret the ad as expressly advocating the defeat of Clinton and Gore. Such a decision, the ACLU argued, would infringe on freedom of speech. "One incursion into inferential interpretation of speech content will lead rapidly to another," the ACLU gravely predicted.[10] Taking note of the possible danger, Judge Turk threw the case out before it ever was tried, on grounds that the FEC had exceeded the limit of the First Amendment by attempting to require disclosure of CAN's public education campaign.

What such logic ignores is the danger of one-sided group advocacy in the free exchange of ideas. The Fourteenth Amendment of the U.S. Constitution guarantees equal protection under the law. Indeed, the provision has been used widely to extend equal protection in civil rights, pay equity, and voting rights, among other areas. Despite the centrality of political communications, courts have failed to see any danger to freedom of speech from one-sided advocacy. If one set of interests has the money to broadcast an ad while others do not, it represents a serious challenge to the ensuing discourse. There can be little robust exchange of views if only one side has the resources required for policy advocacy.

2. *Broaden Disclosure*: A second approach defines the situation very differently. Rather than seeing no malady, this perspective diagnoses the money in politics issue as a se-

rious problem with a specific remedy: greater disclosure on the part of interest groups. In a media environment, money is central to the public contesting of political ideas, thus more openness and less secrecy are essential as the first steps in establishing minimally equitable grounds for civic discourse.

The logic behind this idea undergirds current reforms on lobbying and campaign finance. Individuals or groups who give money directly to elected officials or their campaign funds must disclose the nature of the gift, its amount, and when the contribution was made. For decades, this type of disclosure has been the bedrock of anticorruption efforts. Since the turn of the century, when bribes and cash payoffs were routine parts of American politics, reformers have argued that outright gifts need not be outlawed, but they must be disclosed so that people can see for themselves who is lobbying Congress and financing campaign efforts.

Over time, past reforms and old rules have been attacked by legions of lawyers and consultants whose job it is to create loopholes and craft new means of influencing politics outside the disclosure requirements. For example, ads that advocate the election or defeat of federal candidates for office must have a short disclosure message indicating who paid for the ad. That way, viewers have some chance to determine for themselves how to evaluate the information source. Unfortunately, the text or voice-over identifying the sponsor of an ad is seen or heard for just five seconds, which is not long enough for many viewers to identify the ad sponsor. In one study of the 1996 elections, only half of the participants in focus groups were able correctly to identify the sponsors of campaign ads they had just seen. In one spot, that of an independent ad on retirement savings accounts broadcast by the American Council of Life Insurance, only 40 percent correctly identified the sponsor.

Twenty percent erroneously believed it was paid for by the Clinton campaign, 20 percent did not know who broadcast the ad, and 20 percent incorrectly believed it was sponsored by the Cato Institute because that organization had been listed on-screen at the beginning of the spot as the footnote for a claim made during the commercial.[11] Moreover, many advocacy ads list stealth campaign sponsors whose names give viewers or reporters no clue as to their actual stake in the advertisement.

At a minimum, effective disclosure of advertising sponsors stands as a first step in allowing for reasoned public discourse. Rather than having disclosure text be on-screen for only five seconds, the sponsorship should be shown continuously throughout the advertisement. Viewers could better determine which organization is sponsoring the ad, and putting them in a stronger position to evaluate its content.

Recent policy battles have seen the rise of issue-advocacy ads, independent expenditure, and stealth campaigns, all with little required disclosure. Indeed, the last decade has seen an explosion of spending on so-called public education campaigns. These can take the form of communications about a candidate running for office or about a piece of legislation currently before Congress. Under current federal rules, unless campaign ads include words like "vote for (or against) Representative Smith," groups running such ads are not required by the Federal Election Commission to register as a political action committee or to disclose contributions and spending.

The rise of issue advocacy and stealth campaigns takes advantage of loopholes in current disclosure rules, and these should surely be tightened. There should be more timely and complete disclosure of independent expenditures and issue advocacy in election campaigns. For example, ads that show pictures or discuss stances of specific candidates in the sixty days before an election should be treated as campaign ads and be subject to current federal rules on campaign expenditures, including the disclosure of contributors.

Communications that address legislation currently before Congress should comply with federal lobbying rules. This means that the amount and timing of such expenditures need to be reported publicly so that reporters and the public can see who is trying to influence the policy process. Current rules have become very strict for disclosing inside lobbying activities, such as gifts, but completely lax for outside or stealth lobbying. Only when the contributions and spending involved in such efforts are revealed can there be accountability for the new forms of lobbying that have arisen in recent years. Otherwise, as witnessed by *Roll Call* and CNN advertising, interests who can afford it will dominate the framing of many issues.

Disclosure reforms receive strong support from the American public. According to a 1996 national survey, three of four Americans (76 percent) believe interest groups running so-called public education campaigns on the issues should disclose who is paying for the ad. Seventy-four percent also believe these groups should be subject to the same campaign finance rules as candidates.[12]

Broadening disclosure does not imply that such lobbying should be regulated. We do not see disclosure as restricting freedom of expression or threatening the free exchange of political ideas. Rather, effective, timely disclosure helps protect democracy. Once group efforts are made public, voters can judge for themselves whether a particular lobbying activity is problematic.

3. *Increase Regulation*: A third perspective defines the problem of money and politics as fundamental in a de-

mocracy, and it therefore proposes the most fundamental type of response—direct regulation of group advocacy. Although disclosure is seen as laudatory, regulation advocates believe that it simply will not go far enough in protecting public discourse. The threat of misleading advocacy and domination by wealthy interests has grown so serious from this point of view that more rigorous regulations need to be put into effect, ironically to protect freedom of expression.

Regulation is needed to restrict the most insidious types of stealth activities being conducted today, both in campaigns and lobbying. Electronic smear campaigns have become a key by-product of new communications technologies and typically are filled with misleading, erroneous, or outright malicious claims.

Recognizing the danger such expressions have for democratic systems, a number of states have either considered or actually passed "truth in communications" codes. In subscribing to such a code, candidates for office (or lobbying groups and organizations) agree not to distribute fraudulent, forged, or falsely identified writing, to personally approve all literature or advertising for his or her campaign, and to immediately retract or correct any claim discovered to be inaccurate.

A Connecticut bill that would adopt such a code passed in the house. Kentucky also has a bill pending that would ban ads using "false, deceptive, or misleading" statements. New Jersey considered but rejected a truth in campaign act that would have created a commission to investigate complaints that an ad contained "any false statement of material fact." The penalty would have been $5,000 for the first offense and $10,000 for each subsequent offense.

In an effort to deal with independent expenditures, South Dakota considered but did not pass a similar bill requiring individuals who run ads mentioning a candidate at least ten days before an election to provide a copy of that ad to the candidate. Some states have developed rules aimed at media consultants. Michigan, for example, has a bill that passed the State Senate that would fine consultants up to $1,000 for producing ads in violation of disclosure laws.

A few states have passed rules regulating ad content and other types of political communications. Montana has a statute making it unlawful for a person to make a false statement about a candidate's public voting record or to make a false statement that reflects unfavorably on a candidate's character or morality. North Dakota bans statements that are "untrue, deceptive or misleading." Oregon has a statute banning ads with false statements. Unlike other states, this law also has a significant penalty: "if the finder of fact finds by clear and convincing evidence that the false statement of fact reversed the outcome of the election, the defendant shall be deprived of the nomination or election." Washington requires the pictures of candidates used in ads to be no less than five years old. Political ads also must not contain a "false statement of material fact."

More detailed guidelines come from the National Fair Campaign Practices Committee, an industry organization made up of political consultants. According to its Code of Fair Campaign Practices, candidates for public office have an obligation to uphold basic principles of decency, honesty, and fair play. This includes condemnation of personal vilification and avoidance of character defamation, whisper campaigns, libel, slander, or scurrilous attacks. The code condemns the use of political material that misrepresents, distorts, or otherwise falsifies the facts regarding any candidate as well as malicious or unfounded accusations aimed at creating doubts as to loyalty and patriotism. Appeals to prejudice based on race, creed, sex, or national origin are to be avoided. Candidates are asked to repudiate any individuals or groups that resort to improper methods or tactics. Anyone who feels rules have been violated can file a complaint with the committee, which gets publicized in the industry. Nine states (California, Hawaii, Illinois, Kansas, Maine, Montana, Nevada, Washington, and West Virginia) have statutes modeled after the National Fair Campaign Practices Committee code. Still, these statutes go widely unenforced, in large part because almost all claims remain open to interpretation.

In recent years, Wisconsin has enforced the most sweeping regulation of political communications. According to a previous state law, any group or persons engaged in activities having "the purpose of influencing the election" must register with the state Elections Board and disclose their donors. Ads or other types of communications may not be paid for with corporate or union money. During the 1996 election, state courts ordered off the air several ads critical of state legislators on grounds that the groups involved, such as Americans for Limited Terms, the Sierra Club, and Wisconsin Manufacturers & Commerce, had not disclosed their contributors. The groups have sued and the case is pending in federal court.[13]

At the national level, Congressman Ernest Istook, Jr. (R-Ok.) sought to deal with issue lobbying from tax-exempt nonprofit groups by proposing legislation that would oversee such activities. Groups that are federally funded would be required to disclose their lobbying activities to the federal agency that awarded the grant. This legislative proposal unleashed a tidal wave of bitter criticism from the affected groups. Groups from the National Right to Life Committee to Planned Parenthood protested what they saw as an effort to "gag" their freedom of expression. Although initially favored by some Republican leaders, the sharp outcry over this legislation effectively prevented passage of the bill.

While Congress has debated what to do in this area, still another federal agency quietly but persistently has stepped up its regulatory oversight of group advocacy. The Internal Revenue Service has begun to examine the lobbying and political activities of nonprofit groups with tax-exempt status with an eye toward revoking the tax exemption of groups engaged in blatant political activities. According to federal law, nonprofit or 501(c)3 organizations must not engage in *any* electioneering activities and must avoid any substantial amount of political lobbying. The IRS goal is not to limit freedom of expression, but to make sure group expressions are not subsidized by federal taxpayers under the guise of public charities.

In a prominent audit of an abortion rights organization, the IRS reviewed the group's fund-raising letters in order to determine if it had crossed the line separating charitable and political activities. Finding that the group's letters showed a "clear implication" and a "clear preference" for particular candidates, the IRS moved to revoke its tax-exempt status. When those line are crossed, the IRS pronounced, "voter education becomes voter direction."[14]

The IRS also denied tax-exempt status, later upheld in federal court, for a group called the Fund for the Study of Economic Growth and Tax Reform headed by former vice presidential candidate Jack Kemp. The group raised money for an "all-Republican" commission appointed by GOP congressional leaders. Because of the fund's close ties to Republican legislators, the IRS ruled the organization had crossed the line into lobbying and therefore did not deserve tax-exempt status. In the subsequent court test, a U.S. District judge found "that the Fund clearly supported a one-sided political agenda and did not operate exclusively for non-exempt purposes."[15]

These decisions are of obvious interest to a wide range of tax-exempt organizations because of the unmistakable signal that the IRS is cracking down on blatantly political groups. Overall, right now the IRS has about thirty charities under review for excessive political activities. In addition, there have been other cases, such as one involving the application of the Christian Coalition to become tax-exempt, which the IRS has not approved because of concerns over the group's electioneering activities.

Running through each of these regulatory threads is the assumption that the problem of money in politics has become so serious that we must go beyond simple disclosure to direct regulation of political advocacy. In the same way that the Food and Drug Administration regulates claims for food and medicine so as to protect the public, some feel it is time to safeguard political discourse from the most insidious elements that have arisen with new lobbying strategies. Only in that way can the public dialogue so essential to democracy be protected.

The Reform Dilemma: Squeezing the Money Balloon

At one level, the money problem in politics is almost inherently unresolvable. If you squeeze the money balloon in one place, the cash merely rushes to a new part of the balloon. Or, if you squeeze it hard enough, the balloon suddenly bursts open, which throws cash everywhere with few outside controls. This basically is the system the United States had before the Watergate scandal of the 1970s.

Past efforts at controlling the power of money always

had unanticipated consequences. Reforms always generate unforeseen responses because of the creativity of interested individuals and the inherent ambiguity of laws. It always is hard to anticipate how people will react in the future to a new set of rules.

Squeezing the money balloon is complicated because there are competing reform principles such as equity, freedom, and representativeness that conflict with one another. It is possible to pass laws that encourage free political expression, such as raising contributor limits in campaigns, that may aggravate the resource inequity of American politics. It is also possible to create new accountability measures that attempt to regulate the truthfulness of group advocacy that dampen freedom of expression. These fundamental contradictions mean in practice that one cannot solve every aspect of the money in politics problem through legislative means.

But this does not mean that reform is impossible. There are a number of formal and informal changes that would improve public discourse. For example, journalists must come to terms with their responsibilities for monitoring the voices of the new heavenly chorus. Groups could and should receive the same scrutiny reserved for candidates. Stealth campaigns must be vigorously investigated to see who funds campaigns that are simultaneously hidden and public. Alone among major players in the political system, reporters have the credibility to demand answers to tough questions about group advocacy.

In the absence of other safeguards, the press must work to encourage coherent discourse and accountability in group conflict. The most egregious lies and misstatements in group advocacy must be exposed, publicized, or, at a minimum, simply ignored. Journalists need to cover public lobbying, without amplifying questionable claims by self-interested parties. Simply being aware of the pitfalls in press coverage, such as ignoring small organizations or paying disproportionate attention to large ones, would go a long way toward improving the public dialogue.

Interest groups themselves must understand the need for some self-regulation and self-restraint. Democracy has survived in the United States for more than two centuries because of voluntary limits on group conduct and a general agreement to play by widely shared rules of the game. Strangely enough, increased amounts of group activity may not improve the quality of debate but rather demean it, as interests have great incentives to construct self-interested and parochial stories.

At a minimum, groups must stand for truthfulness in public claims and tolerance for opposing viewpoints, and they must eschew illegal or unethical tactics. Unfettered group competition damages the system in the same way overgrazing ruins the village commons. As they put forth their arguments, groups must recognize their own role in protecting the overall system in which they operate.

Even with improved press oversight and self-restraint on the part of groups, some legal changes are required to safeguard the contemporary system. Stronger disclosure laws are necessary to insure a rough fairness of contemporary discourse. In the absence of information on who sponsors expensive ads or mails slick brochures, neither elites, reporters, nor the public know who is behind particular claims or how such communications should be evaluated. Truth and accuracy provisions in mass communications need to be strengthened in order to make sure that discourse is conducted in an honest manner. Narratives, of course, will still matter, but baselines of accuracy and disclosure must exist. Not all claims are equally valid, and some legal remedies may deter those who violate well-defined standards of honesty. Only by staying attentive to Schattschneider's warning about the upper-class bias of the heavenly chorus, both in traditional American politics and in its new, high-tech manifestations, can we protect the gritty, day-to-day give and take that constitutes American democracy.

Notes

Chapter One

1. Quoted in Michael Lewis, "Bill Clinton's Garbage Man," *New York Times Sunday Magazine*, September 21, 1997, p. 58.

2. See Darrell M. West, *Air Wars: Television Advertising in Election Campaigns, 1952–1996*, 2nd ed. (Washington, D.C.: CQ Press, 1997).

3. Susan Libeler, "The Politics of NAFTA," in Alan Rugman, ed., *Foreign Investment and NAFTA* (Columbia: University of South Carolina Press, 1994), p. 26.

4. Ibid., p. 42.

5. Ambler Moss, Jr., ed., *Assessments of the North American Free Trade Agreement* (New Brunswick: Transaction Publishers, 1993), p. iii.

6. Jill Abramson and Leslie Wayne, "Nonprofit Groups Were Partners to Both Parties in Last Election," *New York Times*, October 24,

1997, p. A1; and Leslie Wayne, "Papers Detail G.O.P. Ties to Tax Group," *New York Times*, November 10, 1997, p. A27.

7. See "The Big Picture: Money Follows Power Shift on Capitol Hill," (Washington, D.C.: Center for Responsive Politics, 1997). Also see Jill Abramson, " '96 Campaign Costs Set Record at $2.2 Billion," *New York Times*, November 25, 1997, p. A18.

8. E. E. Schattschneider, *The Semi-Sovereign People* (New York: Holt, Rinehart, and Winston, 1960).

9. Alexis Simendiger, "A Slow Trip on Fast-Track," *National Journal*, September 27, 1997, p. 1897.

10. Jill Abramson with Steven Greenhouse, "Labor Victory on Trade Bill Reveals Power," *New York Times*, November 12, 1997, p. A1.

11. Katharine Seelye, "President Spends a Weekend with Big Donors," *New York Times*, November 2, 1997, p. 26.

12. See, for example, Allan J. Cigler and Burdett Loomis, "More than 'More of the Same,' " in Allan J. Cigler and Burdett Loomis, eds., *Interest Group Politics*, 4th ed. (Washington, D.C.: CQ Press, 1995).

Chapter Two

1. William Greider, *Who Will Tell the People?* (New York: Touchstone, 1993), p. 335.

2. *Ibid.*, p. 335, emphasis added.

3. *Ibid.*, p. 338ff.

4. William S. Safire, *Safire's Political Dictionary* (New York: Random House, 1978), p. 787.

5. Ron Faucheux, "The Grassroots Explosion," *Campaigns and Elections*, December/January 1995; Greider, *Who Will Tell the People?* p. 339.

6. Figures from http://www.campaign-reform-org.

7. Among others, see David Shenk, *Data Smog* (New York: HarperSanFrancisco, 1997).

8. E. E. Schattschneider, *The Semi-Sovereign People* (New York: Holt, Rinehart, and Winston, 1960), p. 68, italics in the original.

9. *Ibid.*, p. 35.

10. Paul E. Peterson, "The Rise and Fall of Special Interest Politics," in Mark P. Petracca, ed., *The Politics of Interests* (Boulder: Westview, 1992), p. 340.

11. Jonathan Rauch, *Demosclerosis* (New York: Times Books, 1994), p. 39.

12. Frank Baumgartner and Bryan Jones summarize various studies in their book, *Agendas and Instability in American Politics* (Chicago: University of Chicago Press, 1993), p. 177.

13. Kay Lehman Scholzman and John T. Tierney, *Organized Interests and American Democracy* (New York: Harper and Row, 1986), p. 155.

14. Mark Petracca, "The Rediscovery of Interest Group Politics," in Petracca, ed., *The Politics of Interests* (Boulder: Westview, 1992), pp. 22, 25.

15. Hedrick Smith, *The Power Game* (New York: Random House, 1988).

16. Peter H. Stone, "Follow the Leaders," *National Journal*, June 24, 1995, p. 1642.

17. Paul Herrnson and Clyde Wilcox, eds., *Risky Business: PAC Decisionmaking in Congressional Elections* (Armonk, N.Y.: M. E. Sharpe, 1994), p. 258.

18. Jeffrey Berry, *The Interest Group Society*, 3rd ed. (Boston: Little, Brown, 1997); David Vogel, *Fluctuating Fortunes* (New York; Basic Books, 1989), p. 293ff.

19. Robert H. Salisbury, *Interests and Institutions* (Pittsburgh: University of Pittsburgh Press, 1992).

20. Frank Baumgartner and Bryan Jones, *Agendas and Instability in American Politics*, pp. 6–7; Andrew McFarland, *Cooperative Pluralism* (Lawrence: University Press of Kansas, 1993), p. 70ff.

21. Frank Baumgartner and Bryan Jones, *Agendas and Instability in American Politics*, pp. 100–1.

22. James Thurber, *Divided Democracy* (Washington, D.C.: CQ Press, 1991), pp. 340–1.

23. Lee Fritschuler, *Smoking and Politics*, 4th ed. (Englewood Cliffs, N.J.: Prentice-Hall, 1989).

24. Frank Baumgartner and Bryan Jones, *Agendas and Instability in American Politics*, p. 236.

25. *Ibid.*, p. 191.

26. David Rochefort and Roger Cobb, ed., *The Politics of Problem Definition* (Lawrence: University Press of Kansas, 1994), p. 5.

27. Chris Bosso, "The Contextual Bases of Problem Definition," in Rochefort and Cobb, *The Politics of Problem Definition*, 182–203.

28. Paul Light, *The President's Agenda* (Baltimore: Johns Hopkins University Press, 1985).

29. Frank Baumgartner and Bryan Jones, *Agendas and Instability in American Politics*, p. 25 ff.

30. Chris Bosso, *Pesticides and Politics* (Pittsburgh: University of Pittsburgh Press, 1987).

31. David Vogel, *Fluctuating Fortunes*, 295–97.

32. Jeffrey Berry, *The Power of Citizen Groups* (Washington, D.C.: Brookings, forthcoming).

33. Gary Mucciaroni, *Reversals of Fortune* (Washington, D.C.: Brookings, 1995), pp. 180ff.

34. Ralph Nader, "Minimal Media Coverage of Auto Safety Initiative," *Liberal Opinion*, March 27, 1995, p. 26.

35. James Thurber, *Divided Democracy*, 1991; William E. Browne, "Organized Interests and Their Issue Niches," *Journal of Politics* 52 (May), 1990, pp. 477–509.

36. William E. Browne, *Cultivating Congress* (Lawrence: University Press of Kansas, 1995); John Wright, *Interest Groups and Congress* (Boston: Allyn and Bacon, 1996); David Whiteman, *Communication in Congress* (Lawrence: University Press of Kansas, 1996).

37. James Thurber, *Divided Democracy*, p. 336.

38. David Rosenbaum, "A Financial Disaster with Many Culprits," *New York Times*, June 5, 1990, p. C1.

39. The lasting symbolic stain of the savings and loan debacle can be seen in the continuing problems faced by Sen. John McCain (R-Ariz.), one of the Senate's "Keating Five," who accepted campaign funds from Charles Keating, a major S&L player, and attended meetings to press his interests. Despite his status as a former Vietnam prisoner of war and no record of seeking special favors for Keating, McCain remains under the "Keating Five" cloud, which might well affect his credibility as a presidential candidate. It might also help explain McCain's fervor in pushing campaign finance reform.

40. Theda Skocpol, *Boomerang* (New York; Norton, 1996); Burdett Loomis, *The Contemporary Congress* (New York: St. Martin's Press, 1996).

41. Robert H. Frank and Philip J. Cook, *The Winner-Take-All Society* (New York; Basic Books, 1995).

42. David Vogel, *Fluctuating Fortunes*.

43. Jeffrey Birnbaum, *The Lobbyists* (New York; Times Books, 1993), p. 4, emphasis added.

44. Quoted in Jonathan Rauch, "The Parasite Economy," *National Journal* April 25, 1992, p. 981.

45. Personal interview; source guaranteed anonymity.

46. Thomas Ferguson, *Golden Rule: The Investment Theory of Party Competition and the Logic of Money-Driven Political Systems* (Chicago: University of Chicago Press, 1995), p. 29.

47. *Ibid.*, p. 30; Burdett Loomis and Eric Sexton, "Choosing to Advertise: How Interests Decide," in Allan J. Cigler and Burdett A. Loomis, eds., *Interest Group Politics*, 4th ed. (Washington, D.C.: CQ Press, 1995), 193–214.

48. Kay Lehman Schlozman and John T. Tierney, *Organized Interests and American Democracy* (New York: Harper and Row, 1986).

49. John Wright, *Interest Groups and Congress* (Boston: Allyn and Bacon, 1996).

50. See Oscar H. Gandy, *Beyond Agenda Setting: Information Subsidies and Public Policy* (Norwood, N.J.: Ablex Publishing, 1982); also, Andrew Rich and Kent Weaver, "Advocates and Analysts: Think Tanks and the Politicization of Expertise in Washington," in Allan J. Cigler and Burdett A. Loomis, eds., *Interest Group Politics*, 5th ed. (Washington, D.C.: CQ Press, 1999).

51. Richard L. Hall and Frank Wayman, "Buying Time: Moneyed Interests and the Mobilization of Bias in Congressional Committees," *American Political Science Review* 84 (1990), pp. 797–820.

52. Jeffrey Berry, 1984, *The Interest Group Society* (Boston: Little Brown, 1984), p. 118.

53. Wright, *Interest Groups and Congress*, p. 88; Whiteman, *Communication in Congress*, p. 40.

54. Whiteman, *Communication in Congress*, p. 47.

55. Lester Milbrath, *The Washington Lobbyists* (Chicago: Rand McNally, 1963); Raymond Bauer, Ithiel de Sola Pool, and Lewis Dexter, *American Business and Public Policy* (New York: Atherton Press, 1963).

56. William Muir, *Legislature* (Chicago: University of Chicago Press, 1982), p. 23.

57. Alan Rosenthal, *The Third House* (Washington, D.C.: CQ Press, 1993), p. 114.

58. Wright, *Interest Groups and Congress*.

59. Schattschneider, *The Semi-Sovereign People*, pp. 2–3, his italics.

60. Gary McKissick, "Issues, Interests, and Emphases: Lobbying Congress and the Strategic Manipulation of Issues," paper presented at the 1995 Political Science Association meeting, Chicago. For an appli-

cation of the narrative idea to group conflict over Western public lands, see John Tierney, "Clashing Interests, Values, and Narratives in the Politics of Western Public Lands Policy," paper presented at the annual meeting of the American Political Science Association, Washington, D.C., August 28–31, 1997.

61. Bill Buford, *New Yorker*, June 24/July 1, 1996, p. 11.

62. Kenneth Kollman, *Outside Lobbying* (Ann Arbor: University of Michigan Press, 1998); Hedrick Smith, *The Power Game* (New York: Random House, 1988); and Frank Baumgartner and Beth Leech, *Basic Interests* (Princeton: Princeton University Press, 1998).

63. Jeffrey Birnbaum, *The Lobbyists*, pp. 5–6, emphasis added.

64. *Ibid.*, p. 4.

65. Richard Fenno, *Home Style* (Boston: Little, Brown, 1978), p. 144.

66. Grant Reeher, *Narratives of Justice* (Ann Arbor: University of Michigan Press, 1996), p. 31.

67. *Ibid.*, p. 31.

68. Jay Clayton, *The Pleasures of Babel* (New York: Oxford University Press, 1993).

69. Marion Just, Ann Crigler, Dean Alger, Timothy Cook, Montague Kern, and Darrell M. West, *Crosstalk* (Chicago: University of Chicago Press, 1996).

70. Deborah Stone, "Causal Stories and the Formation of Policy Agendas," *Political Science Quarterly* 104 (1989), pp. 281–301.

71. Clayton, *The Pleasures of Babel*, p. 27.

72. See Emery Roe, *Narrative Policy Analysis* (Durham, N.C.: Duke University Press, 1994).

73. Deborah Stone, "Causal Stories and the Formation of Policy Agendas," p. 283.

74. Legislators and other policy makers should not be considered easy targets for even the most attractive narratives. They spend their days reacting to individualized stories and generally resist the temptation to "govern by anecdote," as one Republican lawmaker put it.

75. George Lakoff, "The Contemporary Theory of Metaphor," in *Metaphor and Thought*, Andrew Ortony, ed. (New York: Cambridge University Press, 1993), 202–51; Murray Edelman, *The Symbolic Uses of Politics* (Urbana University of Illinois Press, 1964) and *Constructing the Political Spectacle* (Chicago: University of Chicago Press, 1988).

76. Edelman, *Constructing the Political Spectacle*, p. 33.

77. John Kingdon, *Agendas, Alternatives, and Public Policy*, 2nd ed. (New York: HarperCollins, 1995).

78. Stone, "Casual Stories and the Formation of Policy Agendas," p. 283.

79. John Nelson, "Political Myth-Making in Post-Modern Times," University of Iowa unpublished paper, no date.

80. In an academic paper, John Nelson plays off of a Katha Pollitt poem as he implores members of his own scholarly audience to reconfigure the metaphors that shape their cognition of politics. He cites the lines, "What if the moon / was never a beautiful woman? / Call it a shark shearing across black water. / An ear. A drum in the desert. / A window / A bone shoe . . ." to prompt people to use Pollitt's form to rethink the metaphor of politics and governance. For his own offering, Nelson composed: "What if the government / was never a machine or a man? / Call it a seduction among strangers / An eye. A drum in a forest. / A movie. A blue sky." See John Nelson, "What If the Government Was Never a Machine or a Man? Myth as Cognition and Communication in Politics," University of Iowa unpublished paper, no date.

81. Murray Edelman, *Political Language* (New York: Academic Press, 1977).

82. See Dan Morgan, *Merchants of Grain* (New York: Viking Press, 1979).

83. Kingdon, *Agendas, Alternatives, and Public Policy*, 2nd ed.

84. See Rochefort and Cobb, eds., *The Politics of Problem Definition.*

85. Ken Shepsle, "The Changing Textbook Congress," in John E. Chubb and Paul E. Peterson, eds., *Can the Government Govern?* (Washington, D.C.: Brookings, 1989), pp. 238–66; and Richard Fenno, *The Power of the Purse* (Boston: Little, Brown, 1966).

Chapter Three

1. Darrell M. West was an expert witness in this case on the side of the Federal Election Commission.

2. See Richard Fenno, *Home Style* (Boston: Little, Brown, 1978).

3. Ronald Hrebenar and Ruth Scott, *Interest Group Politics in America* (Englewood Cliffs, N.J.: Prentice Hall, 1982), p. 63.

4. Hrebenar and Scott, *Interest Group Politics in America*, p. 69.

5. Lee Fritschler, *Smoking and Politics*, 4th ed. (Englewood Cliffs, N.J.: Prentice Hall, 1989).

6. Jill Abramson with Barry Meier, "Tobacco Braced for Costly Fight," *New York Times*, December 15, 1997, p. A1. Microsoft is another

example of a company that after years of little spending on lobbying has started to spend more money to enhance its corporate image. See Catherine Yang, "Microsoft Goes Low-Tech in Washington," *Business Week*, December 22, 1997, pp. 34–35.

7. Quoted by Jessica Lee in "Tobacco Wrote Its Own Deal in Budget Law," *USA Today*, August 29–September 1, 1997. Also see Paul Raeburn, "Smoke and Mirrors?" *Business Week*, August 25, 1997, pp. 36–37.

8. Cited in Tom Konda, "Ads on Issues Go Back Decades," *New York Times* letter to the editor, November 1, 1993, p. A22. Also see Thomas Konda, "Political Advertising and Public Relations by Business in the United States," Ph.D. diss., University of Kentucky, 1983.

9. Herbert Schmertz, *Good-Bye to the Low Profile* (Boston: Little, Brown, 1986).

10. Thomas Patterson, *Out of Order* (New York: Vintage Books, 1994) and James Fallows, *Breaking the News* (New York: Vintage Books, 1996).

11. See, for example, William P. Browne, "All-Direction Lobbying," in Allan J. Cigler and Burdett A. Loomis, eds. *Interest Group Politics* 5th ed. (Washington, D.C.: CQ Press, 1999).

12. Darrell M. West, "Activists and Economic Policymaking in Congress," *American Journal of Political Science* 32:3 (August 1988), pp. 662–80.

13. S. Prakash Sethi, *Advocacy Advertising and Large Corporations* (Lexington, Mass.: Lexington Books, 1997).

14. Figures qutoed during an interview with advertising managers at *Congressional Quarterly* and *National Journal*, August 4, 1997.

15. Quoted in Eric Sexton and Burdett A. Loomis, "Marketing as Advocacy: Advertising by Elites for Elites," paper prepared for presentation at the Midwest Political Science Assocation, Chicago, Illinois, April 14–16, 1994, p. 9.

16. John Kingdon, *Agendas, Alternatives, and Public Policies* (Boston: Little Brown, 1984).

17. For additional details, see Sexton and Loomis, "Marketing as Advocacy: Advertising by Elites for Elites," pp. 7–8.

18. Valerie Heitschusen, "Strategic Lobbying by Interest Groups: The Role of Information and Institutional Change," paper presented at the Midwest Political Science Association, April 15–17, 1993.

19. Hrebenar and Scott, *Interest Group Politics in America*, p. 83.

20. Allan J. Cigler and Burdett A. Loomis, "Contemporary Interest

Group Politics: More than 'More of the Same,' " in Allan J. Cigler and Burdett A. Loomis, eds., *Interest Group Politics*, 4th ed. (Washington, D.C.: CQ Press, 1995), p. 395.

21. Hedrick Smith, *The Power Game* (New York: Random House, 1988), p. 240.

22. Quoted in David Hosansky, "Hill Feels the Big Clout of Small Business," *Congressional Quarterly Weekly Report*, January 10, 1998, p. 59.

23. Amy Fried, *Muffled Echoes: Oliver North and the Politics of Public Opinion* (New York: Columbia University Press, 1997), pp. 206–7.

24. Cigler and Loomis, "Contemporary Interest Group Politics: More than 'More of the Same,' " p. 396.

25. Fried, *Muffled Echoes: Oliver North and the Politics of Public Opinion.*

26. Cigler and Loomis, "Contemporary Interest Group Politics: More than 'More of the Same,' " pp. 396–97.

27. Elizabeth Drew, *What It Takes* (New York; Viking, 1997), p. 78.

28. Quoted in Drew, *What It Takes*, p. 78.

29. See Federal Election Commission press release, "PAC Activity Increases in 1995–96 Election Cycle," April 22, 1997.

30. Deborah Beck, Paul Taylor, Jeffrey Stanger, and Douglas Rivlin, "Issue Advocacy During the 1996 Campaign," Report by the Annenberg Public Policy Center of the University of Pennsylvania, September 16, 1997.

31. For this and following material, see Herbert Alexander, *Financing Politics*, 4th ed. (Washington, D.C.: CQ Press, 1992).

32. Darrell M. West, *Air Wars: Television Advertising in Election Campaigns, 1952–1996*, 2nd ed. (Washington, D.C.: CQ Press, 1997).

33. Sheila Kaplan, "Tobacco Dole," *Mother Jones Magazine*, August 4, 1997; World Wide Web site, http://www.ctyme.com/dole/tobacco.htm.

34. Larry Sabato and Glenn Simpson, *Dirty Little Secrets* (New York: Times Books, 1996).

35. Eliza Newlin Carney, "Stealth Bombers," *National Journal*, August 16, 1997, pp. 1640–43.

Chapter Four

1. See Theda Skocpol, *Boomerang: Clinton's Health Security Effort and the Turn Against Government in U.S. Politics* (New York: Norton, 1996); Haynes Johnson and David Broder, *The System* (Boston: Little, Brown,

1996); Bob Blendon, "The Gridlock Is Us," *New York Times*, May 22, 1994, p. 15; and Mollyann Brodie and Robert Blendon, "The Public's Contribution to Congressional Gridlock on Health Care Reform." *Journal of Health Politics, Policy and Law* (Summer 1995), pp. 403–10.

2. David Broder, "As Predicted, This Is One Heckuva Battle," *Providence Journal*, July 26, 1994, p. A9.

3. Michael Hayes, *Lobbyists and Legislators* (New Brunswick, N.J.: Rutgers University Press, 1981) and Theodore Lowi, *The End of Liberalism* (New York: W. W. Norton, 1969).

4. Mark Peterson, *Legislating Together* (Cambridge, Mass.: Harvard University Press, 1990).

5. Interview with William Gradison, March 13, 1995.

6. Interview with top White House official who requested anonymity, spring 1995.

7. Monica Borkowski, "How the House and Senate Bills Stack Up Against the President's Original Proposal," *New York Times*, August 3, 1994, p. A18.

8. Bob Woodward, *The Agenda* (New York: Simon and Schuster, 1994).

9. Thomas Rosenstiel, "Press Found Putting Stress on Politics of Health Reform," *Los Angeles Times*, March 26, 1994, p. A24.

10. Darrell M. West, "Public Gives News Media Mixed Evaluations," Brown University press release, November 1993.

11. Michael Kagay, "Top Woe: Health or Crime," *New York Times*, August 7, 1994, p. 24.

12. Thomas Rosenstiel, "Press Found Putting Stress on Politics of Health Reform," *Los Angeles Times*, March 26, 1994, p. A24.

13. *Well-Heeled: Inside Lobbying for Health Care Reform* (Washington, D.C.: Center for Public Integrity, 1994), p. 83.

14. It is difficult to get precise spending figures because of the unwillingness of groups to disclose their exact spending and the fact that various organizations count different types of production expenditures in their ad totals. Figures released to news reporters are not entirely reliable because several groups announced intentions for million-dollar ad campaigns only to fail in their fund-raising efforts. News reports also varied substantially even for major groups.

15. Interview with Ben Goddard, March 20, 1995.

16. This ratio was determined by adding the expenditures of groups opposed to the president's program (approximately $41.5 million) versus

those in favor ($18.8 million). Opponents included the Pharmaceutical Research and Manufacturers Association, Health Insurance Association of America, American Medical Association, American Dental Association, Christian Coalition, Republican National Committee, and Single Payer Across the Nation. Proponents included the Kaiser Foundation/ League of Women Voters, Health Care Reform Project, AFL-CIO, American Conference for Health Care Workers, AARP, Democratic National Committee, and Group Health Association. There were a number of other organizations who spent less than one million each on health care advertisements. In addition, there was variation in how aggressively various groups opposed the Clinton program. The Health Insurance Association, for example, ran ads criticizing specifics in the Clinton program, while pharmaceutical interests used ads emphasizing their concern that support for basic research to improve drug treatment and medical care would erode under the Clinton reform.

17. Interview with Christine Heenan, February 9, 1995.

18. Interview with William Gradison, March 13, 1995.

19. Interview with Ben Goddard, March 20, 1995.

20. Interview with Mark Isakowitz, March 20, 1995.

21. Interview with top White House official who requested anonymity, Spring 1995.

22. Interview with top White House official who requested anonymity, Spring 1995.

23. Philiip Hilts, "Coalition Opposing Health Plan Is Called Front Group for Insurers," *New York Times*, October 20, 1993; Michael Weisskopf, "Grass-Roots Health Lobby Financed by Insurers," *Washington Post*, October 20, 1993, p. A1.

24. Quoted in *Well-Heeled: Inside Lobbying for Health Care Reform*, p. 49. Also see Woodward, *The Agenda*.

25. Interview with Ira Magaziner, March 9, 1995.

26. Howard Kurtz, "For Health Care Lobbies, a Major Ad Operation," *Washington Post*, April 13, 1994, p. A1.

27. Interview with Christian Heenan, February 9, 1995.

28. Quoted in *Well-Heeled: Inside Lobbying for Health Care Reform*, p. 48.

29. Interview with William Gradison, March 13, 1995.

30. Interview with Ben Goddard, March 20, 1995.

31. *Ibid.*

32. Elizabeth Kolbert, "New Arena for Campaign Ads: Health Care," *New York Times*, October 21, 1993, p. A1.

33. Interview with Ben Goddard, March 20, 1995.

34. Lorenzo Benet and Lyndon Stambler, "Spin Doctors," *People*, April 11, 1994, pp. 105–7; Margaret Carlson, "Harry and Louise," *Time*, March 7, 1994, p. 41.

35. Kathleen Hall Jamieson, "The Role of Advertising in the Health Care Reform Debate: Part One," University of Pennsylvania press release, July 18, 1994, p. 18.

36. Kolbert, "New Arena for Campaign Ads: Health Care," p. A1.

37. Interview with Ben Goddard, March 20, 1995.

38. Quoted in Adam Clymer, "Hillary Clinton Accuses Insurers of Lying About Health Proposal," *New York Times*, November 2, 1993, p. A1.

39. *Ibid.*

40. Dana Priest, "First Lady Lambasts Health Insurers," *Washington Post*, November 2, 1993, p. A1.

41. Quoted in Douglas Jehl, "Clinton Joins Counterattack on Health Insurers' TV Ads," *New York Times*, November 4, 1993, p. B20.

42. Michael Weisskopf, "Health Reform Advocates Add Visibility to Insurance Industry Group's Message," *Washington Post*, November 4, 1993, p. A8.

43. Interview with Ben Goddard, March 20, 1995.

44. Darrell M. West, *Air Wars: Television Advertising in Election Campaigns, 1952–1992* (Washington, D.C.: Congressional Quarterly Press, 1993).

45. David Broder, "Junk Journalism," *Washington Post*, February 23, 1994, p. A17.

46. Kathleen Hall Jamieson, "The Role of Advertising in the Heatlh Care Reform Debate: Part Two," University of Pennsylvania press release, July 25, 1994.

47. Mollyann Brodie and Robert Blendon, "The Public's Contribution to Congressional Gridlock on Health Care Reform," *Journal of Health Politics, Policy and Law* (Summer 1995), pp. 403–10; and Lawrence Jacobs and Robert Shapiro, "Don't Blame the Public for Failed Health Care Reform," *Journal of Health Politics, Policy and Law* (Summer, 1995), pp. 411–23.

48. *Well-Heeled: Inside Lobbying for Health Care Reform*, p. 28.

49. Dana Priest, "Health Groups Launch Ad Blitzes Criticizing Increased Federal Role," *Washington Post*, January 25, 1994, p. A8; and

David Broder and Richard Morin, "Clinton's Health Plan: A Turn for the Worse," *Washington Post*, National Weekly Ediiton, March 7–13, 1994, p. 15.

50. Interview with top White House official who requested anonymity, Spring 1995.

51. Interview with Ben Goddard, March 20, 1995.

52. One limitation of these surveys is that the health care ad exposure questions measured ad viewership as yes or no, not the frequency of exposure such as the number of days in the last week health care ads were seen. This makes it impossible to test hypotheses concerning the link between frequency of ad exposure and views about health care reform.

53. After reviewing an earlier draft of this research, Health Insurance Association of America executive vice president Charles N. Kahn III wrote to us that these publicly available data "make it difficult, if not impossible, to evaluate the Harry and Louise series" because the *New York Times* survey "attempted to capture recall at a time when the ads weren't even on the air." Personal communication to the author, September 13, 1994. He pointed out that ad "recall diminishes quickly after ads are taken down." The HIAA conducted over 25 focus groups and 11 national public opinion studies of health care reform, but they were unwilling to make their data available to us.

54. Quoted in *Well-Heeled: Inside Lobbying for Health Care Reform*, p. 18.

55. For example, it was no accident that Bush's effective advertising campaign in 1988 came on the heels of Michael Dukakis's capture of the Democratic nomination. The Massachusetts governor was the least well known major party nominee in recent years, and the absence of information about him gave Bush the opportunity to shape public opinion through the media. See West, *Air Wars: Television Advertising in Election Campaigns, 1952–1992*, p. 86.

56. Since it is likely that other factors beyond media exposure influence views about health care, we included controls for several other factors in each equation. For example, partisanship and ideology are important to how people respond to policy controversies, so they were included as control variables in the analysis of the *Washington Post*/ABC News and *New York Times*/CBS News polls. Ideology was not asked in the Harvard study. In addition, people have different views about health care and different exposures to ads and news based on their educational attainment, race, age, and sex. As an illustration, well-educated people

are more likely than others to recall seeing ads. Therefore, it is crucial to include these items as control factors in the regression analyses.

57. West, *Air Wars: Television Advertising in Election Campaigns, 1952–1992*, p. 26.

58. Broder and Morin, "Clinton's Health Plan: A Turn for the Worse," p. 15.

59. Questions about news exposure were not asked in the *Washington Post*/ABC News or *New York Times*/CBS News polls, so it is impossible to test whether news or the ads influenced people's impressions.

60. West, *Air Wars: Television Advertising in Election Campaigns, 1952–1992*, pp. 98, 111. However, one must be cautious in comparing these items, because an open-ended question obviously is much tougher than a close-ended one. With the former, you have to recall a specific ad from memory without having a question to prompt your answer. That fact notwithstanding, there is little doubt that the Harry and Louise ads achieved a high degree of visibility for a policy advocacy campaign.

61. Kathleen Hal Jamieson, "The Role of Advertising in the Health Care Reform Debate: Part Three," University of Pennsylvania press release, August 1, 1994, p. 2.

62. In reponse to inquiries from the authors, HIAA released the geographic breakdowns for airing the Harry and Louise ads. Their figures show that overall just 11.4 percent of the ad broadcasts were in Washington, D.C., and 88.6 percent were in other parts of the country. But this does not address Jamieson's critique that the most of the ads targeted the major media markets of Washington, New York, and Los Angeles and the home states of crucial members of Congress.

63. Public opinion pollster Bill McInturff wrote to us on August 18, 1994, after seeing an earlier draft of our research, that his studies on behalf of the Health Insurance Association of America showed "the Harry and Louise spots were effective" with the general public. The specific evidence he cited came from a February 1994 survey in which 1) "People who had seen the Harry and Louise spots were eight percent to fifteen percent more likely to be familiar with the mandatory alliances and other elements of the HIAA-sponsored advertising," and 2) "People who recall seeing the Harry and Louise spots were consistently less supportive of specific elements of the Clinton plan (mandatory alliances for example) and overall provided the Clinton health plan with less favorable ratings." Our results, based on the *New York Times*/CBS News survey of March 1994, support the first point of increased familiarity based on

ad exposure, but not the change in evaluations of mandatory alliances. McInturff did not cite any other specific instances of ad impact in his three-page response to our paper, and HIAA would not release their survey or focus group data.

64. Interview with Ben Goddard, March 20, 1995.

65. Interview with Mark Isakowitz, March 24, 1995.

66. Orval Hansen, Robert J. Blendon, Mollyann Brodie, Jonathan Ortmans, Matt James, Christopher Norton, and Tana Rosenblatt, "Lawmakers' Views on the Failure of Health Reform: A Survey of Members of Congress and Staff," *Journal of Health Policy, Politics and Law* 21:1 (Spring 1996), p. 143.

67. Interview with William Gradison, March 13, 1995.

68. Elizabeth Kolbert, "R.I.P., Louise, Victim of the Health-Plan Advertising War," *New York Times*, March 17, 1994, p. B8.

69. Transcribed by authors from tape of the ad.

70. Don Wright, "Cartoon," *New York Times*, July 3, 1994.

71. Robin Toner, "Making Sausage: The Art of Reprocessing the Democratic Process," *New York Times*, September 4, 1994, p. E1 of "Week in Review" section.

72. Ira Magaziner, "Straight Talk on Health Care Reform," Speech at Brown University, May 28, 1994.

73. Interview with William Gradison, March 13, 1995.

74. Interview with Ira Magaziner, March 9, 1995.

75. Michael Weisskopf, "Harry, Louise to Hit Road During Health Hearings," *Washington Post*, May 24, 1994, p. A1; Michael Weisskopf, "Politicians Pursue Interest Groups to Deliver Health Care Votes," *Washington Post*, May 13, 1994, p. A3; and Steve Colford, "Harry & Louise vs. Billary," *Advertising Age*, February 14, 1994, pp. 1, 40.

76. *New York Times*, "Insurers Halting Ads Against Health Plan," May 25, 1994, p. A22.

77. Interview with William Gradison, March 13, 1995.

78. Interview with top White House official who requested anonymity, Spring 1995.

79. Interview with William Gradison, March 13, 1995.

80. Quoted in Robert Pear, "Getting Even with Harry and Louise, Or, Republicans Get a Taste of Their Medicine," *New York Times*, July 10, 1994, p. 2 of "Week in Review" section.

81. James Fallows, "A Triumph of Misinformation," *Atlantic Monthly* 275:1 (January 1995), pp. 26–37; Thomas Scarlett, "Killing Health Care

Reform: How Clinton's Opponents Used a Political Media Campaign to Lobby Congress and Sway Public Opinion," *Campaigns & Elections* (October/November 1994), pp. 34–37; and Haynes Johnson and David Broder, *The System* (Boston: Little, Brown, 1996).

82. Michael Hayes, *Lobbyists and Legislators* (New Brunswick, N.J.: Rutgers University Press, 1981); and Theodore Lowi, *The End of Liberalism* (New York: W. W. Norton, 1969).

83. Interview with top White House official who requested anonymity, Spring 1995.

84. Darrell M. West, "Activists and Economic Policymaking in Congress," *American Journal of Political Science* 32:3 (August 1988), pp. 662–80.

85. Rick Wartzman, "Truth Lands in Intensive Care Unit as News Ads Seek to Demonize Clintons' Health-Reform Plan," *Wall Street Journal*, April 29, 1994, p. A16.

86. Interview with top White House official who requested anonymity, Spring 1995.

87. Interview with Christine Heenan, February 9, 1995.

Chapter Five

1. Stephen Engelberg, "100 Days of Dreams Come True for Lobbyists in Congress," *New York Times*, April 14, 1995, p. A12.

2. Ed Gillespie and Bob Schellhas, *Contract with America: The Bold Plan by Rep. Newt Gingrich, Rep. Dick Armey and the House Republicans to Change the Nation* (New York: Times Books, 1994); and Michael Weisskopf, "Playing on the Public Pique," *Washington Post*, October 27, 1994, p. A1. Also see James G. Gimpel, *Fulfilling the Contract and Legislating the Revolution* (Boston: Allyn and Bacon, 1996).

3. Mark Peterson, "Political Influence in the 1990s: "From Iron Triangles to Policy Networks," *Journal of Health Politics, Policy and Law* 18: 2 (Summer 1993), pp. 395–438.

4. Eric Schine, "From the Folks Who Brought You Harry and Louise," *Business Week*, April 17, 1995, p. 37; Richard Dunham and Mary Beth Regan, "The GOP's Designated Pitcher," *Business Week*, March 27, 1995, p. 66; Richard Wolf, "Fulfilling Contract, GOP Turns to Selling It," *USA Today*, February 17, 1995, p. A4; and Ira Teinowitz, "GOP Contract Winning in PR, Ad Area," *Advertising Age*, April 10, 1995, p. 1.

5. Richard Berke, "Republicans Rule Lobbyists' World with Strong Arm," *New York Times*, March 20, 1995, p. A1.

6. Quoted in Dan Balz, "GOP 'Contract' Pledges 10 Tough Acts to Follow," *Washington Post*, November 20, 1994, p. A1.

7. However, it later was revealed that Frank Luntz, one of the pollsters for the contract, had not actually conducted polls on each plank but had relied on publicly available opinion data. See Frank Greve, "Pollster May Have Misled GOP on Contract," *Seattle Times*, November 12, 1995.

8. Interview with Barry Jackson, May 22, 1995.

9. Interview with Ed Goeas, May 2, 1995.

10. Interview with Barry Jackson, May 22, 1995.

11. *Ibid.*

12. *Ibid.*

13. Interview with Leigh Ann Metzger, May 26, 1995.

14. Interview with David Mason, May 4, 1995.

15. *Ibid.*

16. Interview with Christie Carson, May 12, 1995.

17. Interview with Ed Goeas, May 2, 1995.

18. Interview with Leigh Ann Metzger, May 26, 1995.

19. Quoted in Dan Balz, "GOP 'Contract' Pledges 10 Tough Acts to Follow," *Washington Post*, November 20, 1994, p. A1.

20. Interview with Grover Norquist, May 18, 1995.

21. *Ibid.*

22. Quoted in Elliot Krieger, "GOP's Contract: What It Means Depends on How You Look at It," November 20, 1994, p. A1.

23. Quoted in Dan Balz, "GOP 'Contract' Pledges 10 Tough Acts to Follow," *Washington Post*, November 20, 1994, p. A1.

24. Interview with Grover Norquist, May 18, 1995.

25. Interview with Barry Jackson, May 22, 1995.

26. C-SPAN II, "The Future of the Democratic Party" conference, April 12, 1995.

27. Interview with Ed Goeas, May 2, 1995.

28. Tarrance Group/Lake Research, Inc., "Battleground '96: Key Points and Charts," unpublished report, 1995.

29. Interview with Barry Jackson, May 22, 1995.

30. Berke, "Republicans Rule Lobbyists' World with Strong Arm," p. A1.

31. Richard Berke, "G.O.P. Seeks Foes' Donors, and Badly," *New York Times*, June 17, 1995, p. A1.

32. Quoted in Berke, "Republicans Rule Lobbyists' World with Strong Arm," p. A1.

33. Engelberg, "100 Days of Dreams Come True for Lobbyists in Congress," p. A12; and George Miller, "Authors of the Law," *New York Times*, May 24, 1995, p. A21.

34. Engelberg, "100 Days of Dreams Come True for Lobbyists in Congress," p. A12.

35. Interview with Keith Apel, May 10, 1995.

36. Interview with Grover Norquist, May 18, 1995.

37. George Miller, "Authors of the Law," p. A21.

38. Engelberg, "100 Days of Dreams Come True for Lobbyists in Congress," p. A12.

39. Dunham and Regan, "The GOP's Designated Pitcher," p. 66.

40. Wolf, "Fulfilling Contract, GOP Turns to Selling It," p. A4.

41. Interview with Barry Jackson, May 22, 1995.

42. Interview with Keith Apel, May 10, 1995. Also see Howard Scripps, "PR Arm of Contract Folds Tent, Moves On," *Cleveland Plain Dealer*, April 8, 1995, p. 12A; and Joan Lowy, "Republican 'Contract' Has Publicity Machine," *Rocky Mountain News*, January 1, 1995, p. 74A.

43. Benjamin Sheffner, "Contract's Private PR Enterprise," *Roll Call*, February 23, 1995.

44. Interview with Keith Apel, May 10, 1995.

45. Interview with Christie Carson, May 12, 1995.

46. Interview with Grover Norquist, May 18, 1995.

47. Jeffrey Birnbaum, "The Gospel According to Ralph," *Time*, May 15, 1995, pp. 28–35.

48. Interview with Grover Norquist, May 18, 1995.

49. Teinowitz, "GOP Contract Winning in PR, Ad Area," p. 1.

50. Interview with Christie Carson, May 12, 1995.

51. Interview with Leigh Ann Metzger, May 26, 1995.

52. Owen Ullmann, "Corporations 1, Attorneys 0," *Business Week*, July 17, 1995, p. 8.

53. Interview with Christie Carson, May 12, 1995.

54. Interview with Leigh Ann Metzger, May 26, 1995.

55. Ullmann, "Corporations 1, Attorneys 0," p. 8.

56. Interview with Leigh Ann Metzger, May 26, 1995.

57. *Ibid.*

58. Interview with Neil Cowan, May 26, 1995.

59. Interview with Leigh Ann Metzger, May 26, 1995.

60. Schine, "From the Folks Who Brought You Harry and Louise," p. 37.

61. Interview with Ben Goddard, May 17, 1995.

62. *Ibid.*

63. *Ibid.*

64. *Ibid.*

65. *Ibid.*

66. Interview with Leigh Ann Metzger, May 26, 1995.

67. Interview with Barry Jackson, May 22, 1995.

68. *Ibid.*

69. Interview with Neil Cowan, May 26, 1995.

70. Interview with Leigh Ann Metzger, May 26, 1995.

71. *Ibid.*

72. Interview with Neil Cowan, May 26, 1995.

73. Interview with Ben Goddard, May 17, 1995.

74. *Ibid.*

75. Ann Devroy and Helen Dewar, "Product Liability Pits 'Two Goliaths,' " *Washington Post*, March 21, 1996, p. A1.

76. John Harris, "Clinton Vetoes Product Liability Measure," *Washington Post*, May 3, 1996, p. 1; and Neil Lewis, "President Vetoes Limits on Liability," *New York Times*, May 3, 1996, p. A1.

77. Larry Light, "Air Assault on Excess Awards," Business Week, April 29, 1996, p. 6.

78. Teinowitz, "GOP Contract Winning in PR, Ad Area," p. 1.

79. Richard Berke, "Republicans Spurning The Big-Business Label," *New York Times*, May 11, 1995, p. B11.

80. Engelberg, "100 Days of Dreams Come True for Lobbyists in Congress," p. A12.

81. *Ibid.*

82. Quoted Balz, "GOP 'Contract' Pledges 10 Tough Acts to Follow," p. A1.

83. *Ibid.*

84. Interview with Grover Norquist, May 18, 1995.

85. *Ibid.*

86. Steven Holmes, "Interest Groups Howl As Ax Falls on Budget," *New York Times*, May 12, 1995, p. A22.

87. Case cited in "Outrage of the Week," Democratic Policy Committee newsletter, October 31, 1997.

88. Alan Miller and Glenn Bunting, "Funding of Gingrich PAC Raises Questions," *Los Angeles Times*, January 29, 1995, p. A1.

89. *Ibid.*

90. *New York Times* ad, "Is Newt Gingrich Above the Law," July 11, 1995, (full-page ad sponsored by *Mother Jones*).

Chapter Six

1. See, for example, Kirk Victor, "Down to the Wire," *National Journal*, March 5, 1994, pp. 526–30; and David J. Lynch, "Strategic Errors Offset Contributions," *USA Today*, October 16, 1995, p. 1.

2. In reference to high stakes, see Paul Schulman, *Large-Scale Policymaking* (New York: Elsevier, 1980); and Jeffrey Berry, *The Interest Group Society*, 3rd ed. (New York: Longman, 1997).

3. *Business Week*, "McCain on the Record," October 20, 1997, p. 111. Also see Seth Schiesel, "Cable TV Lacks Competition, F.C.C. Notes," *New York Times*, January 14, 1998, p. D6.

4. Mike Mills, "Media Groups Try Paving Way to a Favorable Cable Bill," *Congressional Quarterly Weekly Report*, May 30, 1992, p. 1523.

5. *Ibid.*

6. *Ibid.*, p. 1524.

7. *Ibid.*, pp. 1523–29.

8. Mike Mills, "Bush Asks for a Sign of Loyalty; Congress Changes the Channel," *Congressional Quarterly Weekly Report*, October 12, 1992, p. 3149.

9. Mike Mills, "Senate Action on Cable Bill Provokes a Clash of Titans," *Congressional Quarterly Weekly Report*, January 11, 1992, p. 51.

10. Mills, "Bush Asks for A Sign of Loyalty," p. 3149.

11. Mills, "Media Groups Try Paving Way to a Favorable Cable Bill," p. 1523.

12. Robert H. Frank and Philip J. Cook, *The Winner-Take-All-Society* (New York: Basic Books, 1995).

13. Victor, "Down to the Wire," p. 526.

14. Lynch, "Strategic Errors Offset Contributions," p. 1.

15. Kirk Victor, "They're in a League of Their Own," *National Journal*, May 27, 1995, p. 1307.

16. Quoted in Victor, "Down to the Wire," p. 527.

17. The specific interests of the burglar alarm industry allowed it to

concentrate attention on very specific issues. Their persistence and focus resembled the approach of medical savings account advocates, most notably the Golden Rule Insurance Company, as noted in chapter 7.

18. See Richard Fenno, *Home Style* (Boston: Little, Brown, 1978), for the importance of explanation for members of Congress.

19. Kirk Victor, "Media Monsters," *National Journal*, March 2, 1996, 480–84.

20. Jeffery Berry, "The Dynamic Qualities of Issue Networks," paper presented at American Political Science Association meetings, September 1–4, 1994, Chicago, Ill., p. 12.

21. Berry, "The Dynamic Qualities of Issue Networks," p. 14.

22. See *Economic Impact of Deregulating U.S. Communications Industries*, WEFA Group, Burlington, Mass., and Bala Cynwyd, Penn., February 1995. Their reproduction of figure 6.2 cites the Apple Corporation as source.

23. Victor, "Media Monsters," 484.

24. J. H. Snider and Benjamin Page, "The Political Power of TV Broadcasters: Covert Bias & Anticipated Reactions," paper presented at the annual meeting of the American Political Science Association, Washington, D.C., August 28–31, 1997. The story of the defeat of free television time is told by Michael Kranish in "Networks Help Scuttle Free Ads," *Boston Globe*, December 25, 1997, p. A1.

25. *Economic Impact of Deregulating U.S. Communications Industries*, p. 103.

26. *Ibid.*, p. 24.

27. *Ibid.*, p. 26.

28. Mark Landler, "AT&T Assails a Study by Economist," *New York Times*, September 2, 1996, p. C5.

29. *Ibid.*, p. C5.

30. The Regional Bell Operating Companies, "Presentation of Findings from a Suvery of 1005 Adult Americans," The Mellman Group/Public Opinion Strategies, March 1995.

31. John F. Persinos, "Telecom Ad War," *Campaign and Elections*, October/November, 1995, p. 34.

32. *Ibid.*, p. 34.

33. *Ibid.*

34. *Ibid.*, p. 35.

35. Mary Jacoby, "Tale of 'Astroturf Lobbying' Gone Awry," *Roll Call*, September 28, 1995, p. 1.

36. Interview, anonymity guaranteed.

37. In surveys by various organizations (CBS, CNN/*USA Today*, Roper, NBC) in 1995–96, health care concerns usually fell within the top five concerns of the public, but telecommunications issues, no matter how generally defined, received no consideration as a major problem. See *The Public Perspective*, April/May, 1995, p. 52; and October/November, 1996, p. 2.

38. Kirk Victor, "Cable's Comeback," *National Journal*, December 17, 1994, p. 2963.

39. Interview, anonymity guaranteed.

40. Victor, "Cable's Comeback," p. 2966.

41. Mark Llander and Geraldine Fabrikant, "Even Before Deregulation, Cable Rates Are on the Rise," *New York Times*, April 12, 1996.

42. Quoted in Kirk Victor, "Here's a Train that Roared by Quietly," *National Journal*, February 10, 1996, p. 316.

43. Gene Kimmelman, quoted in Edmund L. Andrews, "Telecommunications Bill Signed, and a New Round of Battles Starts," *New York Times*, February 9, 1996, p. A1.

44. *Providence Journal*, "Controls Eyed for Cable's High Rates," January 19, 1998, p. A10.

Chapter Seven

1. See, for example, Dave Skidmore, "Understanding the Kassebaum-Kennedy Health Care Bill," *Washington Post*, August 13, 1996, p. A13.

2. Charles Jones, *The Presidency in a Separated System* (Washington, D.C.: Brookings, 1994).

3. Deborah Stone, *Policy Paradox* (New York: Norton, 1997), p. 138.

4. *Ibid.*, p. 138. Also see Gary J. McKissick, "Issues, Interests, and Emphases," paper presented at the Midwest Political Science Association meeting, Chicago, April 6–8, 1995.

5. Charles Cook, "Republican Pollster Diagnoses Medicare Message Problem," *Roll Call*, November 30, 1995, p. 8.

6. One analysis of the labor strategy, generated by the Business-Industry Political Action Committee, questioned its effectiveness. See Richard I. Berke, "Issue Ads' by Labor Fell Short in 1996, Business Group Says," *New York Times*, August 7, 1997, p. A16.

7. In fact, former speaker Tip O'Neill labeled tampering with Social

Security as touching the third rail of American politics. Veteran congressional correspondent Adam Clymer played off the subway metaphor by observing that "tinkering with Medicare is like throwing yourself in front of the train." See Clymer, "Of Touching Third Rails and Tackling Medicare," *New York Times*, October 27, 1995, p. A11.

8. This story is best told by David Maraniss and Michael Weisskopf in *Tell Newt to Shut Up* (New York: Touchstone, 1996), chap. 10. The following discussion depends in part on their reporting.

9. *Ibid.*, p. 129.

10. John Kingdon, *Agendas, Alternatives, and Public Policy*, 2nd ed. (New York: HarperCollins, 1995).

11. Richard Cohen, "Setting the Stage for an Epic Drama," *National Journal*, July 22, 1995, p. 1904. Also see Maraniss and Weisskopf, *Tell Newt to Shut Up*, p. 135.

12. Morton M. Kondrake, "Polls Show GOP Gain in Medicare Marketing Wars," *Roll Call*, August 3, 1995, p. 6. The Kaiser Family Foundation commissioned the Harris poll.

13. Robin Toner, "G.O.P. Medicare Effort Avoids Deadly Detail," *New York Times*, August 2, 1995, p. A1.

14. Martin Gottlieb and Robert Pear, "Beneath Surface, New Health Bills Offer Some Boons," *New York Times*, October 15, 1995, p. A1.

15. *Ibid.*, p. A1.

16. Adam Clymer, "Both Parties Wage Medicare Debate on the Air," *New York Times*, August 16, 1995, p. A13.

17. Robert Pear, "Doctors' Group Backs Plan of Republicans on Medicare," *New York Times*, October 11, 1995, p. A1.

18. Colette Fraley, "Historic House Medicare Vote Affirms GOP Determination," *Congressional Quarterly Weekly Report*, October 21, 1995, p. 3206.

19. *Ibid.*, p. 3206.

20. Juliana Gruenwald and Robert Marshall Wells, "At Odds with Some Workers, AFL-CIO Takes Aim at GOP," *Congressional Quarterly Weekly Report*, April 13, 1996, pp. 993–98.

21. *Ibid.*, p. 996.

22. By one count, twenty-seven or thirty-two Republicans targeted were freshmen. See "Labor Group's Ads Target 32 Republicans," *The Hotline* (http://www.politics.now.com), September 10, 1996.

23. Adam Clymer, "GOP's Freshmen Out on the Stump," *New York Times*, August 7, 1996, p. A9.

24. Jonathan Weisman, "Republicans Battle Unions on Hill and on

Airwaves," *Congressional Quarterly Weekly Report*, August 10, 1996, p. 2252.

25. Quoted in Alissa Rubin, "Time Short for Hard Choices on Medicare, Social Security," *Congressional Quarterly Weekly Report*, October 26, 1996, p. 3058.

26. Observers calculated that 9,753 changed votes in select House races across the country would have returned Democrats to majority rule, according to *Providence Journal*, "Democrats Lift Ban on Noncitizen Donations," January 11, 1998, p. A5. For a more general discussion of the political climate, see Richard Cohen, "Setting the Stage for an Epic Drama," *National Journal*, July 22, 1995, p. 1904.

27. John Kingdon, *Candidates for Office* (New York: Random House, 1968).

28. Gary Jacobson, "The Congressional 1996 Elections of 1996," *Extension of Remarks*, January, 1997, pp. 2–14.

29. George Hager, "Clinton, GOP Congress Strike Historic Budget Agreement," *Congressional Quarterly Weekly Report*, May 3, 1997, p. 993.

30. Elliot Carlson, "Medicare: Is the Sky Really Falling?" *AARP Bulletin*, September 1997, p. 2.

31. *Ibid.*, p. 2. This story cites Harvard University's Richard Parker and the Brookings Institution's Steven Hess.

32. Quoted in Carlson, "Medicare: Is the Sky Really Falling?" p. 2.

33. Murray Edelman, *The Symbolic Uses of Politics* (Urbana: University of Illinois Press, 1964).

34. George Hager, "Groping for a Record to Run On," *Congressional Quarterly Weekly Report*, May 3, 1997, p. 1038.

35. See for example, the "Heritage Foundation Backgrounder," by Carrie J. Gavora, who labelled the Medicare budget as "disastrous" because it would promote savings and expand coverage in expensive ways. From http://www.lead-inst.org/heritage, May 12, 1997, p. 1.

36. Adam Clymer, "Senate Passes Health Bill with Job-to-Job Coverage," *New York Times*, April 24, 1996, p. A1.

37. *Ibid.*, p. A1. Also Kevin McShane, "The Health Insurance Reform Act of 1996," paper written for the University of Kansas Washington intern program, May 9, 1996.

38. Steve Langdon, "Dole Could Determine Outcome as Bill Moves to Conference," *Congressional Quarterly Weekly Report*, April 27, 1996, pp. 1170–72.

39. David Rosenbaum, "There's Been No Rush for Medical Savings

Accounts, but Idea Is Gaining Favor," *New York Times*, December 24, 1997, p. A11.

40. National Center for Policy Analysis press release, "Misplaced Criticism of MSAs," May 6, 1996. The funds can be left in the MSA to grow, tax-free. Thus, after several years, the accounts may be quite large and capable of absorbing all but the largest medical expense. Hence the catastrophic insurance policy may be activated only infrequently. For a profile of Rooney, see Amy Borrus, "Not Your Usual GOP Crusader," *Business Week*, December 8, 1997, p. 41.

41. Robert Dreyfuss and Peter H. Stone, "Medikill," *Mother Jones*, January/February, 1996, pp. 5–11.

42. *Ibid.*

43. Marilyn Moon, Len M. Nichols, and Susan Wall, "Medical Savings Accounts: A Policy Analysis," The Urban Institute, March 1996.

44. Robert Pear, "Health Insurance Skirting New Law, Officials Report," *New York Times*, October 5, 1997, p. A1, 16.

45. The rapid adoption of MSAs, however, did not occur in the initial year; less than 10,000 new MSA accounts were established, in part due to substantial restrictions in the Kennedy-Kassebaum bill.

46. Benjamin Page, *Who Deliberates?* (Chicago: University of Chicago Press, 1996), p. 5.

47. *Ibid.*, p. 124.

48. Darrell M. West, Diane Heith, and Chris Goodwin, "Harry and Louise Go to Washington," *Journal of Health Politics, Policy and Law* 21: 1 (Spring 1996), pp. 35–69. Also see James Fallows, "A Triumph of Misinformation," *Atlantic Monthly* 275:1 (January 1995), pp. 26–37. For a more historical perspective, see Thomas Konda, "Political Advertising and Public Relations," Ph.D. thesis, University of Kentucky, 1983.

49. William E. Browne, *Cultivating Constituents* (Lawrence: University Press of Kansas, 1995); David Whiteman, *Communication in Congress* (Lawrence: University Press of Kansas, 1996); John Wright, *Interest Groups and Congress* (Boston: Allyn and Bacon, 1996).

50. Christopher Lasch, *The Revolt of the Elites* (New York: W. W. Norton), p. 170.

51. *Ibid.*, p. 170.

52. Adam Clymer, "White House Says Plan Endangers Health Bill," *New York Times*, June 10, 1996, p. A10.

53. Benjamin Page, *Who Deliberates?*, p. 9.

54. See Mark Rodwin, "The Neglected Remedy," *American Prospect*,

September-October, 1997, p. 45ff, who argues for institutional channels within managed care plans for consumers to express their concerns. On many policy issues, even when the scope of conflict expands, there is precious little chance for consumers to voice their position effectively, even if there is such a position.

55. Benjamin Page, *Who Deliberates?* p. 9.

56. Jane Mansbridge, "A Deliberative Theory of Interest Representation," in Mark Petracca, ed., *The Politics of Interests* (Boulder: Westview, 1992), p. 54.

57. John Judis, "Pool Sharks," *The New Republic*, April 29, 1996, pp. 10–11.

Chapter Eight

1. David Truman, *The Governmental Process* (New York: Alfred Knopf, 1951).

2. Mancur Olson, *The Logic of Collective Action* (Cambridge, Mass.: Harvard University Press, 1965).

3. James Sundquist, *The Dynamics of the Party System*, rev. ed. (Washington, D.C.: Brookings, 1983).

4. Saul Alinsky, *Rules for Radical* (New York: Random House, 1971).

5. E. E. Schattschneider, *The Semi-Sovereign People* (New York: Holt, Rinehart & Winston, 1960).

6. Raymond Bauer, Ithiel de Sola Pool, and Lewis Dexter, *American Business and Public Policy* (New York: Atherton Press, 1963).

7. Theodore Lowi, *The End of Liberalism*, 2nd ed. (New York: Norton, 1979).

Chapter Nine

1. E. E. Schattschneider, *The Semi-Sovereign People* (New York: Holt, Rinehart & Winston, 1960).

2. Kay Lehman Schlozman and John T. Tierney, *Organized Interests and American Democracy* (New York: Harper and Row, 1986).

3. Jerome McKinney and Michael Johnston, *Fraud, Waste, and Abuse in Government* (Philadelphia: Institute for Study of Human Issues, 1986).

4. Jill Abramson and Leslie Wayne, "Nonprofit Groups Were Part-

ners to Both Parties in Last Election," *New York Times*, October 24, 1997, p. A1.

5. Richard Davis, "Electronic Lobbying: Interest Groups and Grassroots Mobilization," paper presented at the annual meeting of the American Political Science Association, Washington, D.C., August 28–31, 1997.

6. David Shenk, *Data Smog* (New York: HarperSanFrancisco, 1997).

7. Jamieson is quoted in David Broder, "Junk Journalism," *Washington Post*, February 23, 1994, p. A17.

8. A. Trevor Thrall, "Look Who's Talking: Money, Power, and Interest Group News Coverage," paper presented at the annual meeting of the American Political Science Association, Washington, D.C., August 28–31, 1997.

9. For a similar point about think tanks, see Andrew Rich and R. Kent Weaver," "Advocates and Analysts: Think Tanks and the Politicization of Expertise in Washington," in Allan J. Cigler and Burdett A. Loomis, eds., *Interest Group Politics*, 5th ed. (Washington, D.C.: CQ Press, 1999).

10. Amicus curiae brief of ACLU filed in the Fourth Circuit, U.S. Court of Appeals, docket no. 95–2600, filed January 22, 1996. Darrell West was an expert witness in this case hired by the Federal Elections Commission.

11. Darrell M. West, *Air Wars: Television Advertising in Election Campaigns, 1952–1996*, 2nd ed. (Washington, D.C.: CQ Press, 1997), p. 102.

12. *Ibid.*, p. 192.

13. Amy Keller, "Wisconsin Regulates 'Election-Related' Issue Ads," *Roll Call*, September 4, 1997.

14. Damon Chappie, "The IRS's 'Story of M' May Affect '96 Politics," *Roll Call*, April 15, 1996, p. 1.

15. Damon Chappie, "Judge Denies Tax Exemption to All-GOP Group," *Roll Call*, March 9, 1998, p. 1.

Index